MEMOIRS

Also by Harold Wilson

NEW DEAL FOR COAL (1945)

IN PLACE OF DOLLARS (1952)

THE WAR ON WORLD POVERTY (1953)

THE RELEVANCE OF BRITISH SOCIALISM (1964)

PURPOSE IN POLITICS (1964)

THE LABOUR GOVERNMENT 1964–1970 (1971)

THE GOVERNANCE OF BRITAIN (1976)

A PRIME MINISTER ON PRIME MINISTERS (1977)

FINAL TERM: THE LABOUR GOVERNMENT 1974–76 (1979)

THE CHARIOT OF ISRAEL (1981)

MEMOIRS

The Making of a Prime Minister 1916–64

HAROLD WILSON

WEIDENFELD AND NICOLSON
AND
MICHAEL JOSEPH

Copyright © 1986 by Lord Wilson of Rievaulx

First published in Great Britain by
George Weidenfeld & Nicolson Ltd
91 Clapham High Street
London SW4 7TA

and

Michael Joseph Ltd
27 Wrights Lane
London W8 5TZ
1986

Second Impression November 1986

The author would like to thank Brian Connell for his great help in
putting the book together.

ISBN 0 7181 2775 7

British Library Cataloguing in Publication Data

Wilson, Harold, 1916–
    Memoirs: the making of a Prime Minister
    1916–1964.
    1. Wilson, Harold, 1916– 2. Prime
    ministers—Great Britain—Biography
    I. Title
    941.085′6′0924   DA591.W5

Filmset by Cambrian Typesetters, Frimley, Surrey. Printed and
bound in Great Britain by Butler & Tanner Ltd., Frome, Somerset.

Contents

Illustrations

(*Unless otherwise indicated, the photographs belong to the author's collection*)

Prologue

When the Labour Party scraped back into power in the general election of February 1974, with 301 seats, we were left in a minority of thirty-two in the House of Commons. I told my wife that if we managed to hold out, I would serve two more years as Prime Minister and stand down on my sixtieth birthday, 11 March 1976. Mary had played no part in this determination, although she made no attempt to dissuade me. She had been completely loyal during my thirty years in politics.

The second general election of 1974, in October, which returned us with an overall majority of four, only strengthened my resolve. I could now buttress my claim that we were the natural party of government. I was under no personal strain; in fact I do not think I had to take more than five days away from business through sickness during the whole of my public life. There was, however, one factor which bulked large in my thinking. I was afraid of growing stale while still in high office. There continues to be much speculation as to my true reasons for standing down and it is perhaps as well to make this a matter of record.

I was one of the very few Prime Ministers who had never come under the control of the Treasury. I had fought them to a standstill all my political life. I had experienced their methods in Whitehall as a wartime civil servant before I had even stood for Parliament. It had been a long stint and I had become confident in my experience. Nevertheless, problems do tend to repeat themselves, both in diplomacy and in the economy. Two things can happen. Either you take the same decision because it worked the previous time round or you take a different decision largely on the grounds that it did not work as well as it should have done the previous time.

We would look very hard at the elements of a political crisis and, although there appeared to be a very attractive and possible solution, I would feel called upon to say, 'No, we can't do it that way, we will have to do it the other way. I have been through all this before.' I had studied Gladstone, my only superior in longevity in office, and I had seen others brought full circle at the end of their time. I am perhaps the only Prime Minister who has looked at affairs in this manner and I was determined that it was not going to happen to me. Our problems were going to need a fresh mind at the top. My successor, and I had a pretty clear idea of who it was likely to be, would still take a little time to emerge in full command and in the interim I proposed to keep affairs on an even keel. We had accomplished much in office and I was intent on bequeathing a strong administration.

There remained the constitutional obligation of finding a suitable opportunity to inform the Queen of my intentions. I had been most fortunate in my relationship with the Monarch. Perhaps something in my very different background helped. As a result, we were on easy conversational terms from the very start. She was fascinated at the account I was able to give of what life was like in the 'back-to-back' houses she had seen in Leeds and in the industrial villages of the North. She was always full of information about her tours around the country and particularly the impressions formed on her foreign visits, and – what she enjoyed most – her visits to Commonwealth Countries. I do not wish for one moment to lessen the dignity of the occasion, but we just used to sit and chat.

Life has been made much easier for an incoming Prime Minister these days. Much of the stiff formality of the past has gone. When you are summoned to the Palace after an election, you have to answer one simple question: 'Can you form a Government?', to which there are three answers: 'No, Ma'am, I'm sure I can't', 'Yes, Ma'am, I'm sure I can', or 'I'll go away and try'. On my four occasions I was able to say 'Yes'. The Prime Minister is even relieved of the formal duty of kissing hands. On his first visit he does not do so and on his second visit, accompanied by the first members of his Government, although they do, he does not. He is assumed to have done it the day before, which is not the case.

Thereafter the regular and principal contact is the weekly audience, usually on a Thursday afternoon about 6.30 pm. A day or two beforehand, the Queen's Private Secretary and the Prime Minister's Principal Private Secretary exchange notes about the points each party would like to bring up, but otherwise the audience takes place exclusively *à deux*. After a quick lowering of the head from the neck, you are invited to sit down and the door is closed behind you. The Queen might have a small piece of paper with a note on it on a side table to which she might refer, but she makes no notes and the atmosphere is purely conversational. The audience would last about forty minutes. Sometimes we would have a cup of tea or coffee, but not always.

My first period in office had coincided happily with the coming to manhood of the Prince of Wales. At one audience, when I was telling the Queen that I was about to leave for Australia to attend the memorial service for Harold Holt, who had been tragically swept out to sea while swimming, the Queen asked me whether I thought it would be a good idea if Prince Charles went out with me. He was still quite young but I thought it an excellent proposal, so she called him in. 'Charles,' said the Queen, 'the Prime Minister has very generously said that he will take you to Australia. Now you will do exactly what he tells you. If he says go to bed, you just go to bed even if you have to break off in the middle of a sentence.' He was a delightful companion and made a great impression in spite of the sadness of the occasion. Our relationship was very agreeable and I hope I gained his confidence.

When the question of his further education arose, I used to have him at meetings at 10 Downing Street with representatives from the academic world and had several conversations with the Queen on the subject. I had put forward the idea that he should go for at least one term to my old college, Jesus, where there a great number of Welshmen. I also thought that he should spend a period at the University of Wales, and this took place in due course. In the end it was determined that he should spend the main part of his time at university at Trinity College, Cambridge, and thereby hangs a small tale.

The post of Master of Trinity was becoming vacant and I had learned that the appointment was in the Queen's gift on the recommendation of the Prime Minister. I was holding a diplomatic reception at 10 Downing Street for a distinguished foreign visitor and the guests included senior members of the Opposition, among them Rab Butler. At an appropriate moment I took him into a corner in one of the big state rooms and said, 'Rab, look, I am not playing a trick on you to get rid of a very distinguished opponent in the House, but I would hate to hear afterwards that you would like to have gone to Cambridge and that you were not given the opportunity.' He expressed his appreciation and said that he would like a little time to think about it. About eleven o'clock that night the telephone rang at Number 10 and he was on the line. He had probably been talking to his wife and said: 'I suppose I am too late. Have you offered it to anyone else?' 'No, I have not,' I said. 'I have thought it over,' he went on, 'and we'd love to accept it.' His family had long been connected with Trinity, and Charles had a very happy time there.

The Queen always showed a keen interest in visitors from abroad. Her office used to ring up mine to say that she had thought of inviting some particular personality to a function at the Palace and should she arrange to have him sit very close to me or would I prefer to chat with him upstairs afterwards. In my turn, I would always keep her well informed about any interesting figures who were passing through London. On one occasion I mentioned to the Queen that the American Vice-President, Hubert Humphrey, was coming to London. Her response was immediate: 'Would he like to come to Windsor?' she asked. I said I was sure he would. We were both invited to stay the night. Dinner took place at a long narrow table, with twenty or thirty guests, and she placed Humphrey opposite me. In spite of his ebullient public manner, he was rather a shy person, which made it difficult to think of him becoming President. That evening he was in tremendous form and she was charmed by him.

He and I made our way upstairs to bed together. Our rooms were along a very long corridor leading to the royal apartments. Hubert was saying what a marvellous evening it had been and how tremendously he had enjoyed it. 'Let's have another drink,' I said. There is a little ante-room in the corridor where you could ring a bell and one of the Palace servants would bring refreshments. 'The Vice-President and I would like another whisky,' I said. Hubert stretched himself out on a long settee with his feet up and I was on a chair more or less at his side. 'This has been the most wonderful evening of my whole life,' he said. 'Here we are, me from my father's drug store in Minneapolis and you from a relatively humble background in Yorkshire, sitting here in Windsor Castle – drinking the Queen of England's whisky.'

She was very warm and gracious when we lost the 1970 election. The outgoing Prime Minister has to go and more or less hand over the keys to Number 10. Obviously she could not say that she was sorry that I was out, but she asked after Mary and hoped that I was going to have the opportunity for a rest after the very arduous campaign. When I came back for my second two terms of office in 1974, our relaxed intimacy was immediately renewed.

One harmless element in our easy relationship was that the timing of the Thursday audience coincided with the publication of the last edition of the *Evening Standard*. It became something of a conversational gambit for the Queen to ask if I had seen some particular news item. Quite often I had been so busy with government and parliamentary business that I had not had time to pick it up, and this small advantage used to please her.

However, there was one occasion when I had glanced at it when it had reprinted a scurrilous story from Paris about President Giscard d'Estaing. This asserted that it had become a habit of his to tour the streets of Paris in the late evening in a non-government limousine looking for lighter ladies of the town. This time I had the advantage. 'I haven't seen the *Evening Standard*,' said the Queen, 'have you?' 'Yes,' I said. 'May I suggest that you send for it.'

She must have done so because about a week later I was required to inform her that I had to pay a brief visit to Paris. Giscard was the current six months' chairman of the EEC heads of government and I needed to have a discussion with him about the terms of Britain's membership of the Common Market, which I was trying to renegotiate.

'Ho, ho,' said the Queen in high good humour, as if my ulterior motive was to engage in the French President's alleged extra-mural activities. The meetings in Paris were much more formal than that. I had an extremely sumptuous dinner at the Elysée with Giscard and went back to the embassy, where I was staying. Whether something I had eaten at dinner had not agreed with me I do not know, but I was as sick as a dog.

I returned to report formally to the Queen and she said, 'Well, and how did it go?' I gave a general account: 'I think we made some progress and they understand our position, but I don't know whether we can carry it through without the rest of the members of the Common Market.' 'And what about ho ho?' she said. 'Ma'am,' I was obliged to reply, 'there was no ho ho.' I had to tell her the sad story about my being sick and she was terribly disappointed.

One of the agreeable entries in a Prime Minister's diary is the annual autumn visit in attendance on the Queen at Balmoral. She is very happy with the informal life she is able to lead there and Mary and I were much privileged on our visits. There had been one occasion when she suggested that we should go over and have lunch with the Queen Mother at Glamis. 'You don't need your detective,' the Queen said, 'let me drive you over.' She rather enjoyed getting away from her bodyguards, but of course they always followed on in close attendance. Since then, I understand that security has been further tightened up.

In September 1975 we were there for our last visit. She had built another little chalet in the grounds, I think to mark her silver wedding anniversary, and this time she really did leave the detectives behind and drove Mary and me a mile or so down to the chalet. The Queen filled up the kettle and Mary helped her to lay the table. After a most agreeable tea, the Queen passed an apron to Mary, put one on herself and they both proceeded to wash up the crockery.

In that sort of atmosphere it seemed to me that the time had come to inform the Queen of my resolve. Her sense of constitutional propriety is too great for me to be able to report any direct reaction, but I was left with the impression that she had enjoyed our two-way seminars over the years and that I might still have second thoughts on the matter. The following month Speaker Thomas was at Chequers for the weekend and I also informed him.

I recount all this at some length to establish that when the time came, it was no sudden unpremeditated decision. Jim Callaghan, though older than me, had emerged as my clear successor. He annoyed me when one of his first acts was to sack Barbara Castle, whom I had always regarded as one of the most effective members of my Cabinet. If George Brown had reasserted himself on the political scene I might well have had second thoughts, but the way was clear and my mind was made up.

The formal announcement nevertheless caused a stir. The House of Commons effervesced, but I met with great friendliness on the part of most Conservatives, although one of their backbenchers saw fit to stand up and ask what was my reason for going at such short notice. I was able to turn to Speaker Thomas and say, 'I think I told you, Mr Speaker, several months ago.' The Speaker is not normally reported in *Hansard*, but George Thomas said very loudly and deliberately, 'That is correct.'

The Tory press was less generous and full of speculation. There was one particularly unpleasant story that I had been speculating in Italian funds and I had to get my lawyers to look at it, although we never troubled to take court action. In the first place I did not have any money to speculate with and, if I had, it would not have been in Italian funds. I simply do not know how such stories arise.

I am often asked whether I heaved a great sigh of relief at laying down the burden of office. I did not propose to make a nuisance of myself on the back benches and was chiefly concerned to rebuild our home life and concentrate on the second volume of my account of my years in office, which later appeared under the title of *Final Term*. I did not want historians to have to rely on what they read in an entirely hostile set of newspapers or even in *The Times*. There was hardly a single editor or writer who had a clue about how government was run and I was intent that the record should be put straight.

I shall return to those years with further insights in due course, but it seems to me that a purpose might be served in establishing an account of those events and influences in my life which brought me from modest circumstances in a Yorkshire mill village to the post of Prime Minister at the age of forty-eight: that is what this book is about.

1

Sparks in the Playground

My boyhood political hero, Philip Snowden, MP for Colne Valley, where I was born, began his autobiography with the words 'I am a Yorkshireman.' It is a distinction to which I also lay claim, although I find it difficult to tabulate our common characteristics. A judicious calm perhaps, nothing volatile, puffing at a pipe and eyeing a situation or a person quizzically, and never coming to hurried conclusions. In a long public career I do not think I have ever lost my cool except on rare occasions for specific effect. An intense feeling of family loyalty is bred in all of us, reinforced in my young days by regular chapel-going and a sense of community which found expression in countless voluntary organizations. We also have a capacity for protracted hard work, and a sturdy and uncomplaining defiance of the setbacks that afflicted too many livelihoods.

We were suffused with an intense regional pride. By tradition we were solid dyers and weavers of wool. We used to look down on the Lancastrians on the other side of the Pennines because their staple was cotton, a weak yarn compared with wool. Our chief joy was to beat them at cricket and the ultimate disaster, almost involving a period of mourning, was to suffer the occasional defeat. When Huddersfield Town won the League Championship three years running and the Cup Final in two of those years, we felt we were the Lords of Creation. When I was at school the Wars of the Roses were still a living legend, although we were hazy about the facts. We were happy that the conflict continued in our favour.

Boyhood instinct was happily reinforced forty years later, after I became Prime Minister, when a national newspaper commissioned Garter King of Arms, Doyen of the College of Arms and Britain's unchallenged arbiter of heredity, to trace me back in the male line

9

as far as it existed. Garter was able to prove that my Yorkshire ancestry went back to at least the late fifteenth century. This was something of a relief since I had feared that there might have been an infiltration of Scottish blood caused by the successive raids of marauding Scots, bent on rape and pillage, into north Yorkshire.

All my ancestors in the male line up to the late nineteenth century had been born within five miles of Rievaulx, the beautiful Cistercian Abbey near Helmsley in north Yorkshire. When I was made a Knight of the Garter I had to discuss the preparation of my coat of arms. We discovered that the Abbey had never been so favoured, but that an early Abbot, St Aelred, did have one. So part of his escutcheon was duly incorporated in mine.

I do have to admit to one break in the succession, although the protagonists were able to renew their true loyalties. In later years Aneurin Bevan once cross-examined me about my origins. At a Party Conference he had met my father, who regaled him with stories of Lib–Lab successes in the Manchester area in and after 1906. 'I thought', said Nye, 'that you were a Yorkshireman but your Dad has been telling me all about Manchester. Where were you born, boy?' With a Yorkshireman's natural pride, I said, thinking of Sheffield's steel, 'Yorkshiremen are not born; they are forged.' 'Forged were you?' said Nye in that muscial Welsh lilt of his, 'I always thought there was something counterfeit about you!'

Nye was much given to hyperbole and he thought he had spotted the skeleton in our family cupboard. My father, Herbert, and my mother, Ethel, were both born in Manchester. This needs explanation and indicates something about the temper of those times. The Helmsley Archaeological Society took a similar interest in my ancestry when I became head of government and engaged in an even more detailed study of my genealogy. They confirmed the long Rievaulx connection but were also able to pinpoint the trans-Pennine pilgrimage. Following the Poor Law Act of 1830, which in those days was as great a social reform as those of the Lloyd George and Attlee Governments, the burghers of Helmsley, the market town some two or three miles from Rievaulx, implemented its provisions by building and staffing a workhouse.

My great-grandfather applied to become its director, but on the first and second ballots he tied with another candidate. The salary was £1 per week. When a third ballot also ended in a tie, he was offered the post on condition that he agreed to a weekly pay of eighteen shillings. This he accepted. He seems to have fulfilled his duties with such diligence that a few years later he was promoted to the more prestigious position of Master of York workhouse. His daughter, my great aunt, was still matron there when, as a boy, I visited our old family home.

York was a thriving city in the mid-nineteenth century. It almost became the railway centre of Britain. George Hudson, the 'Railway King', was born there and, as he built new lines and bought others in an attempt to create a national system, he planned that all the main routes would converge on York. Unfortunately, in the slump of the early 1850s, he resorted to paying dividends on the Eastern Counties railway out of capital and was disgraced and indeed imprisoned. The York city fathers thought so highly of him that they had decided to erect a statue in his lifetime. The plinth was already in place when he was sentenced. York responded by replacing him with a local worthy, George Lehmann, whose contribtion to society had been to invent the crossing of bank cheques.

The slump also affected my grandfather, James, born in 1843 and apprenticed to a draper in the city. More than a century later, when I received the purely honorary freedom of York, intensive research failed to determine whether my grandfather had become a freeman, as was normal in those days when an apprentice completed his indentures. He probably crossed the Pennines a little too early. He it was who made his way into Manchester, where he prospered modestly in the drapery trade. He also made a good marriage to a Miss Thewlis, whose brother, Alderman Herbert Thewlis, became Liberal Lord Mayor of Manchester at the beginning of the century. He was the only individual on either side of my family who was at all wealthy. He had an umbrella factory in Stockport, the best place in the world for such an enterprise.

My father was one of six children. There was no question of his staying at school long enough to seek entry to a university and at the age of sixteen he got a job in the dyestuffs industry with the firm of Levinstein in Manchester, continuing his education at the Manchester College of Technology. It was during this period that he met Chaim Weizmann, the founder of modern Israel, who was working, though obviously at a much higher level, in dyestuffs and associated chemical products. The industry was facing formidable competition from Germany in the early years of this century and my father had to endure prolonged periods of unemployment, during which he became involved full time in political activity.

In this he has been preceded by his elder brother Jack, who had been Keir Hardie's election agent in 1895 and again in 1900. He was the founder secretary of the ATTI, the Association of Teachers in Technical Institutions, and an active though moderate socialist. He made his way in life and in 1917 was appointed by the then President of the Board of Education, H.A.L. Fisher, to be the first His Majesty's Inspector of Technical Colleges. The first inspection he carried out was at Bradford Technical College, which in due course became Bradford University, where I was Chancellor for many years until I stood down quite recently. It was also Fisher, by that time Warden of New College, Oxford, who gave me my first real job as 'Extraordinary Lecturer in Economics'.

In 1906 there was a general election as a result of Balfour's extraordinary resignation and the formation of Asquith's Liberal Government. At that time, polling day was decided, constituency by constituency, by the returning officer. In Manchester's case, this was the Lord Mayor, no less than my great uncle Thewlis, who could select any day he chose over a period of some three weeks. The good alderman chose a Saturday, to make sure of getting the working-class vote out for the Liberal candidates, Winston Churchill and T.G. Horridge. There was something of an undeclared Lib–Lab pact in the area, and my father was on the election staff of the Labour candidate for Gorton, John Hodge, who was elected one of the twenty-nine members of the Independent Labour Party.

In 1908, Churchill was appointed President of the Board of Trade, the second of five Presidents this century who later became Prime Minister. The others were Lloyd George, 1905–8; Baldwin in 1922, the author 1947–51, and Edward Heath 1963–4. Under the archaic laws which then governed British politics, any MP promoted to the Cabinet had to resign his seat and seek re-election. At this by-election, my father, again out of work due to the uncertainties of the international dyestuffs trade, was deputy election agent to Churchill, who was defeated by Joynson-Hicks, but took refuge in Dundee, where he was successful and able to take up his duties at the Board of Trade. My great uncle, no longer the Lord Mayor, was Churchill's constituency President. The defeated candidate consoled himself with draught after draught of Thewlis whisky – 'My whisky, Herbert,' the aggrieved umbrella tycoon said to his nephew.

When Churchill announced his forthcoming retirement from Parliament in 1964, the Prime Minister, Sir Alec Douglas-Home, called me in to discuss how Parliament might best recognize the occasion. I suggested that the Party Leaders, together with the Father of the House, should pay our tributes to Winston in Parliament, have the relevant sections of *Hansard* bound in the traditional parliamentary green leather and go along to present them to him. In the course of my tribute I referred to my uncle's whisky, adding that he was a strict teetotaller. An angry letter came to me from his daughter, a hospital matron in Lancashire, who said that on the contrary her father was the biggest soak in the county.

After a further period of unemployment, my father got a job in Huddersfield, thus returning to his geographical origins, working first for a Colne Valley firm, Leitch & Company, and later in the dyestuffs factory of L.B. Holliday & Company. Major Holliday was an employer of the Gradgrind school. He would say to my father, who was a departmental manager: 'You know what I have told you. You have got to sack a quarter of your men every month to keep the others on their toes.' My father managed, with some difficulty, to evade this instruction, save where drink or careless-ness caused danger to fellow workers. My parents moved into a small two-up and two-down terraced house, 4 Warneford Road, Cowlersley, where I was born on 11 March 1916.

My father's affairs were beginning to stabilize and before long we moved into a larger house not far away at 40 Western Road, which is the first home I really remember. It was a substantial stone-built, semi-detached residence, with a little passageway between it and the next house, leading to a garden. There was a cellar, where my mother did all the laundry, and my room was in the attic, where in due course I was able to set up my Hornby train set. My elder sister Marjorie, seven years my senior, had her bedroom on the first floor, next to our parents.

At the age of four I joined the most junior class at New Street Council School, Milnsbridge, which was only five minutes walk away, although I had to cross the very busy Leeds to Manchester road to get there. It was a miserable year. Every one of us, boys and girls, were terrified of the class mistress, who was head of the infants department. Looking back on it I would have to conclude that Miss Oddy was either an incompetent teacher or a sadist, probably both. Her educational methods were eccentric. One morning she insisted that each of us, before leaving for lunch, should write on the blackboard the longest word we knew. One friend, later a prominent Yorkshire industrialist, was content with 'kite'. I managed to produce the nine-letter word 'committee'. I had picked it out of our exercise books, all overprinted 'West Riding Education Committee'. I do not doubt that psychologists would attribute this early experience to what they might regard as a premature preoccupation of mine with committees, sub-committees and working parties, not to mention Neddies.

In 1923, at the age of seven, I had an operation for appendicitis, in those days a more formidable experience than it has since become. It took place on the day of the general election called by Stanley Baldwin, who was seeking a mandate to introduce tariff protection for Britain's industries. That evening my parents came to see me in hospital as I came round from the anaesthetic. As they lingered, I kept urging them to leave so that they would be in time to vote for Philip — my hero Philip Snowden.

They said that they had ample time and finally left for the polling booth in the Royal Enfield motor-cycle and sidecar my father had acquired. There was a thick fog in the Colne Valley that night and they arrived too late. But Snowden was elected, with a majority of nearly 2,000 and in neighbouring Huddersfield, his Labour colleague, Jimmy Hudson, was in by just twenty-four votes over the Liberal candidate, with the Conservative third. The Labour Party, with support from Lloyd George's small band of Liberals, formed a precarious Government. Snowden became Chancellor of the Exchequer and appointed Hudson as his Parliamentary Private Secretary.

Appendicitis in those days was by no means the five-day wonder it is now and I missed a whole school term, from Christmas to Easter, convalescing. It at least enabled me to catch up on my reading. My sister, Marjorie, had a set of Arthur Mee's *Children's Encyclopedia*, and this I devoured, especially the sections dealing with history. Some months later, when Marjorie and my mother were attending summer Guide camps, my father took me on a week's sight-seeing tour in his motor-cycle to London, my first visit to the capital and one of only three until the outbreak of war. I had a very provincial upbringing.

This first encounter was exhilarating. We stayed in a bed-and-breakfast boarding-house in Russell Square, had tea in the ABC café by Westminster Bridge, and I spent a shilling of my father's money at threepence a time looking through the pavement telescope at Big Ben and the House of Commons. We visited the Wembley Exhibition, listened to the Hyde Park orators, had a look at Buckingham Palace and, as if with some presentment of posterity, my father took a snapshot of me standing in front of the entrance to Number 10 Downing Street.

I must have been a very forward little boy because when we went on conducted tours of the Palace of Westminster, the Abbey, the Tower and St Paul's, I am told that I picked out all the errors in the official guides on the basis of my concentrated readings of the encyclopedia. I repeated the trick on our return trip via Runnymede, Oxford, Rugby and Stratford-on-Avon. I was certainly a bookworm. There were two large bookcases in the downstairs rooms at home and I was allowed, under guidance, to pull out anything that took my fancy. I was also an avid reader of the *Manchester Guardian*, the only newspaper allowed in the house.

I came out top of the infant class and went on to the 'big school', jumping two grades. The main building was solidly built of Yorkshire stone and until very recently still stood, albeit empty. The terrain was sloping and our playground was paved with suitably slippery stone, excellent for sliding, especially in frosty weather. Many of my fellow pupils wore clogs with iron cladding on the soles to enable them not only to raise sparks, but to out-distance those of us who were wearing stout leather boots – there were, apparently, no shoes in those days. I complained at home about the absence of spark-raising clogs, but my mother considered me more suitably shod.

Years later, when I had become President of the Board of Trade, I was set up by the newspapers over a comment I made at a press conference. Wartime clothes rationing was still in force and it required a formidable number of the coupons available to buy a pair of boots or shoes. In answer to a question about this, I emphasized the leather shortage, the lack of skilled operatives in the boot and shoe factories, the rise in the birthrate and full employment. The increased demand meant a shortage of shoes. Then I was unwise enough to add that when I was at school, many of the boys did not wear leather footware, but clogs.

The Conservative press had a field-day. In no time they were reporting me as saying that my schoolmates had nothing on their feet, and that I had gone barefoot. They had a wonderful time asking ex-teachers at the school whether what I had said, as corrupted by the reporters, was true. Teachers who confirmed the facts were simply not quoted. It was many years before the press ceased to deride me as a 'barefoot boy'. Labour ministers must expect this literary style. As Confucius, or perhaps some other philosopher, said: 'What do you expect from a pig but a grunt?'

Our school was also remarkable in having, deep down below the classrooms, a small swimming bath, cold and dank, which was shared with other surrounding schools whose pupils filed along in all weathers to take their turn. In return, we New Street boys would go on successive weekly mornings to the neighbouring Crow Lane school to learn woodwork.

The Wilson family lived a very simple existence. All the holidays I can remember from my young days took the form of the four of us crowding into my father's motor-cycle and sidecar, with me stretched out on my mother's knees and Marjorie on the pillion, and driving to the village of Old Byland, a couple of miles from Rievaulx. We lodged with a friend of my father's whose cousin also owned the pub on the village green. I have often been challenged about premature recollections, but I have a clear memory of first being there at the age of three when the village band assembled to celebrate the formal signing of the peace that ended the First World War in 1919.

Our pastimes were bucolic enough. We went on country walks and I would kick a ball about with the local lads or stage a game of boys' cricket. I set snares for rabbits once or twice, but without success; my grandfather always did it better. We did catch one, but it was a baby, so we let it go. I also remember one disastrous journey home on an August Bank Holiday when we stopped off to buy a copy of the *Yorkshire Evening Post* for the cricket scores. Yorkshire needed some eighty odd runs to win and were all out for something over half that figure. We were taunted for years by our Lancashire relatives over that result.

These happier days came to an end about 1925 when the lord of the manor incontinently expelled all the tenants from their houses, with no suggestion of anywhere else to live. Our relatives were fortunate in finding barrack-style accommodation at Catterick Camp, both father and son having served in the First World War.

The Wilsons attended church regularly. Both my parents were Congregationalists, but there was no church near enough, so at 10.30 every Sunday morning Marjorie and I were taken by them to the local Baptist church, where the minister, the Rev. W.H. ('Pa') Potter, enjoyed a great local influence. Marjorie and I also went to his Sunday School in the afternoon. I would not say there was an atmosphere of religious fervour at home, but this practice was a normal and accepted part of our lives.

My father was very busy on the social side, always organizing parties and get-togethers, and there was a very strong Scout Group which Mr Potter ran as a constituent branch of his church. My father was a Rover Leader, my mother a Guide Captain and Marjorie a Guide. I became a Cub at a very early age and in due course a Patrol Leader in what was the biggest Scout Group in Yorkshire, the 3rd Colne Valley Milnsbridge Baptist Scouts, which was in due course merged to become the 20th Huddersfield. We went camping, organized debates and I even joined the band, playing first the triangle and later the side drum. I happily acknowledge my membership as one of the main elements in my formative years.

The great treat of the week was to be allowed to go and watch Huddersfield Town playing at home during their great days. I would leave home at about 10 am. My mother would give me a shilling. The number 4 tram from Marsden to Bradley went through the town right to the ground and cost one penny each way. Entrance was sixpence, the programme cost twopence, threepence purchased a small portion of fish with an abundant accompaniment of chips 'with bits on' – the fried knobs of batter that floated off in the cooking. The remaining penny provided a 50 per cent increase in my regular weekly pocket money of twopence, of surprising purchasing power in those pre-inflation days.

In 1926 I had a wonderful opportunity, denied to most of my contemporaries, of seeing something of the world. My mother's family, the Seddons, in Openshaw, had a strong railway connection. Her grandfather had been an engine driver on the old Manchester, Sheffield and Lincolnshire railway. This line was later linked to London and renamed the Great Central, and lost money every year until the 1914–18 war, when the profits went to the state. When the Baldwin Government in 1923 returned the companies to private ownership, they formed the four new companies, LMS, LNER, GWR and SR in order to ensure that as far as possible there would be competition to the principal destinations – LMS and LNER on the London–Scotland run, and GWR and SR to the south-west. I remember that in standard three at school (the nine year olds), we had to inscribe in the little notebooks we bought from the teacher for a halfpenny each the constituent companies of each rail merger.

My maternal grandfather had been a ticket clerk on the MS & L and my uncle Harold, after whom I was named, an electrician. Thus, in terms of the trade union movement decades later, my great-grandfather had been a member of ASLEF, my grandfather of the TSSA and my uncle of the NUR, a point I did not fail to make *ad*

17

nauseam, when I had gravitated to politics, in successive speeches at railway union conferences and particularly in late-night sessions in Number 10 when a rail strike was threatened.

Uncle Harold suffered badly from asthma, an uncomfortable ailment for a Mancunian, and at the turn of the century he had emigrated to Western Australia, where he worked on the construction of the trans-continental line. When it reached Kalgoorlie, he left the railway and found a job dealing with gold mine supplies. He also involved himself in politics, joining the Federal Labour Party, which towards the end of the 1914–18 war began to split over the issue of conscription. He opposed the call-up, and this lost the Party votes. After the war, when he stood for the Legislative Council, the elected upper house of the State Legislature, he was the only member elected. The result had been very close, and the leading Party, rather than lose its majority of one, appointed my uncle as presiding officer, or speaker, and in that capacity he was knighted as Sir Harold Seddon. He also persuaded most of the family to join him. My father remained behind, and so of course did my mother. Had she gone, as I told Prime Minister Gough Whitlam several decades later, I might have had his job.

The family had settled more or less in the bush in what is now an overspill of Perth. Early in 1926, grandfather Seddon was taken seriously ill with what seemed a terminal condition. My father said he was prepared to work the shirt off his back to raise the money and insisted that my mother went to pay a last visit. Marjorie was to look after him during Ethel's absence, but she would not have been able to look after me as well, so it was decided that I should go too. Father had now graduated to a family Austin 7 and in May he took us to London, where we embarked on RMS *Esperance Bay*, one of the five liners owned by the nationalized Australian Commonwealth Government Shipping Line.

I hardly need to recount the enchantment of such a long journey, through the Mediterranean, with one-day stops at Port Said and Colombo and the arrival at Perth. We found something of a Seddon family commune, one aunt and her husband, who worked in a department store in Perth, with their five children, a maiden aunt, and grandfather, who was in much better health than we had feared, living on a small farm outside the village of Gosnells, about a dozen or so miles from Perth. They had a few score fruit trees, apples and oranges, and a few chickens, just enough to keep my grandfather busy, with a little outside help in the fruit-picking season, in addition to forced labour for my older cousins and myself. The local school was in the village and each day my grandfather and I used to accompany the older children in the morning and bring them back in the afternoon. We had to cross a tract of country overrun with cactus and brambles and the old man would always break off a thick branch from one of the citrus trees, strip off the leaves and have it handy as a weapon in case we came across any snakes. I took to carrying a small branch myself.

One morning an evil-looking black snake, about five feet long, slithered across the path. My grandfather moved quickly, broke its back with his stick and then hung it up a few feet above the ground on the remains of a dead tree. It was a common enough encounter. On another occasion, we heard a rattling on the corrugated metal roof of the house and my uncle climbed up and shot another snake through the head with his rifle.

I had an even more alarming solitary encounter with a representative of Australian fauna unknown in Yorkshire. I had been sent out on the farm to pick navel oranges for the market when a sub-tropical storm suddenly blew up. I took refuge in a hut consisting of sacking spread on four corner-posts, only to find that my haven was also inhabited by a tarantula, to my mind the largest tarantula ever hatched. I was holding a mattock, a cross between a chopper and a small pick, with which I succeeded in cleaving my adversary somewhere between the tarantulan wind and water.

As if this was not enough, we had another fright. My uncle by marriage was driving my mother and me to Kalgoorlie to stay with my uncle Harold. We were in an open car and were speeding along an untarred sandy road at sixty miles an hour when we hit a brown snake some four feet long as it was crossing the road. It was caught in the wheel, flung high in the air and landed in our car. A sudden slamming of brakes and a skid brought us to a halt on the grass verge and our relative duly dispatched the intruder with the spare car handle from the tool kit. This was the last preliminary to the highlight of our tour which was to attend, seated on that part of the floor allocated to strangers, the session of the upper house of the State Legislature under Uncle Harold in all his dignity. This was the first time I had actually sat in any of His Majesty's Parliaments.

I had been so exhilarated by this first experience of a larger world that, on our return to Cowlersley, I not only composed a lecture, which was duly delivered to all the classes at school, illustrated by the artefacts I had picked up, but I also wrote articles for my favourite publications. The editor of *Meccano* magazine acknowledged my contribution thus:

> Dear Wilson,
> I thank you for your note and the article describing your visit to an Australian gold mine. I regret that I shall not be able to accept this as I have already accepted two articles dealing with very similar subjects. Accordingly I am returning your article herewith.
>
> For a boy of your age the article is remarkably well written and I am sure that with a suitable subject you could write an article of the required standard. I shall be very glad to read any you may care to send me.

I sent the same composition to *The Scout*, whose editor was rather more terse in his response:

> My dear Wilson,
> Thank you very much for letting me see your article on 'A Visit to an Australian Gold Mine'. I am afraid that this is not of sufficient interest to my readers to enable me to make you an offer for it.
>
> If you think of taking up writing, I shall always be pleased to see any articles or stories you care to send me and to publish them if suitable. With my good wishes to you.

I would not wish to prolong these minutiae of boyhood. We are all products of our environment, and in my case the strongly knit family background wove the whole pattern of my existence. The sternly demanding limitations of the life we lived played an essential part in my formation. When I came of age and consequence, my ingrained enthusiasm for the conception of the Commonwealth can be firmly traced to this early experience in Australia. It is not given to many to have their horizons broadened before they know where they lie.

2

Someone for Tennis

Back at Milnsbridge at the age of eleven, my schoolmates and I faced the ordeal of the County Minor Scholarship – what came to be known years later as the Eleven Plus. One bitterly cold February morning, we trooped along to the nearby Crow Lane school to answer papers in English and arithmetic. The sums seemed easy enough, but we had an hour or so in which to do our 'essay'. Each of us was given a photograph of, apparently, a farmer and his wife standing in a field, and we had to write a story around it. I did not know, and I am sure few, if any, of my contemporaries did, that it was the picture known as *The Angelus*.

My own somewhat theatrical explanation must have been inspired by a recent temperance lecture to which we were all subjected from time to time. The man in the picture, I suggested, had been drinking as a result of pressures from intemperate friends and had wasted all his agricultural subsistence in riotous or, as we should say now, conspicuous spending. He therefore had nothing to give his wife to feed their starving offspring.

However that may be, I won the scholarship, one of five in my large class. Another boy who came on to my next school had to leave at the beginning of his fourth year because his father was out of work – eighteen months before he would have sat for Matric. or, as we would now say, O levels. I am happy to say that when I next saw him a few years ago, he was one of the leading professional men in Huddersfield, a churchwarden, councillor and a pillar of the local Conservative Party.

In September 1927, in brown blazers with pale blue piping round the collar, the new generation of scholars, boys and girls, presented themselves at Royds Hall Secondary School in Huddersfield. Opened in 1921, the buildings were in part a gentleman's former residence, I think that of a former woollen manufacturer,

21

and in part a new wing constructed functionally as a school in perfectly good post-war taste.

In my fourth year at Royds Hall, I contracted typhoid fever. Our Scout Group, the Milnsbridge Baptist, had a small camping site a few miles outside town. Two of us were there with the Group Scout master and chapel minister, Mr Potter. I drank a glass of milk from the next door farmer, and accidentally knocked over my friend's glass. Despite his recriminations, I saved him from the consequences. Over a dozen local consumers also contracted the fever. Six of them died in the hospital where I spent thirteen weeks. I was the marginal survivor. My grandfather's comment to my father was: 'That lad is being saved for something, Herbert.'

In January I returned home. The cure had been almost worse than the disease, and consisted of having hardly any food, just boiled milk and water; I came back looking like a skeleton. I was given a small truckle bed in front of the gas fire in my parents' bedroom. Apart from the coal fire downstairs, it was the only heating in the house. On the first Monday morning after my release, I was surprised that my father had not got up at the usual time and asked him why. I heard the whispers, 'Shall we tell him?' While I was in the isolation hospital he had lost his job at L.B. Holliday. Perhaps his poor dismissal rate of unskilled workers was not to the liking of the boss.

The adjustment, not only of the wage or salary earner and his wife, but also of the children in a house struck by unemployment, is hard to describe. There were thousands of families in the region faced with the same predicament in that disastrous slump year. I shall never really know how the family survived. My father must have had some savings, as his ordeal lasted a couple of years. Our food became more simple, although my mother always managed to keep me adequately fed. Our clothes had to last well beyond their date for renewal and our pleasures were curtailed. My parents endured it all with quiet dignity. For years I never forgave myself for asking my father at some scout function in Wakefield if I could have 3s.6d. to buy a sheath knife. I still remember his expression and his words: 'I can't just now – you know how things are.'

I concentrated with even more determination on my schooling. I had missed two whole terms, critical as far as maths was concerned, as we had been taking our first steps in higher geometry and advanced algebra. I would probably have fallen by the wayside if it had not been for a selfless and generous gesture by the maths master, F.S. Wilmut. He was a gentle-voiced man, short and grey, with glasses. He was a born teacher, though with no degree, and hence no hope of promotion. He had quite a large family. Two of his sons were good at sports and in due course became teachers themselves, one of them a headmaster.

Wilmut was an active supporter of the Huddersfield Labour Party. Whether this inclined him towards a family with similar loyalties I am unable to say, but one evening in my third term he took me on one side and asked me if I was game to stay on for half an hour after school each day to catch up. If I was, he would stay with me. The cramming worked and I was a willing pupil. No one was more pleased than he when I received a distinction in the School Certificates examination.

Many years later when I had become active in public life, I was invited to present the certificates at the school's speech day. For some reason, Wilmut had broken all ties with Royds Hall, but he sneaked in at the back of the magnificent nineteenth-century Huddersfield Town Hall, with its wonderful acoustics and echoes of a hundred performances of the *Messiah*. He was thus able to hear my warm references to his kindnesses, although I did not know he was there and he came up to me only at the end of the ceremony.

Our own speech days were a bore. We had to go to the Town Hall in the morning and rehearse the singing, especially those of us who were in the mixed choir, and all of us below the age of fourteen had to scrub our knees as well as our faces. Just before our speech day in 1928, Asquith, who for a few months had attended an older Huddersfield school, died. The visiting teacher was, as I recall, principal of what was then called a Teacher Training College. He was extremely pompous and, after a eulogy of Asquith, turned towards the ranks of boys and girls and said condescendingly: 'Perhaps one of these boys will one day be Prime Minister.' The reaction of half the school was: 'Why not one of the girls?' My own reaction was contempt for his ignorance. Didn't he *know*?

In fact, my ministerial ambitions at that time lay in another direction. Because of my continuing hero worship of Philip Snowden, I simply wanted to become Chancellor of the Exchequer. The first-formers were divided into four groups according to age, with only a month or two between each. I rather gave the game away when we were asked by our English mistress to write an essay as though each of us was a journalist twenty-five years later interviewing himself in whatever capacity he or she had achieved. There was a scratching of West Riding Education Committee pens and after a minute or two my small hand went up: 'Please Miss Whelan, does the Chancellor of the Exchequer live at Number 11 or Number 12 Downing Street?'

She correctly hazarded Number 11 and my essay went on to describe Harold Wilson preparing his budget. For a prospective Chancellor I was extremely forthcoming. The journalist was given a complete outline of my fiscal proposals. The one element I can remember was my firm intention to tax gramophone records. We did not have a gramophone as some of my friends' families had. To me it was a mark of the idle rich, not to say the sybaritic, and my proposed tax of one shilling was undoubtedly intended as a deterrent.

Of my fellow pupils only one made a substantial mark in later life, and that was Roland Spencer. He did not go on to university when I did, but went out to Australia and got a job with the Commonwealth Shipping Line, which was nationalized and then privatized and merged with a number of other companies of which he became the head. Some fifty years later, when I was chairman of the inquiry into the financial institutions of the City of London, he suddenly got in touch again and invited me out to lunch.

In the autumn of 1932, my father, who had never ceased his search for suitable employment, found a job at Brothertons Chemical Works on the Wirral peninsula in Cheshire, hard by the west bank of the Mersey. In November of that year, we moved for good from the Colne Valley to a flat owned by my father's new employer in Bromborough, four miles from Birkenhead on the Chester road. It was a spacious and pleasant apartment, the ground floor of a large house built in 1860 by a Mersey shipping tycoon as a wedding present for his son and daughter-in-law. The move must have come in the nick of time and my father was doubtless hard put to pay even the modest cost of the removal. My sister Marjorie may have been able to help a little. She had been at Leeds University studying chemistry, which she failed, but then she took a teacher training course and became a gifted children's teacher.

My own County Minor Scholarship held good for any state school in the Wirral, or even across the river in Liverpool, including two or three Headmasters Conference or Public Schools. My father decided to consult his elder brother, the former inspector of technical colleges. 'Send him to the new school, Herbert; they have got their name to make. Let them have a go at the lad.'

It was sound advice. Apart from the headmaster of Wirral County School, later Wirral Grammar School, there was no teacher over thirty years old. My main subject was history, and the other two subjects to be taken at principal level for Higher School Certificate were English and French. At subsidiary level I took Latin and maths. I pressed to be allowed to do the latter as I already had a vague feeling that I would one day want to study economics. Doubtless the concern about Number 11 Downing Street, which I had shown five years earlier, must have still been in my mind.

Since the last two years of my school life were spent at a boys' school, I have often been asked how a mixed school compared with a single sex or, as one interviewer once put it, 'a homosexual school'. My answer has usually been that I was glad to go to a mixed school up to the age of sixteen and glad to have gone to a quite 'separate' school thereafter. Perhaps this was just a rationalization of my own experience.

The mixed school has several advantages. Looking back on those days, I would feel that the girls fulfilled a kind of *mission civilisatrice* on the rough lads. There was, of course, a compulsion on our part to show off, especially if the target of one's imagination was in the same form. In the junior school, where it would have been 'sidey' to wear long trousers, it meant we had to scrub our knees. Long trousers were permissible only from one's sixteenth birthday. Again, in soccer or cricket matches between different forms or houses, as well as the summer athletics, our efforts were frequently watched and cheered on by the girls. In class, too, the average boy did not want to appear stupid and perhaps did his homework better in consequence of his female friends.

At the Wirral, I became the only boy in the sixth form and was again exceedingly fortunate in my masters. The history master, Mr P.L. Norrish, a Devonian, who himself became a headmaster at a very early age, shattered me at our first encounter. In Huddersfield I had been studying nineteenth-century history. Now I was told 'we shall be doing the seventeenth century'. It was a useful stretching of my faculties, as I had to take in the political and economic history of 1760–1914 for my final examination at Oxford.

My English master, Mr W.M. Knight, affected a degree of cynicism, but he was a born teacher. 'What paper do you take at home?' he asked me at our first meeting. 'The *Manchester Guardian*,' I told him. We had taken it in our family from the time of my grandfather's arrival in Manchester in 1860, and it was a matter of family pride that we were in part descended from the Taylors of Radcliffe, Lancashire, who were among the paper's founders. 'If you hadn't taken the *Guardian*, he said, 'you would do quite well with the *Liverpool Daily Post*. It is one of the three best papers in Britain.' After being a Merseyside MP for over thirty-five years, I can confirm his judgement.

I also have a warm recollection of Frank Allen, the senior classics master, who was also a fine cricketer and games coach. He had more influence on my teenage political development than anyone else. He was a socialist and probably a pacifist. He took me to hear Sir Norman Angell speaking at Birkenhead shortly after Sir Norman had won the Nobel Peace Prize. His speech made a more lasting impression on me than anything else I heard over the years.

On another occasion Allen took me to Liverpool to see Henry Lytton on his last tour in *The Yeoman of the Guard*. I had long been a devotee of Gilbert and Sullivan. The T'brig Baptists had been well known for miles around for their D'Oyly Carte performances. My father had been secretary of the operatic society, getting more and more anxious about the high charges the D'Oyly Carte company were levying on amateurs, no less than two guineas a time.

Years later, when I was back in Number 10 after our 1974 election victory, I was sitting in a Trinity House luncheon next to the Lord Mayor of London, Sir Hugh Wontner. He asked me if I would like to go to the D'Oyly Carte centenary performance and what part I would like to play in the celebrations. I offered to act as prompter, without the book. We had done it at Milnsbridge. Sir Hugh told me that the D'Oyly Carte company was in great financial difficulties and might have to close. I arranged to meet Miss Bridget D'Oyly Carte, who became Dame Bridget in that centenary year. My secretary, Marcia Falkender, also managed to contact Sir James Hanson, who came in to see me at Number 10. It turned out that he had first attended the operas at Milnsbridge when I was call boy, indeed had played a midshipmate in *HMS Pinafore*. His father had owned the local fairground and a privately operated bus service. When the Attlee Government took over heavy road transport, he and his father became managers of the nationalized road haulage organization in Lancashire. It was the beginning of a remarkable career, but he was unable to save the D'Oyly Carte company.

A renewed interest in Gilbert and Sullivan was not the only debt I owe to Frank Allen. Our Latin sessions were set aside time after time while he deployed his classical knowledge and deep religious faith to widen my appreciation of current political affairs. A year after I went up to Oxford he was killed, at the age of twenty-six, slipping on some scree on a Cumberland mountain, where he had taken a group of boys for the day from the school camp at Arnside.

I did have to make one major adjustment to my lifestyle. Wirral was a rugger school, playing rugby union, not the lethal 'Kick him, he's still breathing' rugby league game I had often played after school in Huddersfield. As the biggest boy around I was directed into the forward line and in the scrum I was penalized a number of times for tactics that would have won acclaim in the thirteen-a-side version of the game. Before I left school, the time came for us to seek outside opponents and a match was arranged with Birkenhead Park School. We calculated our average age at about fourteen and a half and asked them to play their fourth side against us. For some reason they thought we were pulling a fast one and the side they fielded averaged seventeen years in age. At half time we were 37-nil down and the final score was double that. We contented ourselves with the thought that, playing uphill against the wind in the second half, we had not deteriorated, although we were assisted by the fact that one of the opposition had had his collar bone broken in the scrum just before half time.

I was more interested in athletics, actually winning, by a foot, the three mile Junior Cross Country Championship of the Wirral Athletics Club and the Club's silver medal. On the strength of this I was chosen to captain the Wirral junior team in the Merseyside Championships, for medals presented by Mr Fred Marquis, later Lord Woolton, of Lewis's Ltd, the big Liverpool store. We finished in eleventh, twelfth, fifteenth and seventeenth place, and won bronzes as the third team. The two medals are still on my bedroom dresser nearly half a century later.

In my second year in the sixth form I began to get restive. Much of my time was spent in the school library, still largely unstocked, with occasional lessons *à deux* with one or other senior master. I felt I could not face a third year and was pressing to be allowed to try for university. The headmaster, previously head of Wigan

School and himself a physics graduate of Liverpool, was something of an intellectual snob. He decided to send me to Oxford to sit for one of the few places available on open scholarship.

My history master was strongly opposed to this venture. He thought I would probably do so badly that when I went at the proper time in the year following Higher School Certificate, now A-levels, my poor performance would be recalled and would count against me. So strong was his opposition that he refused to let me take time from my planned schedule to revise the little I knew. Three days before I went to Oxford, fearing that my lack of revision would tip the scales still further against me, he allowed me to revise.

I had been entered for the Merton group, which covered six colleges in all. Term had ended and I had one of the students' rooms. It smelled strongly of disinfectant. In the late 1970s, when I was addressing a seminar of American students, I found that the smell had lingered on. All candidates had to face a *viva voce* in the evening and on alphabetical grounds I was the last one. Later, when I had become a don myself and had to interview candidates for college entry, I always found a certain affinity with the last one; since the task was nearly over, one somehow tended to keep him longer.

So it proved in my Merton interview. The questions were pressed hard and the tutor seemed a little surprised at the extent of my reading. It had been my good fortune that my history master was himself working for a London University external degree, writing a thesis on Robert Spencer, third Earl of Sunderland (1640–1702), and he used to borrow the relevant books by post from some university library. I quoted a not very widely known fact about the later years of Charles II and the tutor asked me where I had read it. I had a sudden mental block, and he was just preparing to end the interview when my memory recovered and I almost shouted 'Miss Foxcroft'. This interested him and the interview went on for another ten minutes.

Back home on the following Monday morning, my father opened his *Manchester Guardian* at the door and came into my room saying, 'Open Exhibition in Modern History, Jesus College, Oxford'. I thought he was playing a joke on me, but there it was. The amount of the Exhibition was £60 per year. In those days it was usually considered that £300 would be needed to cover the annual cost of tuition, food and lodging in college, living very austerely. My history master was amazed, my headmaster delighted. He even called me up on to the school platform to receive the plaudits of my rather bored schoolmates.

Soon afterwards I learnt some of the background. The Merton tutor had placed me fairly high, but just below the list of successful candidates, passing the name on to the other colleges of the group. The applicants who had stayed in Jesus and had been viva-ed there did not complete the quota the college had in mind. There was one vacancy. The philosophy tutor at Jesus was Mr T.M. Knox, later Professor and the Principal of St Andrews University. He had worked for a few years at Lever Brothers in Port Sunlight. His father, originally a Congregational minister, was head of the firm's staff training college, a position to which he had been appointed by the two Lever brothers, who had been taught by him in Sunday School.

T.M. Knox telephoned his father to enquire about me. The Rev. Knox did not know very much but recalled hearing my vote of thanks at the school's speech day to the then Chairman of the LMS railway, who had, in his own words, 'delivered' the prizes. He had considered my few words not inappropriate, even humorous, and that, apparently, did the trick.

The next problem was how to bridge the gap between £60 and £300. I had not done particularly well in the Higher School Certificate and just failed to get a county scholarship. Twelve were awarded and I was placed tenth; but since a minimum of three had to go to girls and the top nine were boys, I just missed out. My history master was still suggesting that the Exhibition had been a flash in the pan and that I should stay on for another year. The headmaster, Mr Moir, then took over. He spoke to the county authorities, who not unfairly suggested that I was not yet up to it and also suggested that I should stay on for another year. He continued to fight and managed to obtain a grant. My father said that he would do all in his power to raise the difference, and his firm generously increased his salary by two pounds a week, so I could just manage.

Mr Moir was later able to use this battle to great effect. When I won the Gladstone Memorial Essay prize in my second year at Oxford and the Webb Medley Junior Economics Scholarship in my third, going on to get the top First in Finals, he telephoned the county authorities and said, 'Will you listen to me next time?'

It was during my Higher School Certificate examinations that I first saw Mary. It was the night before and I was feverishly cramming my set books, *Hamlet*, *Cymbeline* and Marlowe's *Dr*

Faustus. I have never been any good at memorizing verse or for that matter prose. I thought any excuse was good enough to lay down my books and get some fresh air. As it happened my father had an interesting appointment that evening.

He had a remarkable gift for mental arithmetic and could multiply any two numbers, each of up to five digits, in his head and give the answers within seconds. Unfortunately, I did not inherit this quality. All I could claim was a certain very limited numeracy. The senior chemist at Brothertons had mentioned this gift to the senior chemist at Lever Brothers, who treated the claim with incredulity, which he was prepared to back with a five-shilling bet.

A match was arranged, to take place in the tennis club nearby, which formed part of the Brotherton complex. The Lever man prepared five pairs of four-figure numbers and Dad was to be allowed fifteen seconds to give the answer to each sum. This was a good enough excuse for me to leave Shakespeare and Marlowe to accompany him and enjoy a few minutes' fresh air beside the tennis-court. The five shillings being duly handed over and the Lever side giving way to Brothertons, I paused to watch the tennis.

Mary, although I did not yet know her name, was on the court. It suddenly became blindingly clear to me that life was not designed for cramming the words of long dead poets, but that there was another world. The following weekend I hung up my running shoes and invested fifteen shillings in a tennis racket and another pound in membership of the club. A week later we both laid up our rackets and began 'walking out' together.

Her name was Mary Baldwin. She had been born at Diss in Norfolk where her father, the Rev. Daniel Baldwin, was the Congregational minister. He had moved from there to Fulbourn in Cambridgeshire, and then to a living in Nottinghamshire, where Mary had become ill. When she recovered, they decided to send her to a boarding-school in Sussex for ministers' daughters. While she was there, her father moved on again to Penrith in Cumbria. On leaving school in 1932, she joined her family and went to the local Gregg school to learn shorthand and typing. There was little employment available in the Lake District, but the school was conscientious with its graduates and found her a job with Lever Brothers, whose employees were allowed to join the Brothertons' tennis club.

One point we found in common was that we both went to the Congregational church at Rockferry, where the minister, Mr

Patterson, was a very fine preacher. We had not met because my parents, Marjorie and I used to go there in the morning, and Mary went to the evening service. Our first point of difference, when I told her about my Oxford scholarship, was that she was strongly pro-Cambridge. Her father had ties with the university and her brother had taken a very good degree there.

I was eighteen years and three months old, but this did not prevent me from informing her that I was going to marry her. I remember it was on the day that King George V opened the Mersey Tunnel, 4 July 1934. I also told her that I was going to become a Member of Parliament and, indeed, Prime Minister. Had she believed one word of all this, it would have been the end of a promising romance. What she would have preferred would have been to go through life as the wife of an Oxford don, a pleasure she was to enjoy for only a few brief months in 1945.

3

Topping the School

In October 1934 I went up to Jesus College, where I speedily learnt what hard work meant. In those days every student had to pass two examinations before qualifying for a degree. Classical students had to pass Honours Moderations after four terms and go on for the rest of four academic years for their finals – Greats. Mathematicians had an exam after one year, two for the less numerate, with two more years for finals.

Historians, economists, students of English language and literature had to face an examination invented by the devil. He could not have been a very learned devil: the exam was relatively simple and the marking easy. Most students essayed it in one term, others took two, before going on to serious work for the final honours school. But though the standard was low, the coverage was very wide: economics with three set books – Hubert Henderson's *Supply and Demand*, R.A. Lehfeldt's *Money*, Hugh Dalton's *Public Finance*; and Latin, with unseens and the mediaeval work *Gesta Francorum et Aliorum Hierosolimitanorum*. I doubt if I have ever worked so hard in my life, but most of us got through; by Christmas we were ready to enter on our final honours course.

I had never lived away from home and my first letters to my parents were full of domestic details and my attempt to maintain the pattern of family life. In the very first I reported:

I share a room with a Welsh Foundation scholar, A.H.J. Thomas of Tenby. He is an exceptionally nice fellow and we get on well. We seem to have similar tastes – both keen on running, neither on smoking or drinking and have similar views on food. Only five Freshers have put their names down for running, including me.

32

We have to have dinner in Hall five times a week. It's a very good one – four courses well cooked, good stuff. But we do not bother with College breakfast or lunch, which one has served in one's rooms. We had it on the first morning but after that we have had ordinary breakfast. We bought some cheese, small tins of paste, a tin of peas, some marmalade, butter, crackers, etc. and have had meat pies, very good ones, this morning; got some tomato sauce too. The books say battels should be kept below £2.5s. by avoiding extravagance but I expect we shall be a long way below that – probably under £2, because the £2.5s. appears to include cigarettes, beer as well as College lunch and breakfast, which are each about 1/6d. to 1/9d.

There are one or two wants:

1   I would like you please to send a travelling rug along, the thickest you have in the house. I am not cold as yet but there aren't many blankets and when the cold weather starts I expect it *will* be cold.

2   Will you send my old red blazer? It'll be useful for hanging about the rooms in, so as not to crease the sports coat. So far I use my grey pullover and hang the sports coat up.

3   I don't want my football boots as yet, and I don't really need a bike, this term anyway. I've only one lecture a week outside and Iffley Road is only a mile away.

4   About laundry. I think that for the first fortnight, I'll just send home my collars, handkies, vests, pants and socks; as shirts would have to go to the laundry at home I'll try them at this laundry first.

Have been to see the chaplain of Mansfield, a really nice fellow named Micklem. He gave me coffee and seemed glad to see me. . . . I am going to Mansfield tomorrow and then he is going to put me in touch with the Oxford Undergrad. Congregational Society and Discussion Group with a view to joining, as I probably shall.

That needs some elucidation. Mansfield was the Congregational theological college in those days, and the Principal, Dr Nathaniel

Micklem, was a substantial figure with whom I maintained close contact. In due course, Mary and I were married by him and her father in the chapel there. It was the one firm link in my upbringing that I never broke and it governed many of my attitudes. I see that in my first letter to my sister Marjorie, dated early in that October, I said:

> I went to a Coll. Discussion Group of the Anti-war Movement and soon made my presence felt. I tried to counteract the Labour element with the Christian lines of argument so to speak, advocating closer co-operation with the churches etc. I thoroughly enjoyed the services at Mansfield College and intend to go there every Sunday.

And so I did. It has often been said that Gladstone was a High Church radical, Attlee a Church of England radical and that I was the first Non-conformist radical Prime Minister. The tradition was very strong in Yorkshire and Lancashire and formed the basis of a substantial body of political opinion. My father had one catch-phrase that he often used to quote: 'What is morally wrong can never be politically right.' It was Morgan Phillips who said that the Labour Party owed more to Methodism than to Marx.

The pull of the apron-strings was still strong during this early period. After only a fortnight, I was writing home:

> My battels are £1.5s.0½d. You see, absence of beer and cigs and entertaining and afternoon tea and toast takes a lot off battel bills. I am just eating College breakfast, two fried eggs on toast, but it is nearly too much for me – *two* eggs.
>
> A.H.J. Thomas seems to get a lot sent from home. Is it worth it? It might pay to send butter (it is very dear here) next week with washing, also two oranges. What about lunch? I like lunches here but think 1/– is a lot for a plate of cold beef. Thomas has had a small boiled ham sent, it's lasting him OK. I suppose you could send a bit of meat of some kind.

The years of scouting also paid a dividend:

> Thomas has had a rough time. He is not very strong and hasn't been going out at all for walks. He fainted during a lecture on Friday. I immediately rendered first aid, while everybody else was clucking and fussing about. He seems all

right now ... I jolly well took charge of the affair. No one else knew any first aid and as it wasn't an ordinary faint, but a kind of apoplectic one, it required very different treatment, so I had to order people about for water. Lucky I took that ambulance course with Mr Jones last year or I wouldn't have known the difference in treatment between a 'white faint' and a 'red' one.

I was still dependent on home to keep my financial head above water. 'Can you please send some more cash?' I was writing in December. 'I shall want £2.5s. for tips, also £1 for fare on Thursday, I must get my ticket on Tuesday for advance luggage. We have had a lot of last minute tests, but I have done quite well. *Economics* I was top with a maximum mark. *French* joint top with one other. *Latin Set Book* joint top.'

I took little interest in political affairs during my first term, because the end-of-term examination involved so much cramming. One meeting of the Oxford University Labour Club was enough for me. What I felt I could not stomach was all those Marxist public school products rambling on about the exploited workers and the need for a socialist revolution. I was no doubt being as intolerant as they were. I had never read Marx – and still have not. It was that whacking great footnote on the second page which turned off any interest I might have sustained. This did not prevent me, when I had entered public life, on visits to the Soviet Union for trade negotiations, quoting yards of Marx at them which I had made up for the occasion. No one protested or sought to correct my version, no doubt considering it was all the fault of translation.

In my second term I went so far as to join the Liberals. Ignorance and vanity persuaded me that I might convert them to a middle-of-the road Colne Valley standpoint. I failed, but not before I had been drafted as Treasurer in my second term at Oxford. Viewed in the light of subsequent events, we were a strange team: Frank Byers, who was President in that term, was later a leading Member of Parliament and a peer; Raymond Walton was Honorary Secretary. He was to become Mr Justice Walton.

My financial efforts took a little time and were surprisingly successful, at least according to the student auditor. College secretaries of the club sent their collective subscriptions to me in cash, which I kept in an old suitcase under my bed in College. In my single term as Treasurer I paid off the whole accumulated debt, between £60 and £70, yet my total receipts, ignoring expenditure, were less than £50. Unfortunately, I had lost this magic touch by the time I became First Lord of the Treasury and neither of the Exchequer Chancellors whom I recommended for appointment showed any similar aptitude.

Not least because of my political ambitions, I wanted to go on to read economics, which in the Oxford of those days meant a Final Honours Course called Philosophy, Politics and Economics (PPE); but my scholarship was in history. The Principal of the College, Dr A.E.W. Hazel, a lawyer who had been Liberal MP for West Bromwich from 1906 to 1908, considered my application, which was subject to a serious snag. The PPE course involved, at the end of the day, a pass-or-fail test in two European languages. I had my distinction in French. The dons ruled that I could transfer from history to PPE if, on returning from the Christmas vacation, I passed an examination in German.

Before I left for the holidays my tutor lent me a book of German unseens. During the vacation, in addition to all the other reading prescribed for us on which we were to be examined when we returned on the first day of term, I had to grind away at these unseens. Came the day for the test and my tutor, Dr Albert Goodwin, later Professor of Nineteenth-century French History at the University of Manchester, chose unseen number 8 for me to do. I felt it right to point out that I had already worked through number 8 at home with the aid of a dictionary. He ordered me to get on with it. 'The College said you had to sit an examination and I was to set it. This is it. Number 8. Get on with it.'

Despite my familiarity with it, and his clear desire that I should get through, I barely passed, and he warned me that I would have to spend a lot more time on the language. In fact, I took the easy way out and bought the Hugo course in Italian, a language much easier for anyone who had studied French and Latin. In the Finals I had the same mark in Italian as French, although I could not have spoken one word of the language.

There was something of a prejudice in the College against economics. Only three of us sat the PPE examination in 1937. Now, I am told, there are more like thirty young men and women taking the course.

The pressure of work was unremitting, but I seemed to thrive on it. 'Have started lectures; they are fine', I wrote to my sister at the beginning of 1935.

So far I have had Lord Elton on 'Political History of the Nineteenth Century', Professor Zimmern on 'Some Fallacies in the Current Discussion of International Affairs', and on 'The Machinery of International Co-operation', and Dr Keith Feiling on 'English History in the Nineteenth Century'. I am going to a few more 'Principles of International Administration' by Professor Sir Arthur Salter and the 'Causes of War' by Dr Mendelssohn-Bartholdy. On Monday night I went to hear Sir Norman Angell on 'Pacifism is not enough'. I was talking to him afterwards: very nice to talk to. He autographed my copy of *The Unseen Assassins*.

I managed to keep reasonably fit. 'Just after breakfast this morning, the cross country captain came in and asked me to run for the varsity second team versus Reading AC,' I wrote to my parents. 'Well I ran. I started badly and after two miles was fourteenth out of a field of sixteen. After we had topped Shotover Hill, I got my second wind and moved a lot better. I caught up seven places in the last mile and finished seventh – the third Oxford man home.'

I continued to run occasionally for the University, both on the track and cross country, never getting near a blue. On another occasion, two or three of us trailing in a rearguard of our own, got lost on that same Shotover Hill. Our captain was Laurence MacIntyre, a New Zealander, whom I was to meet again in later life when he was his country's permanent representative to the United Nations. My track performances were just as undistinguished. My best times, if anyone were to record them today, would probably result in a series of prosecutions for loitering with intent.

In the Northern Counties AAA Championships, where we had staggered starts, I ran behind A.L. Littler of St Helens, who later won an Olympic medal. I eventually became his constituency MP and he came to see me, without knowing anything of my humble athletic record. I greeted him by saying that it was the first time I had seen his face, having in the past seen only his rear view rapidly disappearing into the far distance. My most signal appearance was when I paced Jack Lovelock, who had come down to Oxford in an attempt to break the world record for the two miles. With three others, we each gave him half a mile and he left us all standing, me more than the rest.

I continued to run both academic and athletic horses for quite a while. 'I averaged seven hours per day last week,' I was writing to my parents in May, 'which is very good in summer term and I went to the track four times. I am not wasting time going to see people and messing about in their rooms, for this is more interesting.' I had also been drawn into the circle of one of the major Oxford figures of the time, who was to play a considerable part in my later development:

> G.D.H. Cole's discussion classes are very good. About eight or ten of us in his room on settees while he offers cigs, sits down, smokes, gases and stops for discussion. It's rather good to put questions to a man like him. Tutes with Knox are very fine. We get into all sorts of arguments – we are meant to really. I was slating Locke for something and Knox began defending him. We worked through chemistry to geometry and back to philosophy and in the end he said there was a lot in my criticism. He thinks I have a penetrating mind which should be useful in philosophy.

T.M. Knox was the philosophy tutor at Jesus to whom I had owed my place. I am greatly in his debt. He always found a lot of time for me and was most encouraging. I reported to my parents in the autumn of 1935:

> Knox sent for me on Monday to set me an essay and he mentioned the paper I had done for him the day after coming up. He said I had put in a lot of work on it during the vac. and had showed knowledge of the whole of Kant, whereas very few people get past half way, even in their whole degree course. He had set me two papers, both Final Honours papers 1935 – one on Kant as a special subject, which I am not taking, and one general one on the history of philosophy which I am.
>
> The first question I had done – he said, 'Therefore it must have been your favourite' – was one he had set in the Finals paper. He said that no Modern Greats candidate had done it. As he was very interested in the subject he had questioned them all on it in their *viva*. He found that they had all shirked it either because they had not read so far or had not understood. He said he was very pleased both because I had tackled it and because he liked my treatment. Good old Knox!

38

In my second year I took off virtually two terms to submit an essay for the Gladstone Memorial Prize. The subject chosen was dear to my heart: 'The State and the Railways 1823–63'. As always, Bert Goodwin gave me a reading list, the footnotes and bibliographies of which led me to more and more publications. I gave up athletics and abandoned the Iffley Road running track for two terms of afternoons in the Bodleian Library. In the College vacation I used to travel by the Mersey Ferry from Birkenhead to Liverpool to study in the Picton Library there. With Liverpool's contribution to the early history of the railway, it had many relatively unknown works to add to the Oxford store.

The rules governing the Gladstone Prize laid down 12,500 words as the length, but Bert Goodwin told me that meant not more than 18,000 – an early example of academic inflation. When the text was finished it had to be typed by an agency at the cost of 1s.3d. per 1,000 words – 6.25p in decimal currency, a good indication of our post Second World War monetary inflation. In March of the following year I was telling my parents, 'Handing in the Gladstone tomorrow. Will bring spare copy home with me. The result should be well on its way now. . . . I wish I had a chance – it would be worth winning.'

When the news was published that the Gladstone Prize had returned to Jesus College, ten years after Bert Goodwin himself had won it, I found myself caught by a College custom. At dinner in Hall, any successful prizewinner had to ask the dons' High Table in writing, in Latin, for permission to introduce at his expense the big sconce, a large drinking vessel holding some very potent beer from, I think, a Welsh brewery. On such occasions, the prizewinner has the first draught, wipes the rim and passes it round, a thoroughly insanitary proceeding.

Over the next year and a half I was called upon to repeat this expensive practice on winning the Webb Medley Junior and Senior Economics scholarships. Best College 'old' then cost ninepence a pint. On the third occasion, not really relishing the drink myself, I ordered cider and was roundly condemned by my colleagues who took a sip, diagnosed the drink, and passed it on with appropriate comments, not in Latin but very basic English. The prize was worth £100, a huge sum of money in those days, but I was not being overthrifty, as a high proportion of it had to be taken in books.

Meanwhile, I struggled to understand the mysteries of economics, to say nothing of philosophy. My tutorials were all held in other colleges. My tutor at Jesus, Bert Goodwin, dealt with economic history. However, his range of knowledge did not extend to the specialized subjects. I came back from one vacation and rather naughtily put to him three or four really loaded questions for his elucidation. He just laughed and said, 'I haven't got a clue', or words to that effect. 'If you are going to keep coming up with questions like that, the sooner you get an out-of-college tutor the better.'

He put me on to four of them. Lindley Fraser had just left Queens to become a professor at Aberdeen, but he came to Oxford for a day each week to teach us. I also went to Maurice Allen at Balliol, a very strange person who used to dance round the room a lot when he was going into some great subtlety, but he was a brilliant economic theorist. I also went to R.F. Bretherton of Wadham on economic organization and to R.B. McCallum of Pembroke for political institutions. He was also the Oxford correspondent of the *Manchester Guardian* and at a crucial later point in my career recommended me to the paper for a job.

At the beginning of my third year, I sat with a few dozen contemporaries for the George Webb Medley Junior Economics Scholarship. Who George Webb Medley was I had no idea. I only learned in due course that he was a fanatical free trader who used his wealth to fight for free trade against the protectionist campaign dating from Joseph Chamberlain's day. I found the paper distinctly difficult and was surprised to read on the College notice-board that I had won. That was worth another £100, and I began to feel like a millionaire.

In May I sat for my Finals, getting off to a good start on the Thursday morning with a philosophy paper, which had sufficient questions that I roughly understood. In the afternoon, the economic history paper was more than I could have decently prayed for. The first question was on the subject of my railway history prize, on which I spent rather too much time. My answer criticized one of the examiners who, in a book review, had attributed a particular policy to Gladstone. The facts were that the House of Commons Clerk had, by accident, tabled a Motion for debate and attributed it to him. He had had to move a Resolution withdrawing it and substituting the correct draft.

The next morning I was cut down to size when I saw the economics theory paper. Hardly a question was comprehensible to me. Those I essayed took nearly half the time allotted for the morning, and as I ploughed on with it, I tried almost in vain to finalize a geometric diagram which I hope would prove something or other. After a long struggle, I nearly crossed it out and even contemplated walking out, safe in the knowledge that I was sure of my alpha for the previous day and hoping that the later papers would be easier to deal with. However, I sat it out and was surprised to be told when the results were published that I had been given an alpha plus for the morning's work, the only one given, I was told, since the PPE school had been established. This statement was repeated later by an Oxford don of those days, now a peer, Lord Longford.

I had run closer to the wind than I realized. For a term I had been Secretary of the Oxford Economic Student Group. My predecessor had invited a don from Magdalen, an Englishman who had done all his work in America, to address us. I took him out for a cup of coffee after his lecture and asked him what he thought about John Maynard Keynes, whose new book had come out at the end of my second year, although I had only managed to read about four pages a day of it with difficulty. 'This is the most evil book published in our science in the present generation. Its effect has been unmitigatedly malicious,' my guest pronounced. Thank God I don't have him as a tutor, I thought. I then learned that he was going to be our examiner in Final Underschools. He did at least give me an alpha. In the event, out of eighteen marks (two examiners, nine papers), I had seventeen alphas or alpha minuses and one beta query treble plus.

There remained the *viva voce*, the oral confrontation we all had to go through. Conscious that on a general question on William Pitt in my political history paper I had disguised my ignorance by describing his record on parliamentary reform as 'apathetic', and guessing that the examiners might seize on this looseness of expression, I looked up the whole story in a life of Pitt in the Liverpool Public Library. When the day came, with some forty of us watching the tortures of our colleagues under examination, I was eventually called. The chairman of the examiners began by saying that he had been asked by his colleagues to congratulate me on the 'universal high quality' of my papers, but they had to put a question to me. It was, in fact, the expected one on Pitt. I had been so taken aback by the congratulations that I could only stumble out my carefully researched answer. One of the examiners later told me that a colleague had whispered to him: 'Damn good thing this fellow isn't being viva-ed for his First.'

Later that day, a colleague of mine in College, J.W. Sykes, who only got a Third but went into the Indian Civil Service and rose very high, asked Professor T.M. Knox, my tutor, who was packing his bags to return to St Andrews: 'I take it Wilson has got his First?' 'Yes,' Knox replied, 'he's topped the School.'

I was faced with looking for a job. I had little hope of a Research Scholarship. The George Webb Medley Senior Scholarship of £300 a year, we had been told, would go to one of three of us who had won the Webb Medley Junior. The other two were E.F. Jackson of Magdalen, already a graduate of Birmingham University, who had won it at the beginning of his second year, and J. Taylor of University College, Oxford, who had won it in my year. The funds of the endowment were obviously flourishing at the time. I saw little hope of beating Jackson and, on the kind recommendation of R.B. McCallum, I wrote to W.P. Crozier, the editor of the *Manchester Guardian*, who immediately offered me a vacation job. It was, I discovered, a practice of the paper to recruit temporaries during the holiday period and to offer one or two permanent appointments if they showed promise. In that very paper the Monday before my *viva*, there was an announcement from Oxford that I had been awarded the Webb Medley Senior Scholarship at the full rate of £300. I knew that I must have got my First and that the examiners had passed on the news to the Trustees.

What should have been a period of unalloyed pleasure and promise was marred by domestic disaster. Just when I was achieving academic success, my father lost his job at Brothertons. Mary and the family had shared and rejoiced in my progress. I had spent every vacation at home. Mary had found comfortable digs and was always welcome with my parents. At least once a term, when she was able to find a Saturday and Sunday free from her job at Lever Brothers, they used to pile into my father's car, now a Jowett, and starting at six o'clock in the morning, make the long journey to Oxford to spend the weekend with me, returning on the Sunday afternoon.

Mary and I were firmly resolved to marry, although she was a little shocked when she discovered that I took the occasional glass of beer, and absolutely horrified when she discovered that Dr Micklem was not averse to the same practice. It was merely a question of finding a settled job and secure future, but now this crisis was upon us.

I was finding it necessary to devote some part of my prize money to help pay the rent on my parents' flat, which they were still allowed to occupy. This situation continued for nearly eighteen months, when my father managed to find another job far away at Liskeard in Cornwall. He had been put in touch with two brothers who manufactured explosives for blasting. The rules required that manufacture could only proceed if someone with my father's qualifications were employed to supervise. He made the long journey alone, lived in digs and, in due course, my mother and Marjorie joined him there.

I did not have to take up the *Guardian* offer, but returned to Oxford, where my academic record had opened up a much wider opportunity.

4

Breakfasts with Beveridge

The lifeline had been thrown by Sir William Beveridge, who had just left the London School of Economics to take over the Mastership of University College, Oxford. He was also engaged in a massive research project on 'The Demand for Labour in Great Britain', a sequel to the historic study he had made of unemployment when he was an assistant commissioner with Sydney and Beatrice Webb on the Royal Commission on the Poor Law 1906–9, the year in which he published his classic *Unemployment – A Problem of Industry*, updated in 1930.

He had written to two of his former LSE lecturers, now at Oxford, asking them to nominate a young graduate to act as his research assistant. Both of them recommended me and he wrote to say that I had the job, provided I could finance myself with a research fellowship. In these days of more lavish funding of research projects, often of a less fundamental nature, it seems incredible that a man of Beveridge's distinction had to make this condition. The Webb Medley Senior Scholarship solved that problem. At his suggestion I tabled the title of my projected doctoral thesis as 'Aspects of the Demand for Labour in Great Britain' in order to conform. It has to be said that it is still not written to this day. I can reasonably claim that in a wider sense, I was later working on and seeking to enhance the demand for labour in and between five general elections.

Beveridge duly arrived at Oxford and set about reforming the College, not neglecting the smallest detail, right down to the cooking utensils in the kitchen. He installed vast flat-topped ovens, but all the large cooking pots were round-bottomed, fitting in the circular holes on the existing stoves. The cost of new vessels was a major preoccupation during the first term for the domestic bursar's finances.

44

I found him a devil to work for. The long summer vacation lasted nearly four months; in my first after joining him, he allotted me three weeks' holiday. The rest of the time I was required to spend with him at his cottage at Avebury in Wiltshire, which he claimed was the oldest house in England. All our research work was done in an uncomfortable room we shared above the barn. Early rising was not my forte but Beveridge, after a swim in the coldest water I have ever known, kindly awakened me each morning at seven with a cup of tea. After dressing, without a swim, I put in a stint of two hours' work with him before breakfast, a formidable meal presided over by his cousin and constant companion for many years, Mrs Jessie Mair.

Where Beveridge was difficult to live with, she was almost impossible. I think even he was frightened of her. The worst part of it was that I had to partner her most evenings at bridge, after dinner. Contract was the least of my achievements, and each hand was followed by an acrimonious inquest. The only relief was when we had visitors or occasionally drove into the neighbouring market town for dinner.

In spite of it all, Beveridge himself remained very much attached to her. Only once did she upset him in my presence. She was mowing the quite extensive lawn at Avebury. It was a hot day and he had taken off his brown sports jacket, probably quite an expensive garment for those days, and laid it down just off the lawn. Her petrol-driven lawn-mower got out of control, ran into the rough and took unto itself Beveridge's jacket. When this was abstracted from the machine, the whole of one side consisted of one-and-a-half-inch strips of Cotswold worsted. Beveridge insisted on wearing it, ribbons and all, for the rest of the afternoon and even at dinner.

The first euphoria of being invited to work with the great man was soon dissipated by the boring nature of our research. We were engaged in a study of the unemployment figures for the cyclical period 1927–37. He was not sure whether the downturn had began in 1927 or 1929 and felt that there was a hiccup between the two earlier dates with a small recovery in 1928. He had done his first calculations on his great wooden slide-rule, more than a yard long, made of thin strips of wood mounted on green baize. I preferred to use a small cylindrical Otis King. He then invested in a hand-operated calculating machine with a forward and reverse rotating mechanism. Some months later our task was eased by a grant from the Rockefeller Foundation, providing £350 for one year to pay a young lady to operate this formidable machine. She was always referred to by Beveridge as his 'calculating woman'.

In those days the *Ministry of Labour Monthly Gazette* published the unemployment figures for some ninety-odd separate industries and Beveridge was hoping that we would be able to demonstrate two facts: one, that each cyclical depression and recovery began in the export industries, transmitting misery to the rest of the economy, where the figures lagged behind; and two, that the capital industries began their fall later but declined far more than the consumer industries.

I was fortunately able to obtain some relief from this routine and an additional source of income, when I also began teaching at New College, famous for its Winchester connection. As the PPE school became more popular, the economics tutor, Henry Phelps-Brown, became overworked with too many pupils and the College decided to appoint an 'extraordinary lecturer with teaching duties' at £125 per annum, plus free dining rights. Phelps-Brown approached me and said that he had recommended me as a candidate for the post and would I come to take tea with the Warden, H.A.L. Fisher, the famous historian and former Minister of Education in the Lloyd George wartime administration. He was also successor to the famous Warden Spooner, from whom the word 'spoonerism' was coined.

The tea party, some eight of us, was very formal. Fisher began by saying, 'The conversation will be in French.' The reason for this was that the principal guest was Jean Giraudoux, the famous French playwright, whose son, a New College undergraduate, was in some trouble with the College authorities. At one point, Fisher turned to me and referred to his appointment of my uncle Jack as the first ever His Majesty's Inspector of Education of Technical Colleges, which had occurred in 1917.

Fisher then retired with Giraudoux senior and I was kept waiting for what seemed hours. When the Warden came out, he shook my hand and sent his regards to my uncle who, as I had already told him, had been dead for some years. My hopes fell. I was not even interviewed. Then I learned that the College had already acted on Phelps-Brown's recommendation. The tea party had been a formality.

My first pupil was David Worswick, for many years the distinguished head of the National Institute for Economic and Social Research. He had already graduated in mathematics but was continuing for an extra year in preparation for the Home Civil Service entry examination. The College said that he must take a course of tuition and he chose the economics diploma. In addition, because of pressures on the teaching staff, the third year PPE candidates had had no tuition in 'Economic Organization' – the facts as opposed to the theories – and because of this mistake they simply had to be crammed. I therefore took a regular class, as well as tutorials, two pupils at a time, and a most distinguished group they were. One was Hugh Seton-Watson, later one of the world's leading historians of Russia both in Czarist and post-revolutionary times.

Most of my pupils at New College were Wykehamists. There have always been strong ties between the two institutions. These products of Winchester shared one trait in common: they were all extremely bright and, after a couple of tutorials with me, more or less allowed it to be known that they knew more economics than I would ever know. This was a characteristic about which I had been warned many years earlier by my father, who had a deep knowledge of the Bible, which he used to discuss with me. He developed a strong antipathy to St Paul, whom he used to call the Wykehamist among the disciples, because he was slightly superior and always absolutely certain that he was right. Several Americans also came my way, including a delightful young man named Harlan Cleveland, who quickly graduated to become a presidential adviser on his return to the United States and whom we shall meet again in that capacity.

Many of my pupils reading PPE had been tutored in philosophy right up to the previous term by Richard Crossman. He voluntarily left the College because of his impending divorce. This did not in fact, even in those days, constitute grounds for resignation, although New College under Fisher was stricter than most. What I learned from my pupils was their unbounding admiration for him as a teacher. For example, he was a dedicated Platonist, but if one of his pupils read a pro-Platonic essay, whether hoping to please Dick, or out of conviction, Crossman for the rest of the tutorial annihilated him with the most devastating Aristotelian logic.

This was a good trait in a teacher, although some of my fellow economists, embattled on one side or the other over Keynes' *General Theory*, would have regarded such behaviour as treachery. Many years later I was to find that it was not an endearing trait in a Cabinet meeting. To take one example, Dick was one of the most dedicated friends of Israel, ever since his membership in 1946 of the Anglo–American Commission on Palestine. When during the Six Day War between Israel and Egypt in 1967, such former pro-Arabs as George Brown, the Foreign Secretary, and others supported Israel, Dick became the Arabs' best friend, on the grounds, as he told me, that some of his colleagues were supporting Israel for the wrong reasons.

After two terms at New College I moved to University College. The number of students reading PPE was rapidly increasing and was proving too much for G.D.H. Cole, who, in addition to being Economics Fellow of the College, was Reader in Economics in the University, and had been one of my examiners two years earlier in the Webb Medley Junior Scholarship. Again my pupils included several Americans, among them Stephen Bailey, who was to become a diplomat and American Ambassador to China.

I had long held G.D.H. Cole in high regard and found this closer contact with him most congenial. He was a good-looking man, of medium height with a good head of hair, and most attractive in speech and address, except for the manner of his lectures. I had attended a number of them, which he delivered at great speed, eyes down, without a single note. His special subjects were economic organization and history, and he concentrated on these. I was left to teach economic theory, not the area I preferred.

I took to spending most Tuesday and Wednesday evenings with him, helping with copy for and proofs of his articles for the *New Statesman and Nation*. When the work was finished, he used to pour out for each of us a glass of Irish whisky, which he preferred to Scotch. On one of these occasions he was celebrating his fiftieth birthday. He announced that he had made a resolution, to foreswear all reading of books and concentrate on writing them. He was already publishing at least one a year in addition to his other writings. For the most part they were highly topical and dated rather quickly but some, particularly those on economic history, have survived.

It was G.D.H. Cole as much as any man who finally pointed me in the direction of the Labour Party. His social and economic theories made it intellectually respectable. My attitudes had been clarifying for some time and the catalyst was the unemployment situation. I had seen it years before in the Colne Valley, with members of my class jobless when they left school. My own father was still enduring his second painful period out of work. My religious upbringing and practical studies of economics and unemployment in which I had been engaged at Oxford combined in one single thought: unemployment was not only a severe fault of government, but it was in some way evil, and an affront to the country it afflicted.

Although not a member of the University Labour Club I had by this time joined the Oxford University Labour Party. At that time, the University, as with Cambridge, the combined English universities and learned establishments in Scotland, Wales and Northern Ireland, returned two Members of Parliament. In 1939 we had a by-election caused by the elevation of Sir Arthur Salter to the House of Lords. There was great anxiety and criticism of Chamberlain's 'appeasement' of Hitler. That great entertainer A.P. Herbert stood and defeated the ruling Tory Party's candidate Quintin Hogg, now Lord Hailsham, and still at the time of writing a member of Mrs Thatcher's administration. Labour ran Frank Pakenham and there was great pressure on him to stand down in favour of Herbert under the slogan of 'To Hell with Hogg and Hitler'.

One of the fascinations of Senior Common Room life was the evenings spent with tutors discussing a wide variety of subjects. In New College I had spent a great deal of time with Professor Alfred Zimmerman, Montague Burton Professor of International Relations, originally a Greek scholar. He wanted to know everything, especially about organizations such as Lever Brothers, whose iniquities, as I saw them, were coloured by Mary's accounts of her employers. If Aristotle were alive today, he pronounced, it would be of Lever Brothers and other large industrial organizations that he would be writing.

At University College, I learned a great deal from Duncan Gardner, Professor of Bacteriology, and later Regius Professor of Medicine, and the chemistry tutor, Dr E.J. Bowen. In addition to his teaching duties, Dr Bowen had a part-time assignment. When College Feasts were held, or College or University Clubs had their dinners, or on the last night of term, students were in a celebratory mood. On a tip-off from one of the College servants, he would go along the corridor from the front lodge to the little marble hall, where the death of the former University College student, Percy Bysshe Shelley, is commemorated in a nude statue of him as he lay after being washed up from the sea. On such nights Bowen was armed with a special liquid detergent he made in his laboratory, containing all the substances necessary to remove the ink with which the more intimate parts of the poet had been decorated. This was not the easiest of tasks, as year by year the students became more and more sophisticated in their choice of raw materials.

At the end of my first year's work with Beveridge, I had been able to disprove even to his satisfaction his belief that unemployment was purely frictional and that there was no army of labour genuinely seeking work. The numbers registering for work at the employment exchanges were broadly comparable, except in the depressed areas, with the numbers of unfilled vacancies recorded in the week's register. Beveridge arranged for me to spend a few weeks visiting employment exchanges in the area where unemployment was relatively low and examine the vacancy records in association with Mr A. Reader of the Ministry of Labour's Statistical Branch.

A number of them, mainly in the Midlands, South and Outer London, were in areas which were experiencing, in comparative terms, a mini-boom, partly as a result of the arms orders which began to be placed as Hitler's threats became more strident. The payment of unemployment benefit in those days was conditional on the applicant's proving that he was 'genuinely seeking work'. When he went to the employment exchange to sign on, he was given a card to take to a factory within the exchange area to see if a vacancy which had been notified was still open. An unemployed man was paid eighteen shillings a week, the figure to which benefit had been reduced from one pound in the 1931 'emergency cuts' when the National Government was formed.

I examined literally thousands of these job application cards and kept careful records of them. Not one in twenty led to a job. In most cases, as one would expect, a firm requiring a few more 'hands' would register the vacancy, while being ready to employ any suitable man who came to the factory looking for work, or any available former employee. In some cases the would-be applicant had to walk five or even ten miles, wearing out his boots and having to pay the cost of repairs out of his eighteen shillings, and this in the more prosperous boom towns of Britain.

When I started working with Beveridge, I soon found that, although he was ruthless at getting at the facts and drove me as hard as he drove himself, he had certain ingrained views about unemployment, still derived from the historic study he had made in 1909. At that time, unemployment as a recognized social factor was relatively new, although it had always been there. Indeed I discovered that the word first appeared in the *Oxford English Dictionary* less than twenty years before Beveridge began his studies. Beveridge was the first major figure to subject the problem to serious analysis, based partly on the figures he was able to obtain through the Poor Law Commission and partly through his characteristically humane work at Toynbee Hall in East London, where both he and, later, Attlee first became aware of the 'social problem'.

The main conclusion in his original work had been that unemployment was mostly frictional, seasonal in certain trades, aggravated by technological and structural change, but principally due to ignorance of the unemployed of the jobs that in any normally working society would be available. This had led to his appointment by Winston Churchill to set up the British system of labour exchanges and he become its first director. Even with the elimination of frictional problems, as far as administratively possible, by the time I joined him Beveridge was still not able to recognize that there could be in a modern society a permanent and inbuilt under-demand for labour. Equilibrium as then understood could be maintained at a level far below the full economic capacity of the country, measured in terms of the employable labour force.

True, he had come to accept the trade cycle but the 1930 edition of his book, *Unemployment,* though revised, still consisted largely of a reprint of the 1910 edition. It was again based on voluminous statistics and, as Beveridge himself admitted before he died, reached the wrong conclusions. He had gone so far as to accept the Hawtrey thesis about the monetary causation of the trade cycle and accepted it uncritically. I used to pull his leg, always a slightly dangerous thing to do, about a chart in his book called 'The Birth and Life of the Trade Cycle'. He dated the birth as 1844 with the passing of the Bank Charter Act.

Later, after I had spent a long month digging out all available figures on cyclical fluctuation from before 1815 to 1844, I submitted a paper to him called 'The Ante-Natal History of the Trade Cycle'. I had learnt that, in dealing with this former civil servant, any communication had to be put on paper in the form of a short minute, otherwise, despite one's insistence or persuasion, one would be asked days or weeks or months later why one had not told him. I remember he was particularly excited about the figures on railway construction in my Gladstone Prize essay on railway history, which had a table showing the violent cyclical fluctuation in the construction of track.

He responded to this evidence by conceding that there had been a trade cycle before the date he had ordained and, as a result of our collaboration, he was more than ready to feel that the answer did not lie wholly or even mainly in monetary movements. It was not until more persuasive economists than I were able to influence him that he accepted that there was still under-demand for labour, even in terms of cyclical boom, and under-demand going beyond the figures of the frictional theories.

The summer before the war he was driven on a short tour by one of our colleagues in the University Common Room, the Rev. John Wild, who as a curate in the north-east had been very active in organizing camps for the young unemployed from depressed areas. He was, I think, more than a little shocked when Beveridge commented that the campers seemed very good types, so he could not understand why they did not go out and get work.

Even with the unemployment figures cyclically increasing, Beveridge had not been impressed by Keynes' analysis, because he regarded him as a theorist. Beveridge felt that one could only get at the facts by a lot of hard slogging through the figures and case studies. Both G.D.H. Cole and I tried hard to persuade him to accept some of the basic principles of Keynes' argument, but our efforts were in the main unavailing.

It was during this last pre-war year that I paid what was still only my third visit to London. My father had taken me there in 1923 and my mother and I had made an overnight stop in 1926 before sailing to Australia. The Fabian Society had decided to produce a book on different experiences of public regulation as opposed to public ownership. G.D.H. Cole suggested to them that I should write the chapter on the railways. The meeting at the Society's premises in London was chaired by Michael Stewart, who was to be, a quarter of a century later, Foreign Secretary in the 1964–70 Labour Government. I duly wrote my chapter, but the war intervened and the book was never published.

I had also become the proud possessor of a car. It was a 1931 Austin 7, covered with brown fabric, and it cost me £11 from an Oxford dealer. I used this to drive back to Merseyside in the College vacations to see Mary at Bebington. In the summer of 1939 I took her down to Crawley in Sussex to visit her old school, Milton Mount. Just before the war broke out I sold the car for £3/15s. in part exchange for a seven-year-old, ten-horsepower Wolsey Hornet, which cost £25. I took Beveridge to see it. 'Very noble,' he said, feeling he had to make some comment.

He had also met Mary. She came down for the last Commemoration Ball at University College before the war. Mrs Mair gave two large parties for him at his lodgings. He took part in all the festivities but struck one note of gloom. A number of us were sitting with him when he looked up and pronounced magisterially: 'This is the ball before Waterloo.' Indeed a number of the people there did not survive the war.

He had suggested to the economics section of the British Association that I should read a paper on our joint work at their annual conference, which that year was at St Andrews. Meanwhile, the world was falling apart. Hitler invaded Poland at dawn on 1 September, just as the British Association was embarking on its ritual of the presentation of papers and discussions. There was little to hear but the roar of car exhausts as I read my paper. One distinguished statistician was not however on the road. For him statistical method took priority over Hitler. He stayed to hear my paper and then on sound academic grounds savaged my intrepid venture into the mysteries of correlation co-efficients.

By this time Mary had gone to live with her parents in Preesall, near Fleetwood, where her father had become minister of the local Congregational church. I called in there on my way south, picked up Mary and drove on crowded roads to Oxford.

On the date appointed for my age group, I registered at the local employment exchange under the Military Service Act. As for millions of others, the immediate situation was unclear. Call-up was slow. 'Specialists', as I had been categorized, were not wanted anywhere. The College would not reconvene until the second week of October. After some days, the employment exchange found 'war work' for me. The Potato Marketing Board, one of the statutory producer-dominated cartel schemes of the 1930s, by this time dignified by the title Potato Control, Ministry of Food, was being evacuated to Oxford. An economist would surely be needed.

In fact my services were hardly required. The 'War Book', based on the assumption of immediate bombing by Hitler's Luftwaffe, was temporarily inoperative. That, however, did not prevent our receiving a report, never properly checked, that the whole of the potato lifting of those autumn days had been directed to a small Scottish town, I think Pitlochry. All was soon re-established, but there was no work for 'control'. Established trade channels were functioning normally. Meanwhile, pending approval of a formal appointment, I was registered as a temporary clerk grade III with a weekly pay cheque of just over £3. Mary had also been to the labour exchange and found herself directed to the same organization. She was living in a room over a café, which cost her £2 a week, and had her meals in the restaurant.

When term began, I returned to College, mainly occupied by service trainees and overseas students. I still had my rooms there, but since younger College servants had been called-up or had volunteered, we had breakfast and lunch in the Senior Common Room. Our medical tutor, Dr Gardner, upset some of his colleagues by proposing for membership a new research colleague of his, just arrived from Vienna, named Ernst Chain. I remember thinking that Beveridge and I would not have asked a similar favour for our research assistant. Moreover, this newcomer spoke hardly any English. A few days later we opened our morning papers and found that Ernst Chain had been awarded the Nobel Prize for medicine with Professors Florey and Fleming for inventing some curative with the then unknown name of penicillin.

During those first months of the war, life at Oxford, although with a diminishing undergraduate population, went on much as usual. The College still held its 'gaudy' at the end of the December term, attended by Clement Attlee, himself a University College graduate. The dons crowded round him to get the latest news. All the talk, particularly among older dons who had fought in the First World War, was of Churchill. Should he not be sent for? When will he be sent for? Attlee was dismissive: 'Not Churchill. Sixty-five, old for a Churchill.'

Mary and I had made up our minds that the time had come to marry. The first person I felt should know was Beveridge. We often used to go for a walk together in the afternoon. 'But you can't,' was his response. 'Well, we can,' I said. He insisted: 'No, it is contrary to the College Statutes, which say that no member of the College can get married until they have spent three years there.' 'Well, strangely, what it says only applies to full Fellows,' I replied. 'It doesn't apply to my kind of apprentice Fellow.' 'A fortiori,' he insisted. 'Well,' I said, 'either in Latin or in English, I am only concerned with the text.' Half an half later he was in my room, saying '. . . but you were right. . . .'

On 1 January 1940 Mary and I were married in the Mansfield College chapel. The ceremony was conducted by the Principal, Dr Nathaniel Micklem, and by her father, who came down specially for the occasion with the rest of her family. My best man was Pat Duncan, a classical scholar who had become my closest friend while we were both at Jesus. He later went into the Indian Civil Service and was killed on the North-West Frontier after the war.

Our original plan had been to go to the Isles of Scilly for our honeymoon, but the onset of war made it impossible to organize the journey. Instead we went just a few miles from Oxford to The Old Swan at Minster Lovell. Beveridge imposed a limit even on that. He considered that five days was quite long enough for a honeymoon and required my presence at a conference on employment statistics the Saturday after the wedding. He did relent to the extent of giving us two rather handsome red glass flower bowls as a wedding present. Mary and I settled down in a furnished one-room flat in South Parks Road to await what events would bring.

5

Whitehall in Wartime

In April 1940, I received a telephone call from Stanley Dennison, the Economics Professor at Newcastle, whom I had come to know as a result of my speech to the economics section of the British Association. He was by now working in the Cabinet Office on a wartime assignment as Economic Adviser to Monsieur Jean Monnet, Chairman in London of the Anglo–French Co-ordinating Committee, concerned with the economic and trade aspects of the Alliance. They needed a research statistician. The low salary being offered was made up, as in other cases, by my College.

Mary and I moved to London, where I began work in the extension of the Scotland Yard building, next door to Richmond Terrace, opposite Downing Street on the east side of Whitehall. We rented a small, two-roomed flat in a block in Twickenham, partly furnishing it on the never-never by the grace of the Times Furnishing Company for an outlay of £150. We simply did not have the capital to buy the items outright.

I cannot say that I enjoyed my first experience of working in London. I had brought with me a healthy set of provincial prejudices that all the real work was done in places like Yorkshire, Lancashire and the Potteries, and that London was the Wen where the spivs were making all the profits at the workers' expense. I was comfortable in the company of my academic colleagues and we rather tended to keep to ourselves. Our activities provided an agreeable glimpse of a wider world, but I took no part in the life of the capital and commuted every evening back to Twickenham and Mary.

On 10 May, Hitler invaded Holland and Belgium, pushed back the Allied forces and entered France. On the same day Churchill became Prime Minister. By the 15th, Premier Reynaud was telephoning him early in the morning to report the German breakthrough near Sedan. Monnet's French colleague, Robert Marjolin, immediately disappeared in full military uniform on his way to France to help rescue his and Monnet's relatives. He accomplished this task after hair-raising adventures crossing the fluid front lines, and survived to become the post-war Secretary-General of the Organization for European Economic Co-operation (OEEC).

The collapse of France brought the demise of the Anglo–French Co-ordinating Committee. The British members, Stanley Dennison and myself along with our staff, were merged with the economics section of the War Cabinet Secretariat under Professor John Jewkes. Churchill had moved his own economic team, headed by Professor Lindemann, into Number 10. This was the cause of some friction. I had known Lindemann at Oxford and did not have a great deal of respect for him. His rudeness upset people and some very good Civil Service Permanent Secretaries had a rough time with him. He enjoyed the 100-per-cent backing of Churchill and became a power in the land.

The Jewkes' team concentrated mainly on the economic co-ordination of the principal relevant departments. We were involved almost full time on forward estimates of industrial manpower requirements. With Britain virtually alone, and with American supplies still only a trickle, we were concerned with the manning of the Royal Ordnance factories and the privately owned engineering works, in particular with the transfer to them of skilled workers from factories still producing consumer goods. I did a quick tour of the main areas involved, including some I had visited in my days with Beveridge. There was no marked shortage of labour overall, indeed there was a surplus in some areas. Registered unemployment still totalled 767,000 after nine months of war. But in the principal munitions factories, above all in aircraft and tank production, there was a chronic shortage of skilled engineers and a considerable lack even of semi-skilled.

The members of the War Cabinet Secretariat had to share in the roster of more general duties, and Jewkes and I were on night duty on the occasion of one of the most important transatlantic telephone conversations of the war. The battle of France was over. The British army, by a miracle, had been saved from capture by the Dunkirk operation, but the massed German army, navy and air force were on the French beaches poised to invade. The military assessments at the time set at less than evens our prospects of resisting the onslaught.

57

The British Government had approached President Roosevelt with a request for the loan or sale of fifty over-age destroyers to safeguard the Channel coasts and strengthen the convoy protection of our supplies of raw materials and food from the Americas. Our telephone rang. It was President Roosevelt on the line asking to speak to Churchill. American presidents too often forget the five hours' difference in clock time, as I was to find out to my cost in later years. Jewkes and I had the responsibility of waking Winston, who had gone to bed after, to put it mildly, a pretty thick night. We took the cowards' way out and decided to waken the Cabinet Secretary, Sir Edward Bridges. He phoned Number 10, and a sleepy, very grumpy Churchill replied.

Roosevelt told him that he had been taking soundings in Congress about the transfer of the fifty destroyers, and was satisfied that there was sufficient goodwill towards the project for him to send the ships under an Executive Act, without going through the procedure of legislation by Congress. But he must ask Churchill for an assurance. He was sure, of course, that Britain would successfully resist the planned German invasion from across the Channel, a prospect neither statesman could view with absolute certainty. But should the Germans get a successful foothold, he wanted Churchill's personal undertaking that in such circumstances the ships would be sent back across the Atlantic to American or Canadian ports. Churchill replied: 'Certainly I give you that assurance, Mr President. But that is a fate far more likely to befall the *Narzhi* fleet than the British,' the offending word being spoken *fortissimo*.

Churchill was always the master of the telling phrase. At one juncture he had become dissatisfied with the quality and content of BBC overseas broadcasts to neutral countries, feeling that they were too dispassionate and wanting them to be more specific in describing Britain's growing strength and will to resist, even if this involved taking occasional liberties with the facts. He summoned Sir John Reith, the Director-General, an immensely tall man and a very pious and deeply religious Scot of distinctly grim demeanour. Churchill tried to persuade him that the overseas broadcasts should be more optimistic in tone, but Reith was brooking no interference with his editorial integrity and the meeting ended in stalemate. After Sir John had been shown out, Churchill could be heard grumbling, 'Don't let that wuthering height darken my doorzh again.'

A much more significant occasion involved a confrontation with

General de Gaulle, who was by now installed in London adopting the deliberate attitude of '*La France c'est moi*', a position not yet fully confirmed by the British Government, who still only regarded him as a very distinguished French general who had managed to escape and was providing an essential rallying point for those French armed forces outside their homeland. De Gaulle had discovered that a substantial quantity of gold ingots had been transferred from France to London, where it was being held for the original customer by the Bank of England under their usual conditions of strict security. De Gaulle laid claim to his hoard and came to demand it of Churchill.

I was summoned to take the notes in the Prime Minister's room in Downing Street with only the two principals and their interpreters present. Most of the conversation was conducted in translation, which is wise as it is always an error to negotiate in a foreign language. It gives you more time to think if you wait for a translation. Churchill's French was at best idiosyncratic, but he finally countered de Gaulle's demands with the immortal phrase: '*Mon cher General, quand je me trouve en face de la Vieille Dame de Threadneedle Street, alors je suis tout à fait impotent.*' I think he should have said '*impuissant*', but his message was clear.

I would not claim that I was in any way a member of Churchill's intimate circle. He found me a new element who could write a two-page document in language that he could understand. I did not try to lead or guide him, but I would always indicate what the possible solutions were. He had an intense sense of loyalty towards those who worked for him. To the end of his life, I remained one of 'his boys' and he was always very nice to me, despite my membership of the other Party.

By the autumn, the night bombing of London had begun. For three months, without a break, an average of 200 German bombers appeared over London. Unknown to the British people, and above all to Goering's Bomber Command, Churchill went each night to a deep underground bombproof shelter round the back of the Horse Guards behind Number 10. By his own order, at the end of the war, the shelter had been left unchanged. One small room has a mini Cabinet table. The place cards are still there and Ernie Bevin's set of Cabinet papers are still in his place, with one document deliberately left by him slightly askew. Churchill's bed, bathroom equipment and utensils remain in the same places as when he last slept there.

Churchill also spent far more time at Chequers than is generally realized or than the secrecy in those days permitted anyone to know. This country residence for Prime Ministers is very clearly visible from the air on moonlit nights and on these occasions Churchill was almost always at Dytchley in Hertfordshire. Chequers was the main refuge from London during the air raids and the Government's communication system was extended there. Churchill's bedroom, room 2, and his old-style bath have been left as they were. Almost all subsequent Prime Ministers have refused to commit the sacrilege of sleeping in his bed.

In the Great Hall at Chequers, there is a magnificent painting, attributed to Rubens, of the Aesop fable in which a lion caught in the toils of a net is rescued by a mouse nibbling at the rope. Sitting up late one evening with his cigar, Churchill proclaimed that he could not 'shee the moushe'. (Churchill's inability to pronouce the letter 's' was not an affectation. In his younger days he had feared that it might prove a bar to a successful political career.) He was the only Prime Minister who would have dared to take action to deal with this particular problem. He sent for his paints and brush and remedied the situation. Unfortunately, he did not realize that the picture had been varnished over since Rubens' time. When, in due course, the Churchill Fund set out to raise £1,000 for the endowment of Churchill College, Cambridge, the Chequers Trustees agreed to allow the portrait to go on exhibition. First it was decided to clean the picture of its centuries of varnish and stains. In this they were successful, but Churchill's adornment disappeared in the process.

Our own flat at Twickenham was on the top floor. Mary had become a shelter warden and for safety we had moved our mattresses into the hall on the ground floor. We had a grandstand view of the bombing and, when we saw London all ablaze, I decided it was time to move out. We rented another flat in a house on the green on the other side of the river from Richmond.

Our little cat, who had already sacrificed one of his nine lives when he fell from the top floor window to the ground, was sent to be looked after in a cattery in Richmond while Mary and I were away for a weekend's peace in Oxford. During our absence he was killed in a bombing raid.

During the week, when those of us in the Cabinet Office were on duty, we slept as best we could on mattresses in a makeshift dormitory at the constabulary end of Richmond Terrace, each more or less fully clothed and rolled up in an army blanket. At midnight and at other regular intervals, we were invariably wakened by policemen coming off the beat and stepping over us to their own place of rest. I regret to put it on record but some of them were distinctly light-fingered, with a strong literary bent. Professor Lionel Robbins, the mildest and most charitable of men, could read himself to sleep with the English translation of one of the Greek classics. He had reached volume four, and was clearly enjoying it, only to find one night that his constabulary neighbour had purloined it and, after reading a substantial passage, put it in the pocket of his uniform when he went on duty.

We then learned that a subsidiary office in the Marylebone area had been destroyed. The bomb fell through the roof, passed through every intervening storey and exploded in the basement. At this point, the establishment division of the Treasury, a unit not famed throughout history for its compassion, took pity on us. It was thought desirable to furnish us with weekend accommodation outside London, and several sets of rooms were reserved in an Oxford college. The plan was that those of us free to do so should go there from about Friday lunchtime until the same time on Monday, with the tempting proviso that anyone engaged in a long-term study, or the drafting of a lengthy report, might stay longer. One of our team tried unsuccessfully to extend his weekend from Thursday lunchtime until Tuesday midday.

Jewkes and I were still working on the problem of essential firms who reported failure to reach their production targets due to shortage of skilled manpower. We had also been instructed to adapt our vocabulary. On the initiative of Ernie Bevin, who was trying to educate Parliament and the Civil Service to treat workers as human beings with a dignity of their own, the word 'manpower' was to be substituted for the word 'labour' in all departmental documents and minutes. Even so, the unemployment figures were coming down, with the exception of Northern Ireland, where they remained surprisingly high, despite the call-up.

I was also impressed by another fact. The cities and towns of England, Scotland and Wales were being heavily bombed, but Ulster had remained immune. How far this was due to a Nazi attempt to ingratiate themselves with the Irish of north and south, it is impossible to say, because their aircraft were using Irish air space to reach their targets on the mainland. I accordingly drafted a minute about Northern Irish unemployment which, to my surprise, was sent on to the Cabinet Manpower Committee. The result was a decision to send me across St George's Channel to Belfast to see the relevant officials and ministers and report back.

When I left the plane at an RAF airfield near Belfast, I was surprised to be met by a senior minister and the Ulster Cabinet Secretary, who had come out to the airport. As we sat down for a drink before lunch, I discovered the reason. How was my esteemed uncle, they were at pains to ask. I could not understand what my Australian relatives or my late Technical College Inspector uncle might mean to them. When they made it clear they were referring to Sir Horace Wilson, Neville Chamberlain's *eminence grise* before and at Munich, and indeed right up to the arrival of Churchill in Downing Street, I quickly disillusioned them and our lunch was quite a speedy affair.

During the afternoon and the following morning, I had a number of useful interviews with senior Northern Ireland civil servants, who were delighted that London was at last taking an interest in their high unemployment and the potential their skilled workers represented. As I was about to leave for the flight back to London, I was informed that fog over southern England had halted all flights, so I returned to the hotel. That proved to be Belfast's first night of heavy bombing. Buildings were destroyed very close to the hotel. Not only were the windows of my own room broken but one of the internal walls was blown out of position. Waiting for the plane the next day, I strongly qualified that part of my report dealing with Ulster's immunity from air raids.

The War Cabinet was becoming increasingly exercised by industry's failure to produce the machines of war. There was an acute shortage of skilled engineers. Churchill's characteristically imaginative decision, on becoming Prime Minister, to appoint Bevin to the Ministry of Labour and National Service had led to major changes. Bevin went straight to the union leaders to secure a relaxation in restrictive labour practices and a willingness to accept trainees from government training centres. The major problem was the number of skilled men who had volunteered for the services. In many engineering establishments now responsible for the production of munitions, there was a chronic shortage of skilled men, and far too little was being done in the way of intensive wartime training courses.

There were allegations that there were highly skilled engineers spending their time in the services square bashing and peeling potatoes, while the production of tanks, aircraft and warships languished. A committee was set up under Beveridge, partly to assuage the critics, partly to keep him away from Whitehall. I was released temporarily from the Cabinet Office to act as Joint Secretary. We visited service establishments all over the country. One of them was Roedean, the girls' public school in Brighton, then occupied by the Royal Navy. We were shown the famous notice on the wall of one of the dormitories, enjoining the students that if they needed a mistress during the night, they were to 'press the bell push'. In the early weeks of the naval occupation, we were told, the bell was rarely silent and experts from the electrical artificers' organization had to be called in to disconnect the system.

After several weeks of touring, we submitted our findings. I recall that we gave the navy an alpha plus, the Royal Air Force a beta double plus, and the army a pure Mu.* Reforms were introduced, including the release of skilled engineers from the services to civilian life, and the munition workshops began to increase their deliveries to the services. Beveridge was brought into the Ministry of Labour as an Under-Secretary on manpower questions and produced a characteristically ingenious call-up system for skilled men. For each grade of skill, he had a two-tier call-up age ten years apart, depending on whether the individual was working on war production or not. This led to a speedy redeployment on war work.

Beveridge had been champing at the bit in Oxford. He now saw an opportunity to impose his superior intelligence and experience on the world of Whitehall. At his own suggestion he was asked to preside over a study, mainly by academics, of unused labour in different parts of the country. He had reckoned without his own temperament and the wall of opposition from civil servants. He suffered no fools gladly and that included most of the people with whom he came in contact. He was absolutely certain that he was right about everything. He made no bones about imposing himself and raised a lot of hackles. His highly critical first findings were printed as *First Report*. Sir Godfrey Ince, head of the manpower division at the Ministry of Labour, crossed out the word 'First'.

Contrary to his expectations and desires, Beveridge found himself denied any senior post in the war administration. As a sop, he was sidetracked into a long-range survey of the social services. It was widely understood in Whitehall that this was aimed at ensuring that he would be diverted from current administration.

---

* The Mu was contributed by me. I had tried to remember the Greek alphabet, which I had learned at school (leading me to a gamma minus) but could no longer remember the rest of the letters.

He asked me to act as secretary to this new project, but by this time I was fully involved in other work and had to decline. The Whitehall establishment was delighted that Beveridge had been safely frozen out from any position of influence. They rubbed their hands at the thought that they could now get on and win the war and plan the post-war world without any interference from him. He had been shunted away from the main line to a small local track which, with any luck, would end in a neglected siding.

They underestimated their Beveridge. With only a small staff to help him, he produced one of the greatest and most revolutionary documents in our social history. He certainly was not guilty of underselling his achievement. When he produced his report a little over a year later, he said modestly to me: 'This is the greatest advance in our history. There can be no turning back. From now on Beveridge is not the name of a man; it is the name of a way of life and not only for Britain, but for the whole civilized world.'

He had presented his detractors with a highly embarrassing, forward-looking report, rapidly accepted as a blueprint for post-war Britain. It was seized on in Parliament. He became, for the first time, not a Whitehall expert, but a national figure, in some way the harbinger of the kind of post-war world people wanted to see. Public opinion forced the adoption of his report by Parliament, but he himself, in the words of the inter-war unemployment benefit regulations we had both studied, was again 'genuinely seeking work'. He talked of joining the Labour Party, and sought their support for his nomination to fill a vacancy for the then London University seat. I have always understood that it was Hugh Dalton who did everything in his power to stop this. Dalton had become a powerful figure in the Labour Party. He had worked under Beveridge at the London School of Economics and regarded him as a difficult, bitter man. Instead, Beveridge became a Liberal and was nominated unopposed for the vacant seat of Berwick-on-Tweed.

A political innocent, Beveridge was convinced that the wartime coalition would rush to accept his report. He hoped, with Churchill, that it would continue after the defeat of Germany. He told his intimates that it was certain that the next Government would include him as Chancellor of the Exchequer.

In the general election of July 1945, which resulted in Labour's landslide victory, Beveridge lost his seat in Berwick-on-Tweed and accepted Attlee's invitation to go to the House of Lords. His autobiography was entitled *Power and Influence*. Few administrative theorists in our history have had more influence. Perhaps the best comparison is with Sclater Booth in Disraeli's *Sanitas Sanitas* period. Beveridge sought power, but far from becoming Chancellor in a post-war national government, he had to be content with the post of enthusiastic and path-breaking chairman of two 'new towns' in the north-east.

Beveridge was an administrative genius, probably without parallel in this century. Set him a problem – food rationing in the First World War; the call-up and fuel rationing in the Second World War – and he would retire to a small room and produce an answer. But as a practical administrator he was a disaster, because of his arrogance and rudeness to those appointed to work with him and his total inability to delegate. The few research assistants, including the present writer, who stayed with him, biting the bullet, found him inspiring and constructive in research, impossible in personal relations.

As a result of Beveridge's influence, Britain is a far more intelligently run community. But had he been granted the power he sought, I would have trembled for democracy. In those days the Treasury made all the senior civil service appointments, and Beveridge, with his unrivalled knowledge of the machine, would have appointed his own clique to run the country.

He was a great man *manqué*, and we should remind ourselves of his passing. In the inaugural Beveridge Memorial Lecture, in Beveridge Hall at the University of London, twenty years later, I summed up his achievements in these words:

> Influence, never power, in the conventional sense – but a power to influence the thinking of millions of the urgency, the simplicity and the clarity of his solution to the problem of the poverty of Britain. For a brief moment he saw himself in a role for which his intolerance of human frailty and even his political naïvety would never have fitted him. He must be judged in the succession of great public servants – Sir Edwin Chadwick and Sir Robert Morant – rather than a challenge in his own time to Ernest Bevin or Stafford Cripps.
>
> I have always thought – I once said this to Beveridge at a time when he would have taken it as a compliment – that he would be to this century what Edwin Chadwick was to the social reform of the Victorian Age. Let us judge him then not by the test he might in the short term have applied to himself. Let us respect him as a great contributor to practical, not

theoretical economics, as one of the greatest social reformers in our history, as a man with few peers in his own generation, either in intellectual ability or in intellectual integrity, and as a man who could inspire all who came under his dominating sway with a love of work for its own sake, of the discovery of truth for its own sake and the application of that truth for the betterment of his fellow citizens.

6

Fuelling the Invasion

In 1942 I was approached by the Civil Service Secretary to D.R. Grenfell, Secretary for Mines and himself a former miner, to ask whether I would move over to them to modernize their statistics. In the coal industry, the figures were largely under the control of the Mining Association of Great Britain, the colliery owners' organization. This was the bosses' union, of whom it could truthfully be said that since the boom years of the nineteenth century, almost all of its members had learned nothing and forgotten nothing.

With the outbreak of war, a system of government control had been introduced. Just as the potato marketing cartel had become a Ministry of Food agency, so the coal owners' restrictionist selling schemes were absorbed into the Government's system of distribution. Fuel rationing was introduced and broke down. Many parts of the country were chronically short of coal, yet many pits were idle through shortage of wagons or 'want of trade', as recorded in the weekly returns to the Mines Department.

After the collapse of France in June 1940, the loss of export markets on the continent brought slump conditions to such areas as South Wales, Northumberland and Durham, which relied heavily on their trade with European countries. Pits were idle and men sacked or put on short-time working. The *Ministry of Labour Gazette* for August recorded 58,000 men totally unemployed or working short time. The number at work had fallen from 780,000 at the outbreak of war to below 690,000 and was still falling. By 1941, the number entering the industry was 15,000 a year against 40,000 who were leaving it, often for higher paid work on munitions.

The Essential Work (Coalmining) Industry Order of 15 May

had put a ban on movement to other industries, except with the permission of the National Service Department. In July, Ernest Bevin, Minister of Labour and National Service, appealed to ex-miners to return to the pits, but only a few thousand out of the missing 100,000 did so. In desperation, he introduced compulsory direction under wartime powers – which meant direction from higher-paid to lower-paid jobs. Miners working six full shifts a week were getting much less than their wives and daughters in the munitions factories.

Once a month the Secretary for Mines chaired the Coal Production Council. It became my duty to provide the statistics. At every meeting the coal owners denounced the miners on the subject of absenteeism. Despite the compulsions of the war, the miners were losing more shifts than in peacetime, and much was heard from the Conservative benches in Parliament about their lack of patriotism. In matters of statistics, as in most aspects of life, I have always felt that while there are frequent difficulties in finding the answers to the questions, the important thing is to know the questions to meet the answers. It soon became clear to me that the owners, insofar as they knew what they were about, were putting the wrong questions to the answers. Absenteeism was a question of man shifts lost through men not turning up. The possible working week, which included weekends and overtime shifts, had increased from 5.30 shifts per man in 1938 to 5.91 in 1941. The number of shifts lost without reference to the marked increase in shifts worked was bogus and misleading.

The innumerate owners also made a great deal out of the fall in output per man shift between 1938 and 1941 from 1.12 tons to 1.06, that is by rather more than 5 per cent. The output per man shift worked at the coal face, I pointed out, was only marginally lower, 2.94 against 2.95. The main explanation of the decline in output lay in the proportion of total shifts actually worked at the coalface, which in 1938–41 was down from 38.03 to 35.96 per cent.

Obviously every mine has to have a minimum and virtually irreduceable force on cost work – safety work, winding, pumping, haulage and lines of communication generally. No matter how far total manpower falls there can be no withdrawal of men from these essential duties, irrespective of whether the pit is winding 1,000 or 1,500 tons a day. The loss of men was inevitably borne by the coalface. Between 1938 and 1941, when the manpower of the industry fell by 84,000, it was estimated that nearly 50,000 came directly or indirectly from the coalface, thus lowering the proportion of directly productive workers.

There was a wave of strikes in the coalfields in the spring of 1942, due in part to the fact that, despite a rise in the cost of living index, there had been no increase in wages, and in part to a more general feeling on the side of mineworkers that their hard work and the conditions in which they had to produce coal were not being recognized in the community. Bitter feeling was caused by the high wages paid to relatively unskilled workers in the munitions factories.

There were strikes in Lancashire, Yorkshire, Durham and South Wales in April and May. Emergency wartime powers were used to take over two pits in Yorkshire – Parkhill and Newlands – from the owners. There was a meeting on 26 May of the National Executive Committee of the Mineworkers Federation, which put forward a demand for a national increase in wages of four shillings a week for adult miners over eighteen and half that figure for boys. They also demanded a guaranteed national minimum wage, regardless of pit conditions, of £4/5s. a week. The Joint Consultative Committee for the industry, coal owners and mineworkers, agreed to refer the claim to the Government, whose appeal for a return to work was accepted by most of the miners.

Fresh strikes, again in Yorkshire, Lancashire, Durham and Cumberland, led to the appointment of a Board of Investigation, to be chaired by Lord Greene, Master of the Rolls. Joint Secretaries from the Ministry of Labour and the Ministry of Fuel and Power respectively were Professor D.G. Jack and myself. We began our sittings in June and made our report to the Government ten days later. Meeting at the Law Courts, we heard opening statements by Ebby Edwards for the miners, and a barrister, specially commissioned for the occasion, for the mine owners. Greene's handling of the spokesmen was superb, and it soon became clear that Ebby, even though he overstated his case, was a far more effective advocate than the hired man.

When the evidence was complete, Lord Greene asked me to have lunch with him and immediately expressed scorn at the fact that the owners were represented by counsel, which had led him to the belief that either they had little faith in their ability to make their case, or that they had not done their homework. As for the miners, he felt that Ebby had indeed overstated the argument and asked me: 'They are not expecting us to award them the full four shillings' increase, are they?' I agreed that they were not. He then said, 'Suppose we split the difference and give them two shillings?' With great respect, I told him, that was the one figure to be avoided or the more militant miners in some of the coalfields would blame Ebby for not asking for eight shillings. The wage award was anything but a scientific proceeding. It ought to look as if we had reasons for our recommendations. What about 2/6d.? The phrase 'Greene half-crown' would catch on, as in fact it did, but no one could dramatize the Greene two bob, still less the Greene florin. He took this point.

We then moved on to discuss the demand for a national minimum. 'They are not expecting us to award them that, are they?' he asked. Again I agreed, but, momentarily forgetting my duties as a sober-sided civil servant, I said that this was all the more reason for conceding it. For decades, district had been set against district, brother against brother, both on wages and on the production figures allowed. A national approach would herald a new era. Greene's thinking was almost ahead of mine when he said, 'It means more than that, doesn't it? It means the unification of the industry and that means the nationalization of the industry, because neither Parliament, nor, I guess, public opinion would allow a privately owned monopoly to be created. Well, as for me, after ten days of listening to the kind of evidence we have had, the sooner that happens the better.'

He then asked me what the national minimum should be. I had put together enough material for him to be quite confident about proclaiming a figure. For seven or eight months, in anticipation of a wage crisis, I had been collecting copies of pay-sheets for some thirty or forty collieries in different coal fields. In all I had accumulated several thousands of them. Clearly, I said, it really must be a minimum. If we fix the figure at say 10 or 15 per cent above the lowest wages actually being paid, there would be horrible problems about what we now call differentials and, indubitably, fresh strikes. Eighty-nine shillings for a full week for underground workers and eighty-three shillings for those on surface work would in any one week, by existing methods of pay, leave less than 2 per cent of the workers earning a total less than the suggested minimum.

Lord Greene drafted the report. There was to be a flat-rate increase of 2/6d. a shift for all workers over twenty-one and to all underground workers between eighteen and twenty-one; underground workers under eighteen were to receive 1/3d. to 2/3d. a shift; surface workers under twenty-one were to receive from 9d.

to 2/3d. Underpinning the whole scheme was the national minimum of £4/3s. weekly for all underground workers and £3/18s. for those on the surface.

The recommendations were accepted by the Mineworkers Federation on 23 June and by the Mining Association on 25 June. The miners' leaders then headed a national and district-by-district campaign for maximum output to aid the war effort and particularly to speed the second front against Germany. With the Soviet Union facing the full fury of the Nazi offensive, the minority of communists among Britain's miners worked harder than ever before, and woe betide any of their mates who sought to scamp or skimp their work.

Almost simultaneously with my involvement in the wage settlement, I was busily engaged with John Fulton and other leading civil servants in the old Mines Department in drawing up an entirely new plan for a Ministry of Fuel and Power, covering coal, gas and electricity. Churchill appointed Gwilym Lloyd George, son of the First-World-War Prime Minister, to the post in June 1942.

It was further laid down that coal mining was to be a priority industry which could be chosen in preference to military service. The Coal Board was not to be concerned with wages and conditions of work, which were to be 'dealt with on a national basis by a properly constituted body formed after discussion with both sides of the industry'. The wages and profit structure of the industry would not be fundamentally changed. The proposed organization was 'to continue pending final parliamentary decision on the future of the industry'. In other words, with no general election in wartime, the first post-war general election would decide whether the industry was to continue in private hands to be nationalized. It would depend on whether the Conservatives or Labour constituted a majority in Parliament.

Early in 1943, I was appointed Joint Secretary of a sub-committee of the Anglo–American Combined Chiefs of Staff, chaired by the then Vice-Quartermaster-General, Major-General Alfred Godwin-Austen. My American opposite number in the U.S. embassy in London was Sam Berger, a product of the American Labour movement, who was specializing in trade matters. He was in fact the State Department's first Labour Attaché. He later served in Tokyo and New Zealand and was Deputy Chief of the embassy in Athens, before becoming Ambassador to South Korea and then Deputy Assistant Secretary of State for Far Eastern Affairs.

Our first major task was to ensure that sufficient coal stocks were built up in each of the invasion loading ports. Our second was to release shipping by ensuring that every consumer or handler, such as power stations, gas works, industrial establishments, coal merchants and factors' yards using more than two tons per day, were stocked up with twenty weeks' supply, wherever the lifting capacity was adequate for it to live on stocks.

Our London committee was matched by a parallel body in Washington. Like so many of the organs established in Washington during the war, this committee was duplicated by other bodies charged with precisely the same terms of reference. The respective members were strangers to one another and it was a major task for the British embassy in Washington to provide a measure of co-ordination and to effect introductions between the competing empire-builders. Sam Berger was nearly driven out of his wits by the cross-Atlantic effusions of these different American committees, and it was decided in 1943 that he and I should go over and seek to get agreed estimates, or preferably agreement, on London's figures.

Transatlantic air travel on service planes was becoming a growth industry. We went by train to the Royal Navy seaplane base at Hurn in Hampshire and were flown to Foynes on the west coast of Ireland, to enjoy a peaceful night's rest and, most welcome of all, a sumptuous meal of unrationed food. The next day there was a problem. A head wind was blowing towards us across the Atlantic. Extra fuel would be needed and half the flying boats' prospective passengers had to be left behind to await another day. To their surprise, I was given priority over three senior British civil servants, one a Permanent Secretary, on the simple grounds that I had an American visa.

The wind was rough, the flight was long, and we staggered into Newfoundland waters with twenty minutes of fuel left. We finally splashed down in the Hudson River in New York close on midnight and Sam Berger took me on a tour of the brilliantly lit streets. Officially there was a 'brownout' for fear of U-boats, but no Briton visiting the United States for the first time would have imagined that New York could have been even more resplendently illuminated.

The next day we went on to Washington, where I made contact with the embassy, who were unfailingly helpful, and retired to my hotel to scan my notes. After a few minutes there was a ring. Mr X of the Department of Labour, who had heard I was in town, would like a chat. He was, he said, specifically charged with the duty of recruiting labour for the US coal industry and he would like to know how we were tackling this problem. I was only too pleased to hold a tutorial. A few minutes after he had left there was another ring. Dr Y of the US Bureau of Mines called. He, too, was apparently in charge of the search for potential miners. I naturally said that I had had a visit from his colleague and, no doubt, friend, Mr X. Strangely he had never heard of him. My next caller was Mr Z of the newly created Solid Fuels Administration for War, who was unaware not only of the previous visitors, but ignorant of the fact that their posts existed.

After a fourth and fifth visitor had called, I fled to the embassy and dictated a memorandum on the subject that concerned so many American officials so deeply and had a dozen copies made. At each subsequent conversation, I handed my visitor a copy of the text, all of which were no doubt duplicated and studied by the long line of officials recruited to support each of these key administrators. In many subsequent visits over the years, as Trade Minister and Prime Minister, I failed to gather the impression that anything had changed.

I was booked in at the Hotel Roosevelt, an extremely luxurious place. My suite of three rooms, including a private bathroom, was the most sumptuous apartment that I had ever seen, even more so than the Savoy; but as it was six dollars a night, I soon moved to a cheaper and smaller hotel for 1.50 dollars a night in order to economize on my mission allowance, which was in fact nine dollars a day.

Further meetings were arranged for me by the embassy, and after ten days or so there seemed to be general acceptance of our London estimates of second-front coal requirements. I was in a hurry to get back. There was work to do. Moreover, Mary was expecting our first child, born just six weeks later and named Robin. Then came the bombshell. Yet another new department had been created, the head of which was not only a more powerful figure, with access to the highest levels in the White House, but a formidable statistician who had been going round saying that the British figures were innumerate, illiterate and generally unacceptable. I asked our embassy to arrange a meeting not only between this character and myself, but also with everyone known to them in Washington who had, or imagined he had, the responsibility in this highly contested field. I suggested that they hired one of the larger Washington theatres, if not the Capitol itself.

We went to the appointed place, we waited, but still the great Panjandrum had not arrived. Pulling rank, I thought. Then he came through the door. 'Good God,' he said. I replied in similarly theological terms. It was Harlan Cleveland, the former Rhodes Scholar who had been a pupil of mine at University College. (He was later to become the US Ambassador to NATO and a member of President Lyndon Johnson's Cabinet.) We looked at the mob and withdrew to a private room. Each had confidence in the other. A few minor amendments were made by each of us and we returned to announce our agreement. Whatever criticisms we have read in recent years of Cecil Rhodes' imperialism and his responsibility for the development of South Africa, I was glad that day that some of his diamond-earned fortune had gone to the creation of the Rhodes Scholarship Foundation at Oxford.

Mary still retains a letter I wrote home at this time:

> I had a good time with the Yanks, I admit, and was most hospitably entertained. They seemed to think that I got on OK with them. I was shown, *very* unofficially, a memo from the American head of the CPRB to the head of British Supply Mission saying that the British really ought to send far more like me and less old school tie wallahs. He said my Yorks accent was a great asset and also my direct manner, both much more understood by the Americans. He said my handling of them was superlative and some of them were very difficult. What he said to *me* was that it was a good thing that they hadn't gold fillings in their teeth or I would have had them as well as four million dollars' worth of mining machinery and a US commitment for coal for the Mediterranean.

I also reported that out of the forty dollars I had with me in New York and Washington, I had bought myself a new suit of dark blue tweed, an imitation gabardine raincoat made of spun glass and very light in weight, five good shirts, eight pairs of pants, three pairs of socks and four ties. Nor was that all. I had also had occasion to see Alexander Korda, the film magnate, on some matter. When he learnt of our imminent family arrival he handed to me as a present for Mary a most beautiful pure white silk layette, neutral in colour because I was clearly unable to predict whether it would be a boy or a girl.

The journey back was tedious. We were stuck at Gander for

three days in bitter cold and had to fly back in a Hudson bomber, one of a fleet which was being sent to Europe in readiness for the second front. There were no seats and we were packed tight across the aircraft, my feet beside the other man's haunches and vice versa. The aircraft was not pressurized. We had to breathe through oxygen masks and were warned not to fall asleep lest we lean on our rubber tube and cut off the supply. Weather was bad in the south and we landed in Scotland. After a ten-hour rail journey, we finally reached London.

There was a happy sequel to all this on the night of the Normandy invasion. We had been summoned to the Vice-Quartermaster-General's office for 5 June. It was changed to 6 June when the invasion was postponed through bad weather. During the long night following the first landings, the VQMG turned to me and asked me where I thought all the ships which had been released by our stockpiling operation were by this time. 'I should imagine', I said, 'that they were on their second or third trips to the Normandy beaches.' 'Quite wrong,' he said, 'all fifty of them are in Dover Harbour.' They were anchored there as part of the deception strategy to convince the Germans that either the main invasion, or at the least a second follow-up invasion, would take place across the Straits of Dover, thus forcing them to hold back troops and to that extent weaken their resistance in Normandy.

I had been extremely fortunate, as someone with developing political ambitions, to obtain such intimate knowledge of the governance of Britain before I was even thirty. My work in various departments had given me a clear insight into the ways of Whitehall. I knew how government worked and had acquired a solid antipathy to the overwhelming power of the Treasury, which was to determine many of my subsequent attitudes.

It may well be asked how a junior don managed to make his way in this rarefied atmosphere and what qualities I developed to establish my position. I was first of all numerate, something I had inherited from my father. I always regarded figures as my friend, if used with care. I had a freak capacity for absorbing statistics and applying them to the problem in hand. On any normal appraisal, I had been something of a neophyte to conduct the complicated and intense negotiations in which I had been involved in Washington. I had found that a mastery of the facts solved most of the problems and that even-tempered argument provided solutions. Far from being a recondite art, diplomacy appeared to be susceptible to plain speaking and getting the figures right. It held no terrors for me.

I had also had abundant occasion to see Parliament in action. I had had to sit through countless debates whenever my department was involved and the procedures did not seem to me particularly frightening or difficult. The important thing was to know the facts and to be able to present them. It was as important to be numerate as it was to be literate, although I could appreciate that the great occasion was something special. It was during these visits that I was privileged to hear one of the last speeches of David Lloyd George who, together with Churchill and Aneurin Bevan, was the greatest parliamentary orator of this century. The fire had largely gone out of him, but something of his past greatness was there.

Lloyd George's son Gwilym, my Minister of Fuel and Power, accorded me much intimacy. In the evenings, especially when the 'buzz bombs' confined us to the Ministry, or when I was there as duty officer, he would regale me with stories of the old man. We also had many talks about the politics of the post-war world and my own rapidly forming decision to sit as a Labour candidate as soon as a general election was called. Gwilym, as a Liberal, was on the whole disposed to remain in any national coalition which Churchill could be prevailed upon to form, but he was entirely benevolent and encouraging about my own intentions.

There was a growing demand in the country and in some at least of the unions that the Labour Party should break loose and contest the election as a separate entity. By 1944, Party headquarters at Transport House were becoming restive and the constituency parties, despite being run down during the war, were demanding a clean break. Fearful that Churchill would appeal to the country as soon as the war with Germany had ended, the National Executive Committee began to authorize the constituency parties to adopt prospective parliamentary candidates. The Parliamentary Secretary at my Ministry was Tom Smith, a Labour MP and a former miner. He had taken a friendly interest in my own plans and recommended me to Party headquarters to be placed on their list of possible Labour candidates, which was duly circulated to the constituencies.

There was a gratifying response and I received several invitations. My first selection conference was at Peterborough, held by the Conservatives but high on the list for capture. Seven of us appeared before the Constituency Party Delegate Body. I finished second to a local resident, apparently a French count. His name was sent to Party headquarters, where endorsement was immediately refused on the grounds that he had been a member of the Labour Party for only three weeks. The mystery was how he had ever come to be shortlisted. Because of fears of a snap election, Transport House did not insist on a further meeting of the constituency party, but instructed them to adopt the runner-up. By this time I had been chosen by Ormskirk in Lancashire. The third, fourth and, I think, fifth of my fellow hopefuls at Peterborough had also secured adoption elsewhere and all of them were elected to the House of Commons. So too was the survivor at Peterborough.

Ormskirk was a large, untidy constituency. Most of it was flat, agricultural land with the western part, near Southport, in constant danger of flooding from the sea. Its most important crop every year was potatoes. Many of the electors were council tenants of the City of Liverpool decanted outside the city boundaries, with no councillors to look after their interests on the Liverpool council, and with their own elected representatives not allowed to intercede with Liverpool on their behalf when drains were blocked or the roof leaking. Skelmersdale and Upholland, towards Wigan, were predominantly mining communities with high unemployment as most of the pits were being closed through exhaustion of their seams. Maghull was a mainly owner-occupied estate, with something of a Liberal tradition. Formby, on the coast, was predominantly Conservative with its male population commuting to Liverpool to work in the offices of the cotton-brokers, ship-brokers or shipping lines.

After my adoption, I had tea with my constituency chairman, Mr Fred Sayer. He was a successful Liverpool baker and confectioner. Losing his father when very young, he had been obliged to spend his evenings and weekends touring some of the more depressed areas of Liverpool selling meat pies and other delicacies made by his mother on her stove at home. Later he set up his own bakery and was soon catering for a wide area on Merseyside. During the war he was asked by a local bank manager to take over a bakery chain which had got into financial difficulties. There were aspects in its record of which he did not approve and when he received a substantial gain on selling the enterprise to new owners, he insisted on giving the money to charity. He was frank enough to tell me that he had not voted for me. He had supported a local farmer, thinking that his adoption would attract the quite important farming vote.

The sitting member I had been elected to challenge was the well-known broadcaster, Commander Stephen King-Hall. We were, in fact, friends. He had been recruited by Gwilym Lloyd George to take charge of the Ministry's propaganda drive to raise coal production. There had been something of a mystery about his adoption as a parliamentary candidate early in the war. The constituency had been represented by the redoubtable Sam Tom Rosbotham, a local worthy who had been elected for Labour in 1929 and was one of the few who had gone over with Ramsay MacDonald when the National Government had been formed in 1931.

How Commander King-Hall secured the National Labour reversion was and still is something of a mystery. The Party had folded up its tents and stolen away. The wartime electoral truce provided that the Party represented by the previous incumbent had the right to nominate the successor without opposition. Somehow the Commander had acquired all the documents and perquisites of a defunct organization and he was elected unopposed.

As the war neared its end, the Ormskirk constituency Conservatives were anything but happy about continuing the pact into the new era. At the time of my selection, they were undecided whether to fight or not. Naturally I was anything but loth to see the King-Hall vote split and I was greatly encouraged when one of my constituency party secretaries telephoned to say that the Tories had decided to put up a candidate.

Once adopted, I immediately resigned from the Civil Service. Mary and I went back to Oxford, where there was a fair amount of teaching to do. The College was more or less on a care-and-maintenance basis and I had to take on the position of Junior Dean and Home Bursar in charge of the catering and the Senior Common Room drinks cupboard. In this latter capacity I found a crisis developing over port supplies. In so far as such self-indulgences were allowed, the dons in residence were drinking from the 1895 stocks. The College wine advisers warned that the famous 1907/1908 vintage would have gone off before we reached it and recommended that a considerable number of bottles be sold off at the then replacement price of five shillings. I put up an appropriate notice. I bought only six bottles, since I had but thirty shillings to spare. One we served to undergraduates on the night of VE day, another went on VJ day, three more on suitable anniversaries, and the last bottle we kept and still have.

I also spent five weeks writing my first book, *New Deal for*

Coal, in which I drew on my experience at the Ministry and my work on Lord Greene's committee. I was recommended to a new publisher named George Weidenfeld, who had come to Britain as a refugee before the war and had done valuable work in various secret departments. He has since published nearly all my books. Published on election nomination day in 1945, it attracted unexpectedly flattering attention and provided the basis for the nationalization plans of the Labour Government.

Churchill was still hoping that he could maintain the wartime coalition in being until victory over Japan had been won, and Attlee went so far as to recommend this to the National Executive Committee of the Labour Party. Dalton, ever a trimmer, went along with this proposal up to a point, suggesting that the coalition be maintained until November 1945 and that the position should be reconsidered in the light of the progress made in finishing off the Japanese. Herbert Morrison, Aneurin Bevan and Emanuel Shinwell joined forces to defeat this proposal. When the Germans were conquered and Hitler committed suicide in his bunker, Churchill invited the Labour and Liberal Leaders to remain in the all-Party coalition until Japan had been defeated. The Labour Party Conference decision had been overwhelming. The message to every MP and prospective candidate was 'to your tents, O Israel'.

Despite the split between the Conservatives and the King-Hall faction, the election campaign in Ormskirk was arduous. There were so many small villages and townships to cover, as well as the sprawling and featureless Liverpool housing estates of Croxteth and Dovecot. After one look at my old crock of a car, my constituency chairman lent me his own, driven by a party worker, as there was some anxiety lest the candidate, whose long and turgid speeches always caused him to be late for the following meeting, might be involved in an accident, injuring a cow or even slaughtering a constituent. Looking back, my orations were painfully dull, factual and overweighted with statistics.

I had the help of a number of local speakers, whose task was to keep the meeting going until I arrived. One, I recall, whose political virility far exceeded mine, told me that I was not attacking the Tories as I should. What was needed were more punches in the belly. I heard one of his speeches when I was waiting to be called. After a series of virtually libellous accusations about each and every member of the Conservative Party, he was moved to song:

Sound the bleeding bugles
Beat the bleeding drum
Blast the bleeding bourgeoisie
To bleeding kingdom come
Light the bleeding fires
Higher than bleeding spires
Burn the bleeding so-and-sos
Bleeding one by bleeding one.*

I fear I was a great disappointment to him.

Between polling day and the count there was a delay of three weeks to allow the service vote to be collected and distributed to the constituencies. When counting began on the morning of 26 July it soon became clear that there was a Labour landslide. In Ormskirk the result was declared soon after noon:

J.H. Wilson (Lab)	30,126
A.C. Greg (Con)	23,104
Commander S. King-Hall (Ind)	11,848
Labour majority	7,022

King-Hall had split the Conservative vote for me and I was in on a minority vote.

---

* I have slightly changed the text to 'bleeding' from a more sanguinary adjective.

7

Tales of Three Cities

The electoral landslide had produced 393 Labour Members of Parliament and we received swift notice of the crosscurrents in the upper levels of the Party. We were all summoned to gather immediately in London at a mass meeting held at the Beaver Hall in the City to deal with a manœuvre in power politics engineered by Herbert Morrison.

Clement Attlee had celebrated the declaration of the result with a quiet tea with his wife, Vi, at Paddington Station Hotel, before being duly summoned to the Palace to 'kiss hands'. There were celebrations at the London Labour Party's social that evening, but Morrison and Harold Laski were at work behind the scenes. Attlee was busy appointing the first seven senior members of his Cabinet. He and Bevin, the new Foreign Secretary, had to leave for the Postdam Conference of the victorious Allies within hours to take over the negotiations from which Winston Churchill had been rudely snatched.

At the prompting of Laski, learned but lacking in plain common sense, Morrison was putting forward the bogus constitutional argument that, while Attlee had been the Leader of the Parliamentary Labour Party in the previous Parliament, now there was a new Parliament and a fresh election was needed, Potsdam or no Potsdam. The Chief Whip, William Whiteley, a former Durham miner, and Ernest Bevin, with his massive power base, moved in and convoked us all to the meeting at Beaver Hall.

The Morrison manœuvre was characteristic of him. He would regularly get into a situation where, in the Yorkshire phrase, he would be meeting himself coming back. Not for the first or the last time, he found himself crushed by the sheer bulk of Ernest Bevin. The Chief Whip took the chair. Without any preamble he simply called on 'the Foreign Secretary'. A couple of hundred new MPs were thrilled with the thought that one of their own, a fellow candidate of recent weeks, held that historic post. In the fewest possible words Ernie formally moved that Clem Attlee be confirmed as the Leader of the Parliamentary Party. It was accepted with acclamation. No one would have dared to move an amendment. The Prime Minister and the Foreign Secretary duly left for Potsdam.

I had to get back to my constituency in the car I had borrowed from my chairman. I offered George Tomlinson, a senior figure in the Party and a neighbour, a lift to his home in Farnworth. Perhaps I was driving too quickly, but just near the Watford Gap filling station, the car refused to go any further. Leaving it there for repairs, I was able to borrow another from the garage proprietor's car dump. It was not long before in seeking to apply the brakes, I found that they had retired from active work. There was now no other way of getting back to the north but to drive slowly and run into the pavement, when there was one, in order to stop. It was a nightmare journey. I did not drop George at home until after midnight and then had to drive another twenty-five miles or so to Ormskirk.

At the beginning of August Attlee was back and in two days nominated the rest of his Cabinet appointments and all the junior ministers. Parliament had continued in session to allow members, new or re-elected, to take the Oath of Allegiance and sign the book, which I did on Thursday, 2 August. I then made for Oxford, where Mary and I were still living in our College rooms.

We had been out shopping and were hailed at the College gate by Fred, the Head Porter. 'The Prime Minister', he said, 'has been trying to get hold of you.' I wondered sadly whether a few minutes shopping would mean that history had passed me by. I had the Downing Street telephone number in my head and got through to Number 10. Attlee was brief: 'Forming a government. Want you to be Parliamentary Secretary, Ministry of Works. George Tomlinson will be your Minister. Said you tried to kill him, but doesn't hold it against you. Report to him.'

I never did discover why I had been singled out for preferment, or by whom I had been recommended. Attlee knew me. He was himself a University College graduate and this may have provided its own recommendation as College loyalties are strong. He knew I was a practical economist and was aware of my collaboration with Beveridge. Amid so many new recruits, someone who had spent five years in Whitehall undoubtedly held an advantage.

I was most surprised and flattered. I had taken part in heady small talk with my new colleagues and had very much taken the line that the large new entry was still too inexperienced to be fit for immediate office. I did make one exception – Hugh Gaitskell, with whom I had come into close contact during the war years and whose undoubted talents I had admired. I was distinctly embarrassed to be given an appointment when he was not, but then discovered that he had been seriously ill during the campaign and was not yet fit enough to assume any office.

I wasted no time in reporting for duty. As soon as my presence was announced in the Ministry, I had a call from Sir Percival Robinson, the Permanent Secretary. He had his speech ready. He was glad to welcome me and would like to say something about the relationship between ministers and civil servants. According to his version, ministers spoke for the department in Parliament, but civil servants made the policies. In recent years ministers had tried to interfere with civil servants in the discharge of their duties (he made it clear that he had Duncan Sandys in mind); now it was peacetime. Patronizingly he went on to say that he had heard that I was a statistician and he was arranging for me to see the chart room and meet the head of the statistics branch, Ian Bowen, an old friend of mine in the profession. I saw him without the Permanent Secretary and heard a full account of his frustrations.

My visit to the chart room confirmed my worst fears. The housing programme, for which I found myself responsible, was simply not working, not even the programme of 100,000 prefabs in 1944, to be increased to 150,000 in 1945, which Sandys had inaugurated. Cheerfully, Sir Percival told me that the Ministry was a long way behind schedule in supplying the shells of the houses, but this was not a matter for concern since the Ministry of Health had failed to provide the sites and concrete slabs known as foundations. The building of traditional-type permanent houses was also behind schedule. The production of bricks, for which Works was responsible, was, it was true, far behind the plan, but that did not matter because there was no timber. There was also a shortage of skilled labour. No one was really to blame and certainly not the Ministry of Works, unless it was the statisticians.

Two days later Robinson came to complain that I had been 'interfering' with civil servants. The department had an extraordinary bilateral structure. Each section had at its head a permanent civil servant member of the administrative branch, with an executive officer very much below the salt. I had been told

83

by the Deputy Secretary of my former ministry, Sir Guy Nott-Bower, that I should look out for one of the best civil servants he had ever known, Freddie Smith. Smith had been a great go-getter and log-jam breaker in Nott-Bower's former department, the Ministry of Aircraft Production, to the point where he had even been rebuked by Beaverbrook for his 'piratical tactics'.

I had committed *the* cardinal offence of sending for the executive, not the administrative, grade official. Sir Percival was very patronizing, blaming my youth and inexperience and lecturing me at length on the British Constitution. In response, I told him that I had had more (expletive deleted) government experience than he had. Throughout the war he had filled a relatively minor job at Buckingham Palace. I knew how my department had functioned during the war, and that was how we were going to approach the task of housing the people.

It was not until October that I made my maiden speech in the House of Commons, and I found it a chastening experience. Among my ministerial responsibilities was the rebuilding of the House of Commons and the provision of facilities for its members, a task for which I was clearly unfitted in view of my lack of parliamentary experience and my imperfect knowledge of the chamber. This had been destroyed four years previously when Hitler's bombers, on one of their terror raids on the centre of London, had achieved a direct hit on the Palace of Westminster. The Lower House had been gutted and Westminster Hall had been set on fire.

That was the night when Colonel Walter Elliott, a former minister in Neville Chamberlain's administration, happened to be close at hand and saved one of Britain's most historic buildings. The fire brigade was concentrating on the task of saving the House of Commons Chamber. With no authority apart from the strength of his personality, Elliott went to the officer in charge and formally ordered him to let the Commons burn in order to save Westminster Hall. The Commons was a relatively new building dating from 1834, when the main part of the Palace of Westminster had been rebuilt by Pugin and Barry. Westminster Hall dated back to the reign of William the Conqueror's successor and more than any building in Britain, with the possible exception of Westminster Abbey fifty yards away, enshrines Britain's history over nine centuries. The wartime debates I had witnessed had been held in the House of Lords, who had graciously surrendered their chamber to the 'Commons House of Parliament' and met in the Royal Robing Room adjacent to their own chamber.

It was and is one of the duties of the Parliamentary Secretary of a department to answer those parliamentary questions, which, however important to the questioner and his or her constituency, are less than glamorous in parliamentary terms. A high proportion of these are written questions and answers. The last half hour of each parliamentary day was and is reserved for backbenchers to raise any matter which they want aired, in many cases after they have received what they regard as an inadequate written reply to a question. The usual form is: 'In view of the unsatisfactory nature of that reply, I beg to give notice that I will raise the matter on the Adjournment.'

It fell to my lot to deal with Alfred Edwards, the Labour MP for East Middlesborough who, in the previous Parliament, had frequently inveighed against what he quite rightly regarded as the inadequate facilities provided for MPs to do their job. He was concerned also about the provision of sleeping cars for MPs living or with a constituency at a distance from the House and for the provision in London of cars for backbenchers. This last request has not, even yet, been met more than a third of a century later. Inevitably he had wide backbench support.

At 8 pm *Hansard* records that 'the Parliamentary Secretary to the Ministry of Works (Mr J.H. Wilson) rose. . . .' I made no bones about my inadequacy for dealing with the subject which had been raised. Maiden speeches, by long tradition, are not interrupted by other members, who are otherwise free at all times to rise and ask the speaker in question if he will give way for the interrupter to make a brief point, usually in question form. But there can be no such mercy for a maiden speaker who is a minister and I was interrupted by three members, all Labour: Mr Gilbert McAllister of Rutherglen, Mr Ian Mikardo of Reading and Mr Alfred Edwards himself. At the end of my brief speech, covering just four columns of *Hansard*, Mr Montagu of Islington West also expressed himself as dissatisfied.

The points made by him covered the question of office accommodation and the storage of parliamentary papers and constituency correspondence. He was on to a good point and my reply was totally inadequate. It was, in fact, many years before Parliament began seriously to provide adequate facilities for its members. As late as the mid-1950s, despite having been a Cabinet minister for three and a half years, the only facility I was provided with for housing my despatch case documents was a cupboard on the Ways and Means corridor measuring thirty inches high, fifteen inches wide and eighteen inches deep – smaller than a decent-sized orange box.

Aneurin Bevan, as Minister of Health, had set up a Housing Executive, made up of ministers in the three relevant departments, his own, Works and Lewis Silkin's Town and Country Planning. Freddie Smith and a small number of others provided the executive arm. This was my first close contact with Bevan and I fell readily under his spell. His gifts as an orator in the House were beyond compare; he always spoke without a note, just to the right length, with a generous interlarding of glorious phrases. He was for all that more methodical than he appeared, not only a creature of instinct. He did much more homework than he was credited with and would rehearse the outline of his speeches to himself before he delivered them.

I was finding it extremely difficult to get anything moving in my corner of the Ministry. After a few weeks, the Prime Minister, on, I understand, Nye Bevan's advice, sent for me, with instructions to bring some of the progress charts I had ordered to be prepared. This was really a cover for the cross-questioning he had in mind. Why did the charts show such lack of co-ordination and achievement? What was the bottle-neck? Who was frustrating the policy of the Government? What was all this about the Permanent Secretary?

Being house-trained in Whitehall manners, I demurred, and said that I felt I should not express any opinion with which George Tomlinson might not agree. 'I have spoken to George,' Attlee said. 'He said there were criticisms of Robinson and I should send for you.' I gave him the facts. Attlee took down a piece of paper from the stationery rack and wrote a terse instruction to the Chancellor of the Exchequer – the Treasury was then responsible for the administration of the Civil Service. He was to find another appointment for Robinson. But the Service always looks after its own. Sir Percival immediately became one of the three government directors on the Board of the Suez Canal Company, an appointment to which we had been entitled as a result of Disraeli's *coup* with Rothschild's money seventy years earlier.

We were still confronted with an uphill task. One problem which the new Government faced in tackling housing was the high level of expectations engendered towards the end of the war by the Conservative ministers appointed by Churchill. Winston himself had encouraged the belief that it would not take long for them to reach a housing programme of well over 300,000 homes a year.

Had it not been achieved by private enterprise between the wars? Indeed it had, but it was not until 1933, fifteen years after the end of the First World War, that the housing programme, fed by an abundance of private money which the manufacturing industry could not use in an economy where over three million were unemployed, began to reach substantial proportions. It had taken the greatest slump in British history to create a housing boom, with an unprecedented labour surplus, low wages, cheap materials and low interest rates.

Even so, the houses built between the wars were hardly relevant to the overriding social need for slum clearance and the housing of the less privileged sections of the population. During the whole period, only one out of every fifteen houses built was to clear slums or relieve the chronic degree of overcrowding. Aneurin Bevan was safely within the facts when he said, 'The housing problem for the lower income groups in this country has not been solved since the industrial revolution.'

Churchill had been so carried away by his enthusiasm, or the cunning wording of his brief-writers, that he failed to realize that the pre-war building force of considerably more than a million had fallen to less than 350,000. Many of these had been drafted in the last years of the war into southern England to repair bomb-damaged houses or replace those totally destroyed. Moreover, the building industry had been cosseted during the war with lavish 'cost plus' contracts, whether for building factories, housing for munitions workers, military establishments or for repairs to bombed properties.

Of the twelve and a half million houses standing in 1939, nearly one in every three had been damaged during the war, most of them unrepaired or only sketchily put into a quasi-habitable condition. 208,000 houses had been destroyed, a quarter of a million more had been rendered uninhabitable and another quarter of a million seriously damaged. During the war, 160,000 homes had been created, many of these with a short life ahead of them. Moreover, some 50,000 were requisitioned under wartime emergency powers and had been converted to non-residential uses. The population of Britain was squeezed into about 700,000 fewer houses than there had been six years earlier. Nor were there any estimates to show to what extent effective pre-war housing demand had been reduced by poverty and inability to pay rent and rates, or how many families had been unable even to seek homes of their own because of unemployment and a grossly inadequate dole. Nor had anyone forseen that in the first three years after the defeat of Germany, there would be 11 per cent more marriages and 35 per cent more births than in the three pre-war years.

The Ministry of Works was responsible for 'the building and public works contracting industries, the building materials industries, the supply of timber for the building and associated industries, materials handling, and the constructional engineering industries' and, of course, for all official dealings with the professional organizations associated with these enterprises. I would surmise that very few of the employers in these areas of the national economy had actually voted Labour in the 1945 election, but our job was to work with them; theirs, *nolens volens*, to work with us. In fact their co-operation could not be faulted, although many of them, in public and private, expressed considerable criticism of Aneurin Bevan, and particularly of his decision to concentrate all available resources on building houses for local authorities, with only a small margin for the more profitable construction of houses for sale. Before long my relations with them were as warm as my contacts with the trade unions.

From the outset, I was determined to get out into the country as far as possible. Indeed, my appointment by George Tomlinson as chairman of the newly established National Joint Production Committee for the Building Industry made this essential. Houses were not built in Whitehall, where Nye Bevan reigned in the Ministry of Health, or at our headquarters across the river in Lambeth Bridge House. Regional committees were set up, reporting to my own.

Our predecessors at the Ministry of Works had established a tripartite council of building contractors, trade unionists and ministry staff to discuss all aspects of the post-war housing drive. Together with parallel bodies in each of the regions I decided to make a tour of the whole country, including Scotland, where housing was under the Secretary of State, although our Works writ operated there. I expressed the hope that representatives of both the employers and trade unions at national level would go round the country with me. Union representatives accompanied me to some of the regions, although on the whole preferring to arrange meetings with their local representatives. One of the leading figures on the management side was Captain Holbein, nominated to go all round Britain with me and presumably never to let me out of his sight. We became firm friends.

Health and Works were not the only departments involved in

With my parents and my sister Marjorie, outside our home in Huddersfield

Marjorie and I

Midshipmite in *HMS Pinafore*

(LEFT) Photographed by my father outside Number 10 Downing Street at the age of eight

(BELOW LEFT) Aged eighteen

(BELOW RIGHT) Winner of the three mile Junior Cross Country Championship of the Wirral Athletics Club

(RIGHT) In evening dress after reading the Gladstone Prize Essay, Oxford, 1936

(BELOW) Fellow of University College, Oxford, 1938: I am sitting in the front row (fourth from left) with Sir William Beveridge (seventh from left)

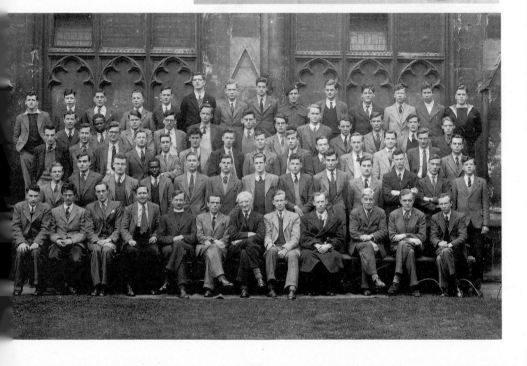

(FAR LEFT) Our wedding day, 1 January 1940. Our best man, Pat Duncan, was later killed on the North-West Frontier

(BELOW LEFT) Outside my committee rooms, Ormskirk, 1945

(LEFT) With my Parliamentary Secretary at the Ministry of Works, 1945

(BELOW) Queuing up for lunch in the canteen with Sir Stafford Cripps, President of the Board of Trade, October 1947

(FAR LEFT) Flying to Moscow to resume trade negotiations with the Soviet Union just after being appointed President of the Board of Trade, December 1947. Amongst the delegation was my Parliamentary Private Secretary Tom Cook (extreme left) and my Principal Private Secretary Max Brown (second left)

(BELOW LEFT) With King George VI, Queen Elizabeth and Princess Margaret, at the British Industries Fair, 1948

(LEFT) In the garden with Robin on my shoulders

(BELOW) Mary and I at home with Robin and Giles

(ABOVE) Arriving at 10 Downing Street with A. V. Alexander, the Defence Minister, for talks on the dollar crisis, August 1949

(TOP) On the steps of Number 10 after Treasury talks on the dollar, July 1949, with (left to right) John Snyder, Lewis Douglas, Sir Stafford Cripps, Philip Noel Baker and Douglas Abbott

the housing programme. Attlee had responded to the vision of the future that the war had engendered by establishing a Ministry of Town and Country Planning and made an inspired decision when he appointed Lewis Silkin to head it. Silkin was an expert in this field and, before the war, had dedicated himself to a crusade to stop urban sprawl along Britain's roads, which at that time it seemed impossible to prevent until London and Birmingham met. With Bevan's full support, on all the major roads which led out from London, he scheduled vast tracts of land as 'no-go' areas for urban development. Instead, to meet the capital's housing needs, he selected eleven development areas, thirty or forty miles from London where good road or rail facilities permitted, for the building of what were called satellite towns or, later, new towns. In due course he extended this scheme to the large metropolitan areas surrounding such cities as Liverpool, Manchester, Birmingham, Coventry and Nottingham. One trembles to think what the face of Britain would have become without Silkin's vision and determination. My visits out of London and the pressures put on me by contractors to persuade Silkin to ease up on his planning controls emphasized the organized strength which he was determined to combat.

The Wilson housing drive was short-lived, but I must have provided commendable evidence of activity. In October 1946, Attlee sent for me again. 'FAO – know what that means?' he said in his usual terse fashion. 'Food and Agriculture Organization of the United Nations, sir.' 'John Boyd-Orr been to see me. Appointing a commission. Sixteen countries. Stanley Bruce [former Prime Minister of Australia and later Viscount Bruce of Melbourne] in the Chair. Boyd-Orr said, "Choose a young minster to head the British team, not a hack from the Min. of Ag. and Fish." Want you to head the delegation. Conference begins Thursday. Washington. Better start packing.'

The Commission began its work at the end of October, adjourned for Christmas, when I came back to report to Attlee, and the agreed statement was signed at the end of January 1947. My Minister of Agriculture adviser in fact proved to be excellent. He was greatly respected by the Americans. The Bank of England contributed one of their bright, if eccentric, young men, Lucius Thomson-McCausland, who later rose to responsible positions in the Bank hierarchy. The key department, the Ministry of Food, was represented by John Wall, later Under-Secretary of the Ministry, knighted in 1968 and created Lord Wall in my last period of office.

The Washington experience provided one of the most valuable training sessions of my life. I knew nothing of agriculture and little of the food problems of the greater part of the world. For over three months I was working twelve hours a day, sometimes more, on these issues. Moreover, apart from my short Washington visit in 1943, I had seen little of the United States. Nor had I any experience of leading a delegation representing a wide variety of Whitehall departments to an international conference.

Despite Bruce's reputation as a tough, even brutal Prime Minister, he shared Boyd-Orr's messianic ideals about the problems of world poverty and starvation. The lead taken by the British delegation was maintained to the end. The committee met each day to consider a fresh chapter. The draft of each was written by Bruce's secretariat, mainly Americans, and was circulated at 7.30 pm for consideration the next day. Most were unsatisfactory, deficient in literacy as English is properly understood and in numeracy bogus to a degree. We produced a re-draft circulated by hand to all delegations at their hotels at 10 pm and in the main it was our draft, with a few agreed amendments, which emerged.

The seventy-five page report of the Commission was laid before Parliament by the Minister of Food in January. Attlee, who had taken a close interest in our work, was present when it was debated in the House of Commons at the beginning of February and expressed his satisfaction at the end of my speech, which this time occupied seventeen columns of *Hansard* and took forty-six minutes to deliver. I summarized the problem in these words:

> Sir John started from the paradox, which has puzzled the minds of ordinary people all over the world, the two simple facts, first that between the two wars farmers and farm-workers were never able to find an adequate market for the food and agricultural raw materials they could produce from the soil, and, on the other hand, the fact that a thousand million people – half the human race – even in 1938, were living at a standard of life far too low to support a decent human existence.

Only a month later, the Prime Minister sent for me again. He was as laconic as always: 'Ernie Bevin. Heart attack. In Moscow. Want you to go and hold his hand. Relieve him all you can. Worried that wartime alliance – Washington, Moscow, London – breaking up. So, if no agreement, he wants you to stay and negotiate trade agreement. Wants to keep door open. I'm appointing you Secretary for Overseas Trade. Stafford approves.* Wants you there Friday. Transport arranged. Better start packing.'

The position of Secretary for Overseas Trade was, with that of Financial Secretary to the Treasury, a junior post a cut above the massed ranks of Under-Secretaries and Parliamentary Secretaries. During and for some years after the Second World War, the department occupied Imperial Chemical House, the head office of ICI in Millbank, overlooking the river. Whenever the Chairman of that company came to see me about ICI business, he always asked me when he could expect the building to be de-requisitioned so that he could get his desk back.

I flew to Moscow via Berlin, in a tatty old aircraft hired from a private charter company. I was taken straight to the British embassy where Ernest Bevin, heart attack or no heart attack, was preparing to give breakfast to the American Chiefs of Staff. Ernie had a congenital attitude veering from deep suspicion to ill-concealed hatred of the Russians and he was critical of what he regarded as the soft attitude of the State Department towards them. 'Just come and watch,' he said to me; 'the Americans don't realize what the Russians are up to.'

He had sent for a school easel and blackboard. Draped over the top was a series of large-scale maps. There was to be no breakfast for the American military until they had had their tutorial. He turned the maps over the back of the easel one by one, directing a wooden pointer at the crucial areas. 'What your State Department does not realize', he said, 'is what the Russian strategy is all about. It's aimed at one thing: access from the Black Sea to the warm waters of the Mediterranean. The Dardanelles, that's what it is all about.' Ernie pulled no punches and the Chiefs of Staff were pretty hungry before they were allowed to sit down to breakfast.

Two days later I went to the airport to see Ernie off. As his aircraft disappeared from sight, I felt lonelier than I had ever felt in my life. I had a small team. John Lockie of the Board of Trade was my principal trade adviser and there were representatives from the Ministries of Food and Agriculture, Supply and the Foreign Office. This first visit in April was in a sense a reconnaissance. Each side wanted to know what the other had available for export and what their principal import demands would be.

* Stafford Cripps was President of the Board of Trade, a post first created in the fifteenth century.

I was dealing with Anastas Ivanovich Mikoyan, prince of trade negotiators and in later years President of the Soviet Union. He was an Armenian, a race noted for their superb negotiating ability as carpet traders. Once, at about four o'clock in the morning, their favourite time for negotiations, he expostulated: 'I am not at all sure whether there is any hope of agreement when you have a Yorkshireman negotiating with an Armenian.' My reply was: 'But then we approach negotiation differently. We tell you what we have, what we want, what we want to charge for our export and what we can afford to pay you for yours. You always ask a higher price, hoping we are soft enough to pay it, and you always offer a low price for our exports, hoping that you can buy more cheaply from us than from other countries. Now let's get down to realities. *This* is our price. . . .'

After establishing a working relationship and exchanging carefully qualified estimates of one another's import requirements and export availabilities, I returned to London to report and to prepare for the serious negotiations. We returned to Moscow in June.

The most formidable encounter during this second visit was when Mikoyan asked my delegation to lunch. Soviet hospitality was always daunting and we had been warned that the aim of our hosts was as clear in their minds as that of a Welsh rugby team on the occasion of the annual clash with England. The Russians have a secret or semi-secret weapon. Usually it is vodka and a great deal of that was on offer. Our Armenian host was determined that we should drink Armenian brandy. We were in no doubt that they had spent part of the morning at least lining their insides with appropriate medicaments, solid as well as liquid, to weaken the impact of the alcohol. We went to the feast with unlined stomachs. The National Hotel had neither food nor anti-alcoholic medicaments. Indeed, because of the chronic food shortage in the Soviet Union, caused by the Nazi scorched-earth policies, there were times when we could not get a meal at all, even bread.

We arrived by car at a luxurious top-people's exclusive restaurant or dining club. Out came the Armenian brandy. 'To Anglo–Soviet friendship and understanding. *Dokansa*. Bottoms up. You do not go all the way? A little sip, that's all? You are against understanding between our two peoples who for so many years resisted the Hitler menace? *Dokansa*. Bottoms up.' There were sixteen courses, beginning with caviare, smoked salmon and various meats. After two hours, thanking our host for his excellent hospitality and preparing to leave, I was met with the reply that the main courses were still to follow. Soon afterwards, X of my team (it is advisable not to identify him) rose to his feet, proposed a toast and fell flat on his back. Two of the Russians and two of my colleagues helped to take him out. When they returned one of ours whispered anxiously: 'There's a hospital ward upstairs with a doctor and two nurses. There are twelve beds' — ominous since that was the number of my delegation and staff at the lunch.

Less than an hour later Y went down, full of honour, fuller still of the best Armenian liquor. I was flashing signals to my colleagues, but every expedient, such as knocking one's glass over or accidentally breaking a glass, invited a refill or a new glass.

At six o'clock the ordeal by food was over. We were taken upstairs for coffee and 'liquid refreshments'. This went on for another hour or two, by which time we were leading three to two, owing to a round of Russian casualties, who were taken to a different place for recuperation. The Lubyanka, we speculated. At last I felt that it was time to leave without incurring a charge of discourtesy. But Mikoyan was equal to the situation. I had to say good-bye and drink a toast to each of his surviving colleagues. Bottoms up again. The score was still three to two and we were in injury time. At this point we turned with anxiety to see a colleague swaying.

It was the Foreign Office representative from our embassy, who had been appointed to look after us. He was a remarkable character, a Scot who would have made a fortune in films in nineteenth-century clergyman roles. We had understood him to be a teetotaller, but he had entered the stakes with avidity. He swayed, forward and back, further and further, close to the fatal forty-five degrees from the vertical. Finally he was flat on his back. We hoisted him to his feet. He beamed at us and began to sway again, then slowly the sways diminished. Jehovah had triumphed, his people were free. We went to our cars with dignity, got back to the hotel, passed through the doors and so to bed. Two hours later, my secretary came in and woke me up. 'They have just brought X and Y back in an ambulance on stretchers,' he said. All I could think of to say was 'Bottoms up, I suppose.' Undoubtedly we had gained prestige. The English and Scots were not soft.

It had become clear during this second visit that, while both sides clearly wanted an agreement, too many factors were still in doubt. On the Russian side there were doubts about the harvest. Since our principal requirements were for wheat and coarse grain, this was crucial. There was another problem for them. The shape of the agreement meant that they would be shipping millions of pounds' worth of grain and in return would be placing orders mainly for engineering equipment which would take a year or eighteen months, in some cases two years, to manufacture and ship. Their negotiations on price, delivery terms and specification would be conducted not with the British Government, but with a considerable number of private enterprise engineering firms. On important items they were not at all clear what they wanted.

Four separate specialized Soviet state trading enterprises, import and export, were brought into the negotiations. One of their urgent needs was transportation equipment. The Nazi invasion and the scorched-earth policy had led to the destruction of railways, locomotives and wagons. In due course they produced a shopping list for locomotives and other equipment and sent it by diplomatic bag to London.

The locomotive bid was sent to the North British Locomotive Company. When their experts looked at the specifications, they had a surprise. The design requirements, they told us, were identical with those used for a shipment of North British locomotives to the Czarist Government in 1915, since when the designs had developed considerably. When we mentioned this to the Soviet purchasing agencies, they said, 'Oh yes, we know. They have given us very good service. Some of them are still at work. No, we don't want to suggest any change in the specifications.' This was the nation which a few years later was to put the first sputniks into outer space.

It was time to return to London and report. We left Moscow in a small aircraft chartered from a private company. After refuelling in East Berlin, we crossed the English coast, which we were mightily pleased to see, and were served with the wine of the country, or rather of Scotland, considerably diluted. One of my colleagues, who was catching up on his sleep, left most of his untouched. It was just as we were landing close to midnight that we had the first hint of trouble, when we saw the liquor splashing about. The aircraft's brakes had failed; we had come to the end of the runway and were ploughing through fields. There was a small stream across our path, its bed some four or five feet below the level of the field. Our wheels and part of the undercarriage holding them had crashed against the far bank. Some of our team were thrown upwards and one, Miss Goddard, a Board of Trade private secretary, injured her head seriously against the roof.

Some kind of emergency exit was opened and we climbed out one by one onto the wing, in total darkness, apart from the headlights from the cars and ambulances which had come to meet us. The worst part was walking along the wing as if blind, as there was no moon, with the water below us, before jumping down onto the grass. I had merely cracked a rib in the crash. In the ambulance I found that an assiduous reporter from one of the popular newspapers, whose directors had strong Conservative inclinations, had hitched a ride to the scene of the crash. There was no light and I heard a voice introducing its owner and his newspaper, asking if Mr Wilson had been injured and where I was. I admitted my presence and said I was hardly hurt at all. He then asked for a statement on the negotiations, which his paper was reporting as having broken down. I replied that I could not make a statement in the dark as he would not be able to take it down. He then asked if I would give him an interview in the airport building. I was obliged to reply that we had all been instructed that we must first been seen by the doctor. 'But I thought you were unhurt,' he interjected. My ribs were, in fact, very sore, as I informed him, and we all had to be cleared medically before making any statement.

His paper duly reported the accident as its main story, featured what they called the breakdown in the negotiations and attributed to me, as though I had volunteered it regardless of those colleagues who were badly hurt, the statement: 'My ribs are hurting, I have got to see a doctor.' This was and is the kingdom of Fleet Street, or that part of it where a Labour minister and not a Conservative is involved.

The next morning, a Saturday, I went at nine o'clock to see Stafford Cripps, who had already done four hours' work. His kind greeting was, 'Things some ministers will do to get publicity.' I was to return to Moscow later in the year, wearing Cripps' hat as President of the Board of Trade.

8

The Halfpenny Clothing Coupon

At the end of September 1947, during the parliamentary recess, Mary and I were able to get away for a few days holiday at Mullion Cove in Cornwall. I did a little fishing with the local boatman, whose judgement, no doubt justified, was: 'You may or may not be a good MP and minister, but you're a bloody awful steersman.' Returning from one trip Mary told me that Number 10 had been on the line. I immediately called back and was told that the Prime Minister wanted me to return and have lunch with him at Chequers. I set off for London at once, calling on my father in Liskeard and arranging with him that if I was not able to return, he would pick up the family at Mullion and bring them to London.

After lunch with Clem and Mrs Attlee, he took me up to the State Drawing-Room and, in his usual clipped way, told me that he was making Cabinet changes. Stafford Cripps was to become Minister for Economic Affairs, supervising all the economic departments, taking this responsibility from Morrison, who would devote himself to the duties of Deputy Prime Minister and Leader of the House of Commons. I was to take Stafford's place as President of the Board. Dalton, of course, remained as Chancellor of the Exchequer.

The press, for once, were unprecedentedly friendly in announcing my appointment, but some reports went too far in referring to the 'youngest Privy Counsellor in history'. I was thirty-one. Churchill had been somewhat older, thirty-three, when he became President of the Board of Trade in 1908, Eden thirty-seven on becoming Lord Privy Seal, Malcom MacDonald thirty-four when he was appointed Dominion Secretary and Gladstone thirty-three as President of the Board of Trade. Lord Henry Petty had been Chancellor of the

Exchequer in 1806 at twenty-five and the Younger Pitt Chancellor at twenty-three and Prime Minister at twenty-four.

The Board of Trade in those immediate post-war years was a vast sprawling department spread over a number of Westminster office buildings. Though it did not challenge either the Treasury or the Home Office in terms of authority or political importance, its duties were closely related to both. The Department of Overseas Trade, which I had just left on becoming a member of the Cabinet, had been responsible equally to the Foreign Office and the Board of Trade. It was usual in British embassies in major trading countries for a representative of the Department of Trade to be appointed to seek out export opportunities and make them known to British manufacturers, in addition to maintaining contact with economic departments of the country to which he was appointed.

We were therefore closely involved in the economic crisis in the late autumn of 1947, which had persuaded Hugh Dalton in November to introduce an interim budget. It brought about his downfall. On his way to the House, he met by chance the Lobby correspondent of an evening newspaper and nonchalantly told him the main features of the measures he had in mind. These were telephoned by the journalist to his newspaper and, as a result of some misunderstanding, were printed and on the streets before the Chancellor, who as usual began with a general statement analysing the country's economic and financial problems, started to outline his specific proposals. While he was speaking, early copies of the newspaper were being passed from hand to hand on the Conservative benches. At first there was no attempt by the Opposition to make capital out of the Dalton gaffe, and Churchill spoke in a sympathetic vein about the indiscretion. But this was not enough for some of his backbenchers. The following afternoon, it became clear that Churchill was going to press the matter hard, involving Dalton's continuance in office.

The uproar began before Attlee had arrived to answer Prime Minister's Questions, but his Parliamentary Private Secretary rushed to his room in the Commons to warn him. The Lords' Chamber is a couple of hundred yards from the Prime Minister's office, and I saw Attlee rushing along the corridor in a very agitated state. Sir Victor Raikes, MP for Wallasey, had tabled a Private Notice Question to which Attlee had to respond. Dalton took full responsibility for this indiscretion and apologized to the House. Churchill magnanimously accepted his statement and expressed his personal sympathy. But later that evening, probably as a result of a meeting of the Shadow Cabinet, Churchill, Eden, Sir John Anderson and the Liberal Leader, Clement Davies, tabled a Motion calling for the appointment of a Select Committee of the House to enquire into the leak. Dalton immediately resigned and Cripps was appointed by Attlee to succeed him.

After a suitable period of penance on the back benches, Dalton was appointed a minister in the Department of Town and Country Planning, but his position and influence were never the same again. The younger members of the Government particularly, and very many backbenchers, were deeply disturbed by Dalton's fall. He had gone to great deal of trouble to take an interest in us and give us wise advice. I have rarely been so upset by any event during my parliamentary life, nor written so sad a letter of condolence from my office down the road. I doubt whether we lost ground in the country as a whole as a result, but one could not fail to see the effect on the Government's own morale.

The most spectacular measure in his budget had been to increase the tax on a packet of twenty cigarettes from 2/4d. to 3/4d. This was regarded, certainly by the press and most smokers, as a penal impost. Attlee responded by forbidding smoking in Cabinet. He probably suffered more from this decision than any of his colleagues, with the exception of the young President of the Board of Trade. From that moment the Cabinet deteriorated as a deliberative body. Moreover, it soon became clear that a further syndrome had developed. The Cabinet cigarette and pipe addicts appeared, at a stroke, to have developed bladder trouble. The smooth flow of Cabinet exchanges was interrupted several times in the course of a morning as one minister after another excused himself and slowly crossed, diagonally, the square ante-room where ministers foregather while awaiting the Prime Minister's summons to take their place around the Cabinet table. In the far corner is a lavatory, and one could see the steady traffic of ministers having a quick drag on their cigarettes or hurried puff on their pipes.

The general situation was even more unsettling. We were in the middle of a crippling economic crisis, threatening the total exhaustion of our gold and dollar reserves until the welcome promise of Marshall Aid became a reality. Starvation in Europe and rationing in Britain, tighter for some foodstuffs than in wartime, added urgency to the Government's plan to expand agricultural production, particularly in livestock. The Russians had enjoyed their first good post-war harvest and access to their surplus of grain was vital. Tom Williams, the Agriculture Minister, was faced with the increasing probability of a mass slaughter of cattle unless we could gain access to these supplies.

After a discussion with Attlee, Bevin and Cripps, it was decided that I should pay a third visit to Moscow with a small delegation, making it clear that I could stay for only four or five days. We were delayed for a day in Berlin through bad weather, so I telegraphed the British Ambassador, Sir Maurice Peterson, asking him to save an evening by asking Mikoyan to dinner at the embassy. Sir Maurice met us at the airport and I asked him if he had sent the invitation. 'Yes,' he replied, 'but Mikoyan would not accept it. No Soviet minister would do such a thing.' On arrival at the embassy we were met with the welcome news that Mikoyan had changed his mind.

We spent a good part of the time sounding him out on broad issues of world policy. It immediately became clear that as Deputy Premier he was very much at the centre of things, quite apart from his departmental duties, and this visit made possible perhaps one of the most frank discussions with a forthcoming and not unfriendly Soviet leader since the war years. Inevitably, he evaded some of the more searching questions with his well-known humour. At one point he said that Britain, and especially its politicians, were too old. I took him up on this. I was thirty-one. How many members of his Government were that age? Indeed, I said, I would select a football team of British ministers, challenge the Kremlin to nominate their team, play in the Dynamo Stadium and beat the hell out of them. When that occurs, he said, he would be on the touchline, cheering on the Soviet team. But Molotov would play. Yes, he would be in goal. He never let anything go past. In a later meeting, Mikoyan was even more frank in describing the execution of a senior minister at a 'Cabinet' meeting.

I had inherited from Cripps his two Parliamentary Private Secretaries, Barbara Castle, MP for Blackburn, and Tom Cook, MP for Dundee East. I had included Cook in our delegation. He was an agreeable companion, moderately to the left, but not extremely so, and a strong critic of communism. More than that he was a highly qualified electrician. I had already made considerable use of the bugs which I knew would have been planted in my suite, though as I did not know their exact location I had to speak loud and clear. Tom was sent to find them and achieved considerable success. What shocked me was his discovery that there was one under the bath. In those days I was prone to sing in my bath from time to time and now a kind of persecution obsession set in. I was afraid to sing lest this could be interpreted as a sign that I was happy with Mikoyan's latest offer.

It was also at this time that I took up pipe smoking. I had never smoked as a young man, partly because of my interest in athletics, but during the war and the bombing of London I had become a cigarette smoker. I never learned to inhale and used to get through each cigarette in a few minutes, without it doing me any good or any harm. It was the Moscow talks which led me to go over to the pipe. I felt, though perhaps this was all imagined, that a cigarette made me jumpy, while a pipe enabled me to slow down. I could just puff away through our interminable sessions, playing out time, resisting the temptation to speed up the negotiations with unwise changes in my price or delivery demands.

Specialist meetings of experts from both sides had been arranged and I had been authorized by the Treasury to be more forthcoming about the limitation of Russian payments due on past debts, including even some repudiated Czarist stock, still outstanding on the Treasury Register as due for settlement. Progress was slow, but I was determined to keep to my timetable.

When the last evening arrived, I gave instructions to our aircrew to go out to Vnukovo Airport to rev up the engines and give notice of our departure time the following day. Then, just before we met the Russians, I received a welcome telegram saying that an agreement had been concluded with the Australians for a large supply of wheat. The price was considerably in excess of what I had been authorized to pay the Russians. Our negotiations with them up to this point had been based on the wheat price; the price of barley, oats and maize were to be an agreed fixed percentage of that on wheat. Now we had the wheat. So when Mikoyan began to discuss the price, I told him, quite nicely, that we did not want his wheat, just coarse grains. I was glad to see him welcome this. 'Your announcement', he said, 'makes things much easier. We are terribly short of wheat. Our people are starving. A limited amount of coarse grains, yes.'

Now it was a question of price. We had been negotiating in terms of American dollars and the limit of my offer price had been agreed with my colleagues in London at $123. One or two of my team thought I should have announced this and stuck to it. My view was that Mikoyan would regard this as an opening bid and seek to raise it. I began the haggle with $97, clearly unrealistic.

Mikoyan suggested an adjournment to allow both sides to review the situation created by the Australian deal.

We had a quick meal at the embassy. Peterson asked whether we had broken off. I told him what had happened. He was worried that the Russians would try to play things slowly while their spies found out what we had, in fact, paid the Australians. He was certainly right and I said that this was why I had insisted on an all-night sitting and an early morning flight. He said he did not intend to lose any sleep over the Russians. He would go to bed. I did not seek to dissuade him.

When the talks were resumed, I said that on reconsideration I felt that $97 was somewhat unrealistic. $108, I said. At the end of the table was the sinister NKVD man, who was never absent from our meetings. Mikoyan challenged me: 'What price have you paid the Australians for their wheat?' 'You ask Gospodin X,' I said, 'he knows everything.' I was hoping against hope that he did not, and my hopes were confirmed when he said, 'Oh well, everyone knows that Australia is a colony of yours. You dictated the price to them.' In other words he did not know, but he soon would.

After a brief homily on the constitutional relationship between Australia and Britain, and a very short lecture on the Commonwealth, I resumed the negotiations. On they went, long into the night. They played every card to keep me long enough for them to find out the Australian price. A note was handed into the room. Mikoyan said he had great news for me. Generalissimo Stalin had done me the honour of inviting me and my colleagues to dine with him the following evening in the Kremlin. I expressed my regrets. I was under strict orders from the British Prime Minister, who had invited a number of his younger colleagues and their wives to have dinner at Number 10 the following evening to meet Lieutenant Philip Mountbatten RN and Princess Elizabeth in honour of their recently announced engagaement. I could not miss it for any competing invitation, however pressing.

At 5 am we settled at $113, shook hands and returned to the embassy. His Excellency had been in bed for six hours or more. For some reason this inspired my colleagues to song. All except myself walked up the embassy stairs singing 'There'll always be an England'. We made for the little room which had been allocated for our planning meetings. The whisky cupboard was locked. This was too much for the representative of the Ministry of Food. Taking a poker, he broke the lock, and our abstemious marathon session – I had forbidden drinks throughout the negotiations – was redeemed by an access of long overdue imbibing. I dictated a short cable to Stafford Cripps and his note of congratulation was handed to us when we refuelled at Berlin. We slept for an hour in our chairs. There was no time for bed.

At breakfast a fully refreshed Ambassador asked me what time we had broken up. When I told him, he replied, 'What did you break down on?' 'We broke up', I told him, 'on signing the agreement.' He was deeply shocked. 'They won't honour it,' he said, and went on to ask how far we had breached the terms of our instructions. We had not. Clearly he was shattered.

His forecast proved to be wrong. In the event the Russians fulfilled every undertaking. Indeed, in one respect, they went further than their commitment. We had agreed, with London's blessing, that at their discretion they could withhold 200,000 of the 750,000 tons for which we had been negotiating if, after six months, they had failed to agree the contracts with British firms for industrial equipment. In fact, although they did fail, they did not invoke this proviso, the reason being, I am sure, not generosity but a desire to obtain currency for spending in free world countries.

Our flight back, with Christmas drawing near, was relatively festive. A message reached me asking me to see Cripps as soon as we arrived in London. He was delighted at the agreement, and rejoiced in telling me that he had sent for Tom Williams, who on hearing the details of the agreement had burst into tears of sheer relief.

During the whole of this period, Mary and Robin had continued to live in Oxford. We remained in our College rooms on Staircase. Then we moved out into a College flat in Banbury Road. This involved me in constant triangular journeys between Oxford, Ormskirk and London. My father and mother had moved to the capital during the war, when he had obtained a job in the Civil Service, and I used his home as a base when Parliament was in session. This was all becoming too much of a strain and we decided we must move our home to London.

Gurney Braithwaite, the Conservative MP, was kind enough to recommend a house in Hampstead's Southway, and we moved in there at the beginning of 1948 shortly before our second son, Giles, was born. In due course we moved to a larger house next door at 12 Southway, and this remained our home until 10 Downing Street beckoned.

However important foreign trade transactions might be to our balance of payments, the Board of Trade was best known to the public as the department responsible for clothes rationing. The miserable ration of twenty-six coupons for the period of six months still continued and the whole population was shabby and ill-clothed. I was keen to abolish or at least ease the rationing system, but in 1948 the economic pressures were all the other way. The first priority had to be given to exports, to pay for the minimum levels of food and raw material imports we were buying with difficulty, whether on government or private account, from the United States and other world stock markets.

The senior officials of the Board of Trade, particularly Sir John 'Henry' Woods, the Permanent Secretary, and Sir James Helmore, his deputy, were keen to see free competition restored, but were averse to making a formal recommendation to end rationing. There were, they urged, only two options – to leave things as they were or to take the mighty risk of complete derationing. I disagreed and embarked on a step-by-step approach. Childrens' shoes were taken off the ration, the coupon rates for adult shoes and waterproofs were halved, as were seamless rayon stockings and inferior woollen clothes, which were not much wanted in the export market of the world. I also pressed shops to hold clearance sales to get rid of excess stocks at half the coupon rates and low prices.

I received little thanks from the Wholesale Clothing Manufacturers' Federation, whose secretary described my actions as 'applying mustard plaster to a broken leg'. Clothing stocks continued to rise, strengthening my conviction that shortage of money was imposing its own rationing system. I therefore tested the market again, by derationing all footwear, all 'non-utility' furnishing fabrics, 'utility curtains' and other items, while reducing the coupons needed for sheets and cotton blankets. Even so, the growing success of our export drive virtually took all nylon stockings off the home market. The problem was that materials woven from wool were in easier supply. Cotton goods, particularly clothing, towels and sheets, were still tight. I derationed the wool products. There was no run on the rest, confirming my monetary theory of the purchasing slump.

I decided to test it by tapping an unusual, but authoritative, source. I contacted Scotland Yard and asked them to send their senior superintendent, appropriately named Mr Yarn, who was dealing, mainly in the East End, with evasions of clothes rationing.

Earlier I had enquired about the black market price of the clothes coupon and had been told it was half a crown. Now the superintendent came to tell me that the current price was a halfpenny. I immediately abolished clothes rationing entirely and the press insisted on taking photographs of me tearing up my ration book. A further bonfire took place three days later, removing the requirement for 900,000 licences and permits and releasing a further 320 officials from my department.

Although far from the most important task of the Board of Trade, its responsibility for the film industry, production, distribution and exhibition, was one of the most exacting. Austerity ruled. The lean and hungry Treasury officials grew even more lean and hungry and saw to it that their meagreness was shared on an even more penny-pinching scale by the Whitehall spending departments. On the face of it, it would not have appeared likely that a dedicated Treasury, led by an even more austere Chancellor, would be pressing money for film-making on an ever-cautious Yorkshire penny bank President of the Board of Trade.

The truth was that Stafford Cripps was not austere when it came to the financing of films. More accurately, Stafford was a soft touch when his wife Isobel came on the film set. She was a warm-hearted lady, a devoted supporter and indeed leader of many good causes. Among these was encouragement in season and out for an immigrant film producer named Del Giudice. Cripps, who was counting every penny for the welfare state, social security, health service and education, was ready to raid the till for Del.

I had announced the establishment of a National Film Finance Corporation, which continued for some forty years before being replaced by a new body which I have chaired for several years.* The Treasury had not yet formally notified the Trade Department of the financial approval which the Chancellor had so readily given. One morning, shortly after dawn, he telephoned me to say that Del did not have the wherewithal to pay the week's wages and virtually ordered me to announce the establishment of the Corporation forthwith. All I could tell him was that the Treasury had still not signified assent. 'You shall have it this morning, my boy,' was his response, and this was formally communicated by the Treasury to my department an hour later.

---

* One thing of which our members are proud is the number of Oscars won by our film colleagues on the Committee.

In the event, Del did not receive a penny. The legislation establishing the NFFC and setting out its powers and its duties, not to mention the ever-present vigilance of MPs whenever government money is being voted for private entrepreneurs, left it virtually proof against ministerial intervention except on broad matters of policy. The Corporation had enough anxieties with Alexander Korda, who had returned to London from his wartime American exile. It was invited to the premiere of his latest film, *Bonny Prince Charlie*. The screening was followed by a lavish party in Korda's lush apartment. The ladies present appeared to be nearly swooning with their appreciation of the film's qualities. Korda turned to me and asked, 'What did you think of it, Mr President?' I replied, 'Well, I enjoyed it, Alex, I always do, but it cost £750,000 [a great deal of money in those days] and it won't in my view make £150,000 at the box office.' I was wrong. I was later told that it had made £151,000. 'Ah,' he replied, 'just wait until you see my next. It is being filmed in the sewers of Vienna.' I groaned, fearing the worst, and pointed out that it was taxpayers' money which he was presumably throwing down the drain. How wrong I was. The film was *The Third Man*.

In the event, we were fortunate with a succession of films; the NFFC financed, among many others, *The Fallen Idol, The Winslow Boy, Maytime in Mayfair, Genevieve, Seven Days to Noon, State Secret* and *Morning Departure*. I felt, however, that direct government aid to the industry was not enough. Cripps had already assisted by imposing a 75 per cent levy, virtually a ban on American films. Hollywood responded with a boycott on the export of productions to Britain, which looked like closing many of our cinemas. I was violently attacked by the organizations representing the distributors and the cinema owners, but held on, as I knew that the American producers would be forced to negotiate.

For good measure, while on holiday in Cornwall, out on a walk from my parents' cottage to Porthpean Beach, I thought up another device, a direct levy on actual cinema takings. Not being sure of Treasury support for this measure, but knowing the vanity of certain Treasury officials of those days and their desire for personal publicity, I called it the Eady Levy, Sir Wilfrid of the llk being in charge of film finances at the Treasury. It is only the provisional, the French tell us, which endures. This very temporary measure lasted for forty years after its establishment, being ended by Mrs Thatcher's government a few months before the time of writing.

Soon after these new systems of encouraging British film production were introduced, I had the opportunity of pressing John (now Sir John) Woolf, son of a legendary figure in the industry, to embark on production. For some reason he felt that he would not be a success – inferiority complexes in the industry are rare – a feeling soon corrected by the acclaim accorded to such film, as *Pandora and the Flying Dutchman*, *Moulin Rouge* and *Day of the Jackal*, to say nothing of the production achievements of Anglia Television, of which he became a founder director.

The restriction on Hollywood productions was not received lightly. The American Ambassador, Lew Douglas, a great friend of Britain, protested to the Foreign Office, who, no doubt agreeing with him, sent him round to the Board of Trade. We were quite willing, having taken action, to negotiate a long-term settlement. Hollywood sent its chief administrator, Eric Johnston, to negotiate. The talks went on for weeks. In the event, an agreement was reached and signed on 12 March 1948. Johnston had pressed for it to be formally dated on the 11th, my thirty-second birthday.

A succession of Hollywood chieftains came over to remonstrate about our quota and levy. The most colourful was Spyros Skouras, whom the most imaginative Hollywood scriptwriter could never have invented. At that time his English was not as good as it subsequently became. He harangued me, politely, forcefully and incomprehensibly for a full fifteen minutes. To help both of us, I asked him very slowly whether he was in fact saying that our policies were proving harmful to Hollywood. 'That', he said, 'is an exaggerated understatement.'

The blood transfusion of Marshall Aid had saved the British economy for only a very brief interval. The monetary theologians of the American State Department had insisted that the funds Britain received must be convertible into other currencies. Europe was starving not only for food, but for the raw materials necessary to get industry moving. When they exported to us it was dollars, not blocked sterling, that they wanted. So Britain's Marshall Aid was quickly dissipated and we faced harsh reality again.

Nevertheless, our economy generally and our exports in particular were achieving a remarkable degree of success. Measured by volume, they had risen from 50 per cent below the pre-war figures in 1945 to almost 55 per cent above. We were paying for 85 per cent of our imports with our own exports. What now hit us was a deep recession in American economic activity. United States orders for British exports fell catastrophically and the international financial markets, already free to react to changing situations, and indeed to speculate freely on the rises and falls in the exchange rates of individual currencies, were taking up positions highly unfavourable to sterling. By so doing, they were compounding sterling's insecurity.

The economic ministers met under Cripps' chairmanship to deal with the crisis in early July. By the middle of the month he was too ill to carry on and went to Switzerland for what he hoped would be a period of convalescence, but also to receive treatment at the Bircher-Benner Clinic in Zurich from his guru, in whom he had complete faith. Attlee announced that Hugh Gaitskell, who had by now made his way in the government hierarchy and was Minister of State at the Treasury, would stand in for Stafford during his absence. It was becoming increasingly clear in London that the exchange rate of $4.03 to the pound could not be held, and Attlee formed an unofficial triumvirate of Gaitskell, Douglas Jay, the Junior Treasury Minister, and myself to deal with the situation.

As the pound came under increasingly heavy attack, the argument began to change from *whether* we should devalue to *when* we would have to do so. The pound was being driven down on world markets by local and, increasingly, world-wide speculation in a one-way market. Sterling was being sold short and no one was willing to buy except at a heavy discount. Our gold reserves had been poured into what seemed a bottomless pit. Treasury officials in the main wanted to defer the actual devaluation until the annual meetings of the World Bank and the International Monetary Fund, but there was strength in Gaitskell's view that we should not be allowed so long a period of grace.

As the situation deteriorated further, we agreed that we should prepare a specific plan of devaluation, involving a new parity of $2.80, and that, as I was due to go to Annecy, close to the Swiss border, for a meeting of GATT and was intending to take a few days' holiday first, I should proceed on to Zurich to hand the document, outlining our plans and signed by Attlee, to Stafford and to explain why we considered early devaluation to be essential. I knew this would not be easy since the Chancellor, a man of rigorously impeccable standards, had stated categorically earlier in the year, when sterling was under heavy speculative pressure, that it would not be devalued.

Great care was taken to safeguard Attlee's letter from loss or theft. I was travelling across the Channel by car ferry for my holiday, before driving to the GATT Conference. After that I would cross the border into Switzerland, but here there was going to be a problem. The worsening financial situation had led to the intensification of Treasury rules on buying foreign currency for holidays. Soft currency areas, including France, were all right. The Swiss franc was the hardest of hard currencies. A special allocation had to be made, and for this purpose a British official in the embassy at Berne was told to drive over to Annecy to hand me the currency I would need. It was considered too dangerous for the devaluation letter to be carried with me on my slow drive to Geneva and subsequent touring. It was therefore arranged that Max Brown, my Principal Private Secretary at the Board of Trade, should fly over the night before I was due to see Stafford and that he should bring with him a tightly sealed copy of the Attlee letter. When I picked him up at his hotel, he told me that he had been so nervous of losing it that he had slept with it under his mattress.

I handed the letter to Stafford. He read it very carefully and, somewhat to my surprise, did not challenge its conclusion. He then sat down and wrote by hand a lengthy letter to Attlee, some three pages, accepting the situation but strongly urging that there should be a general election first. Max Brown took the Cripps letter back with him and awaited me at Dover on my return, whence I went straight to Downing Street to hand it to Attlee. He was in his study. He read it through standing in the secretary's office next to the Cabinet Room. When he came to the reference to a general election, he murmured, with his customary brevity, 'Stafford – political goose'.

As it happened, I had to speak at a public meeting in Oxford at the end of the week. Questions were invited, and I was asked outright when we were going to devalue and, if not, why not. My answer, which gave nothing away, was fortunately not picked up by the press, who were well represented at the gathering. The plan was known only to Attlee and the three relevant ministers, plus of course a few select officials.

Clearly so important a step could not be taken without Cabinet approval. To avoid the risk of a premature leak, the Cabinet was accordingly called to an emergency meeting on the eve of the announcement. Because of the sensitive condition of the money market, Attlee arranged that ministers should come to Number 10 by a series of different routes, some through the Foreign Office, some through the Cabinet Offices in Whitehall and some by the garden entrance. We were further instructed to make ourselves as little recognizable as possible without actually hiring masks or other theatrical disguises. It was Emanuel Shinwell and Tom Williams, the Minister of Agriculture, who provided the most amusement for their colleagues. Shinwell had acquired from somewhere a pair of magnificent mustachios. Tom Williams, who always wore a stiff turned-up collar of the type mainly associated with full evening dress, the kind then known in the north of England as a 'Come to Jesus' collar, was wearing his farmer's jacket and trousers and a somewhat garish sports shirt with what must have been the softest collar he had ever worn.

The sequel was less amusing. When Stafford Cripps returned, he found it necessary to introduce a further round of austerity to keep the national books in balance. The housing programme was cut from 200,000 to 175,000 and he introduced the National Health Service (Amendment) Act which authorized the imposition of a charge of one shilling on each prescription if a fair and workable scheme could be devised. This brought him into direct confrontation with Aneurin Bevan, for whom a totally free health service was the ark of his covenant. Bevan was on the defensive because his estimates had been overspent by £100 million. In those early days it was impossible to calculate what calls would be made on the service when health treatment was no longer rationed by the purse, especially by women who had so frequently refused to see a doctor when ill, because the fee would have had to come out of money for their children's food.

Thus was implanted the schism which was to dog the next eighteen months of the Attlee Government. One weekend at Buscot Park, Lord Faringdon's home in Berkshire, I heard Bevan state that he would resign if the plan for charges went ahead. I made it my business to see Stafford Cripps and plead that no steps should be taken to implement the Act. In turn, I pleaded with Bevan to be gentler with Cripps, who was still in poor health. The corner was turned, and a compromise arranged. In return for the abandonment of the charges, Bevan would accept a ceiling on expenditure and what he regarded as a fairly tolerable indignity, surveillance of health service finances by a special weekly Cabinet committee presided over by the Prime Minister.

In the turmoil of those traumatic weeks, Bevan had not, in fact, resisted the housing cut, which was duly announced as just one element in the post-devaluation 'package'. He also agreed to a further announcement that powers would be put into operation to make a charge of one shilling in respect of prescriptions for medicines. Later he was to say this was his contribution towards providing a convincing post-devaluation package. Once the immediate monetary crisis had subsided, Bevan reverted to his original position and repeatedly made clear to his colleagues his unshakeable resolve never to agree to the imposition of prescription charges. Nevertheless, his public acquiescence was to undermine his case when the battle was resumed.

So we staggered through to the general election of February 1950, when the huge Labour majority was reduced to five. In my own constituency of Huyton, which had been formed from part of the Ormskirk seat after the 1948 boundary changes, I scraped in by 834 votes.

9

Three Resignations

An inquest had to be held into the calamitous election results. Unfortunately, it was masterminded by Morrison, in the then somewhat comfortless rooms of Beatrice Webb House near Dorking. The press were, of course, not present, but Herbert Morrison was, so they were saved the journey. Every newspaper agreed that the conference had been a triumph for him. He sought to reverse the course of the previous five years of Labour Government. There was to be a moratorium on all plans for further public ownership and a deletion from the party programme of all such proposals. Instead, we were presented with a ten-point programme, including a new battle cry: 'Socialism means the assertion of social responsibility for matters which are properly of social concern.' Tautology ruled. Morrison was successfully put in baulk by a triumvirate of Morgan Phillips, the Party's General Secretary, Sam Watson, the usually moderate Durham mineworkers' leader, and Nye Bevan. Attlee hardly troubled to intervene. Years later he said of Morrison: 'I never knew that the poor little man was so full of seething ambition.'

Nevertheless, the battle for power within the Party had been thrown wide open, in political circumstances of particular difficulty. The Conservatives in opposition were asserting their new confidence and increased strength in a Parliament so evenly divided as to frustrate any wide-ranging legislative programme. Bevan himself was highly vulnerable, not only to the Opposition after his apparent wavering in the previous session, but also in terms of the new balance of power in the Cabinet. Hugh Gaitskell has been promoted in the new Government to the high Treasury rank of Minister for Economic Affairs. With Stafford Cripps still in ill health, this precipitated the most serious cataclysm in the six years of the Attlee Government.

Hugh had many fine qualities, including unswerving loyalty to his close band of friends and to the principles of economics as he interpreted them, together with great personal charm. But once he came to a decision, a remarkably speedy process associated with great certainty, the Medes and the Persians had nothing on him. Whether the argument took place in the Cabinet, or later in the Shadow Cabinet or the National Executive, any colleague taking a different line from his was regarded not only as an apostate, but as a troublemaker or simply a person lacking in brains.

In Stafford Cripps, the process was that of a trainee lawyer, a master of speedy reactions in the middle of a cross-examination. Moreover, in his case the master-stroke was always planted in his mind by the Almighty. His equal unwillingness to be moved was due to the fact that he had quickly reviewed the facts and taken a final decision, discussion of which was fatuous, not to say disloyal, indeed a clear case of intellectual dishonesty. With Aneurin Bevan, a policy decision or political attitude emerged from the inner certainty he derived away from the smoky metropolis in the pure Welsh air of the moorlands above Trefil, the Duffryn Valley and the Black Mountains.

Hugh Gaitskell and Nye Bevan were as temperamentally and politically opposed to one another as it was possible to be within a single political party. I had relations of fairly long standing with both of them. I had first come close to Nye during my housing stint at the Ministry of Works, although it had taken time for the relationship to develop. Nye was suspicious of university-trained MPs, particularly those from Oxford and above all economists, but I had broken down that barrier and we had great confidence in each other. I had early developed an admiration for Hugh Gaitskell's qualities and in many way we were intellectual partners. He was more doctrinaire and I was more of a pragmatist.

One other fact soon became clear about Hugh. He was certainly ambitious, and had close links with the right-wing trade unions. It was not long before that ambition took the form of a determination to outmanœuvre, indeed humiliate, Aneurin Bevan. Hugh, for his part, despised what he regarded as emotional oratory, and if he could defeat Nye in open conflict, he would be in a strong position to oust Morrison as the heir apparent to Clement Attlee. At the same time he would ensure that post-war socialism would take a less dogmatic form, totally anti-communist but unemotional.

Had he chosen the housing programme as the principal battleground, instead of the National Health Service, he would probably have stirred up against him a very wide section of the Parliamentary Labour Party. There was more room for deep disagreements about the form the National Health Service should take and, what proved to be crucial, what it should cost. The battle was joined over prescription charges and lasted for more than a year.

It was not only Gaitskell who was aiming to force Bevan into either capitulation or resignation. Herbert Morrison regarded this as a key element in his own private campaign to see Attlee ousted, an event which he was confident would be followed by his own election as Party Leader and thus Prime Minister. What he failed to see was that Attlee, who had an utter contempt for Morrison, had created in Gaitskell the new rising star, who, when Attlee finally quitted the scene, would have little difficulty in seeing off Morrison himself, and so it proved.

I was by no means as fervent an opponent of the proposed prescription charges and did my best to warn Nye about the forces gathering against him. I suppose there were forty-five to fifty MPs who came to be classed as Bevanites, but we did not form a cohesive group, and certainly did not become a cabal. John Freeman, the Parliamentary Secretary at the Ministry of Supply, was one of our number, although neither Nye nor I were particularly intimate with him. Barbara Castle was active, but Nye was not on particularly friendly terms with her. This was largely because he felt that she had been unduly favoured in office while his own wife, Jennie Lee, had received no preferment, an omission I was able to put right many years later. Several of us used to meet from time to time rather than being seen about the House. I would pick up two or three of them in my car and go for a stand-up supper at one residence or the other, including the Bevan establishment in Cliveden Place, but such gatherings were not frequent and not to be compared with the meetings of the 'Frognal Set' being organized by Hugh Gaitskell, Douglas Jay and others.

Nye himself had few illusions about the weeks which lay ahead, but remained stiff-necked in his attitudes. At the end of June he wrote to Stafford Cripps to say that he was no longer willing to attend the weekly dinners which the Chancellor organized for all the economic ministers. Stafford was offended, but his health was now deteriorating. In July his condition became worse, and in October he resigned from the Government. Attlee appointed Hugh Gaitskell to succeed him. Nye was outraged and actually wrote to Attlee, to express his 'consternation and astonishment'. Attlee by now was weary of the guerrilla warfare that was going on and sought a solution by inviting Bevan to move to the Ministry of Labour. Nye was attracted by the proposition but asked for more time to think about it, making it a condition that before agreeing to the appointment, he should receive an undertaking that there would be no further attacks on the social services.

This domestic in-fighting was first submerged and then reinforced by an international crisis. The war in Korea, which had broken out in June 1949, suddenly acquired a menacing aspect when General MacArthur determined to resolve the conflict by bombing mainland China itself, together with a blockade of the entire coast and the employment of President Chiang Kai-shek's forces in Taiwan in an almost unlimited offensive. At the beginning of 1951, the Labour Government initiated an extremely serious two-day debate in the House on the grave international situation, amid anxiety that the Korean war was about to escalate into a world confrontation. On the afternoon of the second day, the Press Association ticker-tape in the Palace of Westminster carried the story that President Truman had said in Washington that General MacArthur possessed delegated authority to use nuclear weapons without reference to the White House.

There was uproar in the Commons when the news spread. Attlee was due to wind up the debate at 9.30 pm, but earlier in the evening he called a Cabinet in his room at the House. He referred perfectly calmly to the report and said that he had concluded that he must fly to Washington, not then a routine operation, and see the President. In other circumstances he would have asked the Foreign Secretary to go, but the state of Ernie Bevin's health ruled that out and a sea voyage would take too long. He would try to contact the President on the transatlantic telephone, a very uncertain means of communication in those days, especially if the President was away from the White House. He would hope to receive confirmation of his planned visit before he wound up the debate. The Cabinet concurred.

At 7 pm Attlee came into the dining-room and sat at the table reserved for ministers. Those of us in the Cabinet clearly could not raise the Washington issue in the presence of junior ministers. None of us felt like raising any other issue, which, in view of his preoccupation with the wind-up speech, might have appeared frivolous. He broke the silence himself, turning to me and saying: 'Just been reading Philip Guedalla. Tell me, which of the popular historians do you prefer, Guedalla or Arthur Bryant?' He concurred with my answer, 'Bryant' and for half an hour the conversation centred round the Peninsular War. At 9 pm the President's agreement came through and Attlee's speech steadied the parliamentary atmosphere.

Attlee succeeded in defusing the crisis in Washington, but at a heavy price as far as Britain's strained economy was concerned. In the communiqué issued at the end of the talks with President Truman, the key clause committed both countries 'to increase their military capabilities as rapidly as possible'. Under American pressure Britain's already crippling arms burden was to go up from £3,400 million to £4,700 million. This squandering of our resources is what brought me out fighting at Bevan's side. The armourers were to thrive, but not the deliverers of arms. I had been a witness of the process. Two wars should have taught the economic innumerates, so many of whom then populated the Foreign Office and Defence departments, what the results would undoubtedly be.

First, there would be vast orders placed slowly at inflated prices, together with damaging interference with our export trade and earnings. Second, in defence terms, there would be sporadic delivery of unrelated products, with a heavy emphasis on those which could be rapidly extrapolated from the machine tools available. These would lie rusting in depots, useless in military terms until the more sophisticated and long-term delivery items were produced months, indeed years, later. All we would get would be a lot more army officers with cars to ride around in.

The expanded rearmament programme created a new tension between Gaitskell, who was preparing his budget, and Bevan, now Minister of Labour, but still obsessed with his cherished health service. They emerged from their corners bare-fisted. Backbenchers and junior ministers took sides and, over coffee in the Tea Room or something a little stronger in the Smoke Room, embarked on their canvassing duties, based on considerable misunderstanding of the real issues and a determination to emphasize personalities rather than politics. So far as the Cabinet was concerned, an immediate crisis was averted by the insertion, pressed by Aneurin Bevan and myself, into the Government's statement on its rearmanent plans of a qualification – what Nye later called the 'cautionary words':

The completion of the programme in full and in time is dependent on an adequate supply of materials, components and machine tools. In particular, our plans for expanding our capacity depend entirely upon the early provision of machine tools, many of which can only be obtained from abroad.

At one point I found myself sharing a taxi with Hugh Gaitskell. I used the occasion to say to him: 'Look, don't always try to neutralize the rest of us by imposing the majority on us. Don't regard the Cabinet as a battleground, try to see it as a levelling out. We might be able to get to a middle position, not every time, but a good deal of it and be able to say, "right, if you will agree to our doing so-and-so, we are not going to object when you do something else." ' That was not the way his mind worked and it had no effect.

Any hopes of a temporary truce were destroyed by a further move on his part when he pressed on the Cabinet what became known as The Branding Resolution condemning Chinese aggression, to be endorsed by the UN General Assembly. A majority of the Cabinet had at first opposed the idea of supporting this Motion, but Gaitskell was reported to be 'so much upset' by the majority view that he told Attlee that he would have 'to reconsider his decision', that is, resign if the Cabinet persisted in supporting the contrary resolution. Reassured by his support, the Foreign Office went again into action and this time won the day. Those of us in opposition felt that it would simply intensify the mass killings in Korea and would drive China into a closer partnership with the USSR – so it proved, for a time.

The main battle was renewed in the Cabinet itself and its committees. The saving clause about the intensity and timing of the arms programme which Nye and I had successfully pressed was ignored by the Treasury, which also continued with their King Charles' Head approval of health service charges. Gaitskell, and Attlee himself, were in no doubt that their adoption would mean the resignation of both Nye and myself. Unfortunately, Attlee was in hospital and Morrison was in charge. Bevan asked why the £23 million involved in the cost of prescriptions could not be taken off the arms programme and warned that he would resign if they were preferred. Gaitskell made it clear that for his part he would have to resign if he were not supported.

On 3 April, Nye Bevan went public. Addressing a meeting in Bermondsey, he had to face angry heckling about the trial of seven East End dockers who were being prosecuted under the Conditions of Employment National Arbitration Order no. 1305. As the interruptions grew and widened, he said flatly: 'I will never be a member of a Government which makes charges on the National Health Service for the patient.' One newspaper, the now defunct *News Chronicle*, reported his words, and the others, without acknowledgement, proceeded to stir the pot the following day. Hugh Dalton, who was active with front and back benches alike, poured ignited oil on the troubled waters when he reported to Gaitskell, whom he regarded as his protégé, that John Strachey was considering joining Nye and myself in resigning. The reply was: 'We will be well rid of all three of them.'

When Cabinet met on 9 April, the last hopes of agreement disappeared with Gaitskell's quite unnecessary, but highly provocative, statement that even if he could find elsewhere the £23 million he sought to save by imposing health service charges, he could find a better use for the money and would still press ahead. Attlee invited Nye and myself to visit him in St Mary's hospital. He was, as usual, laconic and, perhaps because of the treatment he was receiving, not very clear in his enunciation. 'Took a generation to build up this Party,' he said, without indicating who was its likely destroyer. He said he would speak to Gaitskell and then began to discuss the right timing for the general election he was planning.

Gaitskell also went to see the Prime Minister and his account of the meeting testifies to the confusion that will always remain about Attlee's attitude. Gaitskell thought that Attlee had said to him, '. . . in that case – must go', and interpreted this as meaning that Gaitskell must go. 'Certainly,' replied Gaitskell, after which Attlee corrected himself: 'I said he must go.' My own considered judgement after all these years is that he was fed up with all of us.

The following day Gaitskell made his budget speech, including a clear decision to save £13 million (£50 million in a full year) by charges on spectacles and dentures. Specifically addressing the crowded benches behind him, he went on provocatively to say that once he had made up his mind, a Chancellor should stick to it and not be moved by pressure of any kind, however insidious.

Bevan and I had a second meeting with Attlee that night. He said we should attend the Party meeting the following day and pressed us to act carefully. Then the backbenchers got to work, in the Smoke Room, the Tea Room, the corridors, the dining-rooms and in the Bar. Our letter racks in the Members' Lobby were filled many times over. Nye's mail included a letter from John Freeman, supporting his stand and saying that he would also resign if Nye did, although he hoped he would not.

The next morning, Committee Room 14 was packed out, with dozens standing. There had been good news from America in the morning press – Truman's dismissal of MacArthur. Bevan said that in response to many appeals, he had decided to resign immediately, and infuriated Gaitskell by saying that he hoped that other parties to the dispute would show a concern for the unity of the Party corresponding to his own. By this time it was not only the armourers who were thriving, but also the peacemakers, who in a later age of Party autocracy would have been christened 'wets'. Little lobbies permeated the Smoke Room and corridors. Others sought out the parliamentary journalists, most of whose editors and proprietors were utterly hostile to Bevan and for a time laudatory of Gaitskell, until, of course, an election was called, when they returned to the Tory fold.

Even so, the final decision had not been taken. Attlee appointed Ernest Bevin to act as mediator or, if necessary, arbitrator. Ernie had left the Foreign Office, gravely ill, after a hard grind of nearly six years. He had been given the post of Lord Privy Seal, with the idea that he could take on any assignment the Prime Minister chose, subject to his health.

Bevin asked Nye and me to see him. Nye launched into a philippic. I interrupted. I felt that passionate oratory was too much for Ernie and I had, I believed, a simple thought which Ernie would appreciate. The problem had arisen undoubtedly due to Gaitskell's intransigence, but Nye's destruction, I quietly suggested, was being supported if not indeed masterminded by Morrison. That was enough. Had I said 'the devil himself' Ernie might not have responded. 'Morrison did you say? Morrison?' Nye was sufficiently in control of himself to confirm that this was undoubtedly the fact. 'Oh well, in that case', said Ernie, 'why didn't you tell me? I am not having this and I'll see that Clem don't.'

Two days later I was in the Royal Box at Wembley Stadium for the England–Scotland match. Hector McNeil, Minister of State at the Foreign Office, was two or three seats away. Just before the match ended he was called to the telephone. He returned very much upset. He said, 'Ernie died this afternoon.'

Had he lived, the whole course of Labour Party history and certainly the outcome of the Bevan–Gaitskell dispute might have been very different. Even his death was used in a plot to lure me out of the Bevan camp. Since the general election could not be long delayed, it was suggested to me, without quite saying that I must first break with Nye, that Ernie's seat be left vacant and that I should be adopted as its candidate in view of my wafer-thin majority in Huyton. I stuck to Huyton.

When the Finance Bill was tabled, it contained the fateful clause. Bevan was on a speaking engagement in East Anglia. He rang me up to say, 'I am resigning. They've introduced the Bill.' The next day he sent in his resignation letter. To the last he was pressing John Freeman and me not to resign, and Freeman records that he would have stayed on but he felt he had to resign when I did.

Mary remembers how I agonised about my own resignation, walking up and down the bedroom floor all night trying to make up my mind. I was under some pressure to stay in the Cabinet and maintain a presence, if only to fight the battle from within. What formed no part of my thinking, although I have been challenged on it, was the calculation that the Government was disintegrating and that I would do well to put down a marker for the future. At the time it looked far more like an act of political suicide, but the issue on which I resigned was different from Nye's.

His own speech to the House was sadly miscalculated. For once he should have had a script. As it was, banal interruptions and barracking from the Conservative benches, and murmurings from a few on his own side, provoked him to extravagance in his choice of words. One thing was certain: he could not speak for me.

The following morning we went to Ernie Bevin's memorial service and in the afternoon I made my own statement, which was quietly received. I was careful to say that although I personally found it necessary to leave the Government, I intended both inside and outside the House to do everything in my power to support the Party and the Government in the difficult times that lay ahead.

There was a charming sequel. That evening Brendan Bracken sought me out. He had been charged, he said, 'by the greatest living statesman, for that is what Mr Churchill is', to give me a message to convey to my wife. First, Mr Churchill wanted me to know that he had been 'presented' to my wife, otherwise he would not presume to send her a message. This was that whereas I, as an experienced politican, had taken a step which he felt free to turn to such Party advantage as was appropriate, his concern was with my wife, an innocent party in these affairs, who would undoubtedly suffer in consequence. He recalled the number of occasions his wife had suffered as a result of his own political decisions. Would I therefore convey to Mary his personal sympathy and under-standing? Thanking Bracken, I went home. It was about 1 am. I repeated the message to Mary, which was greeted with gratitude and tears. I was enjoined to express her personal thanks. On leaving home the next morning I was told to make sure to see 'the old boy' and deliver the message.

In the early evening, I saw Winston in the Smoke Room on his favourite settee and went up to him, saying I had a message from my wife. He interrupted me to point out that he had on one occasion been presented to her, otherwise he would not have presumed. I acknowledged this undoubted fact and expressed her thanks. Immediately, and with Winston this was not a rare event, tears flooded down his face, as he expatiated on the way that wives had to suffer for their husbands' political actions, going on to recall a number of instances over a long life.

When I reached home this time it was 2 pm, but Mary was still awake. I was asked if I had seen the old boy and thanked him. I recounted the interview. She burst into tears and I was moved to say that whereas two days earlier I had been a minister of the Crown, red box and all, now I was reduced to the position of a messenger between her and Winston Churchill, each of whom burst into tears on receipt of a message from the other.

10

The Attlee Government

Clement Attlee had a curiously negative public image. There was a silly newspaper story about an empty taxi cab stopping outside Number 10 and the Prime Minister getting out. Nothing was further from the truth. He was more than headmaster and still very much Major Attlee. Everything had to be done with regimental precision and loyalty. He was a martinet who could reduce the toughest of his colleagues to silence. I have seen Manny Shinwell, Nye Bevan and Hugh Dalton treated like erring schoolboys.

He was in full control of himself, his Cabinet and the House. His answers in Parliament were concise and clear, with a tight little sense of humour. In the first debate of the 1945 Parliament, referring to Churchill as his 'Right Honourable Friend', he paid an unstinted tribute to his predecessor's war leadership. But he could be sharp with his former colleague. On another occasion, when Attlee was dealing with a particular problem, Churchill intervened to say that the issue had been brought up several times in the wartime Cabinet. 'I must remind the Rt Hon. Gentleman', Attlee replied, 'that a monologue is not a decision.'

Once, when Winston had rushed in with an impulsive attack on a government announcement and found himself committed to an untenable proposition, Attlee told the Cabinet: 'Trouble with Winston: nails his trousers to the mast and can't climb down.' In a warning to ministers about industrial contacts and press attacks, he said, 'A Tory minister can sleep in ten different women's beds in a week. A Labour minister gets it in the neck if he looks at his neighbour's wife over the garden fence.'

His speeches in Parliament were usually very short. Members of the Cabinet summoned to brief him, or calling on some other issue, would find him upstairs in the flat, picking out his text with two fingers on a non-standard keyboard, probably dating from his days as a social worker in Stepney. He would bring Cabinet discussion to a brisk close, before producing a clear summing-up in very few words. Cabinet business was carried through with brevity and discussions kept firmly to the point.

His decisions, personal judgements, terse comments and even his silences created the atmosphere in which all of us, from the most senior minister to the Parliamentary Secretary of Works, had to perform their duties. He was regular in his attendance in the House, regarding his presence there not so much as a gesture to Parliament, but as a means of monitoring the performances of his juniors. I remember one occasion, long after I had become President of the Board of Trade, when I remained seated and failed to answer some particularly banal, would-be funny, supplementary question. 'You're supposed to answer them, you know,' he snapped at me, 'don't sit there. Throw what they say back in their teeth'.

When Clem sacked a minister he was equally brief. One asked him why his resignation had been called for. 'Not up to the job,' said Attlee. To older friends and colleagues he would say, 'Well, you had a good innings. It's time to put your bat up in the pavilion.' One dismissal had a background Attlee would not have wanted to reveal. John Parker was Under-Secretary of State in the Dominions Office. In May 1946 he was answering questions about South Africa. Attlee promptly sent for him and sacked him. 'Not up to the job.' The real reason stemmed from high policy. Attlee was working closely with Field Marshal Smuts in an abortive attempt to civilize the South African system of persecution on the grounds of colour. John Parker's Fabian-inspired attempts to fight the colour bar, the Prime Minister felt, were counter-productive. It was not until nearly thirty years afterwards, when I attended John Parker's constituency party celebration of his forty years as MP for Romford and Dagenham, that I told him and his constituents the circumstances of his dismissal, which he had never known but which were eternally to his credit.

Attlee's most admirable characteristic was his courage, a quality put to the test in the first weeks in office, when Lend–Lease suddenly ceased. Lend–Lease was once described by Churchill as the 'most unsordid act in history'. So in one sense it was. Britain did not have to meet the cost of the supplies of food and raw materials crossing the Atlantic to British ports, but there was a price. As part of the Lend–Lease arrangements, Britain voluntarily surrendered some of her distant markets, such as those in Latin America, to American exporters. There would be no complaint in wartime. It saved shipping, but markets once lost are difficult to regain, and so it proved.

Lend–Lease also involved Britain's surrender of her rights and royalties in a series of British technological achievements. Although the British performance in industrial techniques in the inter-war years had been marked by a period of more general decline, the achievements of our scientists and technologists had equalled the most remarkable eras of British inventive greatness. Radar, antibiotics, jet aircraft and British advances in nuclear research had created an industrial revolution all over the developed world. Under Lend–Lease, these inventions were surrendered as part of the inter-Allied war effort, free of any royalty or other payments from the United States. Had Churchill been able to insist on adequate royalties for these inventions, both our wartime and our post-war balance of payments would have been very different.

The Attlee Government had to face the consequences of this surrender of our technological patrimony, but there was worse to come. Congress had voted Lend–Lease until the end of the war with Germany and Japan and no longer. When the European war ended, most people expected the conflict with Japan to last for another year or so. The atomic bombs on Nagasaki and Hiroshima ended that assumption. Almost within the hour, President Truman, unwillingly no doubt, but without any choice in the matter, notified Attlee that Lend–Lease was being cut off. At that time it was worth £2,000 million a year. There was no possible means of increasing our exports to the United States to earn that sort of sum. Britain was in pawn, at the very time that Attlee was fighting to exert some influence on the post-war European settlement. The only solution was to negotiate a huge American loan, the repayment and servicing of which placed a burden on Britain's balance of payments right into the twenty-first century.

The Truman administration did make some amends. General Marshall, the Secretary of State, made a speech at Harvard in June 1947 half-hinting, but no more, that if the bankrupt European nations would prepare four-year plans for recovery, the US might be prepared to provide the foreign exchange needed. We may never know whether it was a firm proposal, but Attlee and Bevin decided to act as though it was. They accepted an offer which had not been made, and called a conference in Paris which worked throughout the summer.

In the event, the Marshall Plan was decisive in saving Europe, whose nations accepted, country by country, a degree of socialist planning at private-enterprise America's request and expense, without which they could not have survived. In private discussion this appealed to Attlee's not inconsiderable sense of humour and irony. In public his comments were characteristically laconic. Nor did he shrink from unpopular domestic measures. During six years of war, bread had never been rationed but, in 1947, world wheat supplies were inadequate to meet demands, indeed to avert starvation. Once the figures were brought before Cabinet, Attlee was in no doubt what had to be done: bread rationing was announced.

Attlee's strength lay in his ability to preside over a team of five headstrong horses – Bevin, Morrison, Dalton, Cripps and Aneurin Bevan. Bevan was his lock forward, packing more weight than any two others. Morrison was not so much disloyal, as watching for a favourable opportunity to be disloyal. He had the right to be Lord President and Leader of the House, but he was foolish to take the post. When I was a very junior minister, I was told by Aneurin Bevan that Morrison, having no department and only a small, mainly personal staff, would lose out in the long run. He did until, pulling rank, he insisted on the Foreign Office on Bevin's breakdown and proceeded to destroy himself. Cripps was a brilliant lawyer with strong support on the left, but not seriously regarded by Attlee. Dalton, apart from his loud voice, had little to commend him. He crumpled in the 1947 crisis. Attlee simply sat pressing his Cut Golden Bar tobacco deeper into his pipe as the Chancellor whined out his excuses.

Attlee relied heavily on Bevin. Ernie filled a gap which was missing in Attlee's life. Clem had never really met trade unionists and ordinary workers, apart from his time at Toynbee Hall and other East End settlements, and also in the First World War, where his relationship had been that of a major with his rank and file. In the Party he was revered and much respected, but he always seemed to be at a distance. Bevin was a tough leader of working-class origin who had fought Churchill during the General Strike of 1926 and who, all tribute to Churchill, was made Minsiter of Labour in 1940. He knew trade unionists, he had led, or rather commanded, them for more than a generation. He knew employers too, liked and respected many but feared none.

Ernie sat opposite the Prime Minister at the Long Cabinet table. If a few ministers were talking more than they needed to, and Bevin wanted to get in, he just signalled across. One of the problems in government is whom you put on the various Cabinet sub-committees and who you leave off. If my memory is correct, I do not think Attlee had any sub-committee of which Bevin was not a member, even though it might not in any way be concerned with foreign affairs. The two used to meet often, particularly when a difficult Cabinet meeting was coming up. I do not remember a single occasion when the two disagreed in Cabinet, with Ernie acting as the bulldozer whenever necessary.

In many respects, Bevin's foreign policy was sound, often inspired. He was one of the first to see the dangers in Europe, with the Soviet Union asserting an increasing role over her neighbours to the west whom she had 'liberated' from Nazi Germany. He was one of the first statesmen of any country able to read political problems in economic terms and to foresee the imminent collapse of Western Europe if the United States failed to abandon their ancient policy of isolation. He was also one of the first to identify the dangers of Russian penetration of the old Turkish empire. The awesome fact is that by his Palestinian policy he so far angered the White House, even to the point of making at least one cheap anti-Truman jibe, that he could have imperilled his grand designs for Europe in both economic and diplomatic terms.

It is not too strong a phrase to say that Ernie was anti-Semitic. In his policy for Palestine and the Middle East generally, he never accepted the conference commitments and election pledges of the Labour Party. Nor did he for a single moment suggest during this critical period that he paid any account whatsoever to the Balfour Declaration. Commitments entered into by Lloyd George, Baldwin, Churchill and a generation of Labour leaders up to 1945 played no part in his policy, except as tiresome undertakings to be got round or, if he was provoked, challenged head on. The tragic history of the illegal emigrant ships and the Arab–Israeli clashes led directly to the surrender of the mandate. A contributory factor certainly was Ernie's growing *ennui* with the whole subject and, no less, the fact that he was answerable in Parliament not only for the main strategy and the political decisions, but also for the practicalities of control, responsibility for the police, the welfare and, above all, the safety of the troops stationed there.

Bevin proved to be a highly effective parliamentarian, even if brusque both in answering questions and in debate, but he made no secret, at least in Cabinet and private conversations, of the fact that he hated the House. On one occasion after I had joined the Cabinet, I was warning that a particular proposal which a colleague had put forward would lead to trouble in the House of Commons. I made a slip of the tongue and referred to it as "the House of Trouble'. Ernie seized on the phrase and ever afterwards called the lower house of the legislature the House of Trouble.

Ernie could not stand Herbert Morrison, who had been a City boss when Bevin had been head of one of the biggest unions and the two had clashed. I would think that Bevin declared war on Morrison in the 1930s and that they were never going to come together. You could see his hackles rise every time, especially if Morrison tried to encroach on foreign affairs.

Morrison had emerged from the war with a good reputation as Home Secretary in the Coalition Government and he was a figure of sufficient seniority in the Party not to be denied. Attlee kept him at arm's length, did not trust him and was particularly averse to the strong rumours during one period that Morrison was maintaining a liaison with a woman MP, with whom he subsequently broke.

Dalton, with his great booming voice, was a noisy colleague to say the least. He maintained a constant entourage of younger members of the Party, whose careers he would attempt to promote while using them as a source of ideas for himself. Attlee did not understand economics and Dalton did, or made large claims to do so. His book *Public Finance* was one of the first I had been required to read at Oxford. In his own days as an economics lecturer at the London School of Economics, he predated John Maynard Keynes, whom he regarded as a usurper in an area where he was supposed to have a monopoly. My generation was brought up on Keynes and Dalton did not like it. Clem Attlee was altogether above these cults and objected mainly to Dalton's style and bullying in Cabinet.

Stafford Cripps enjoyed a period of high favour. He always made a fetish of appearing very left wing until he had thought it all through. I have always been worried in politics about people who have made their name in advocacy. They are unable to take up a middle position. Either that man is hanged or he gets off, so to speak. Stafford knew very little about ordinary people. He was also very much under the control of Lady Cripps. She was always devising schemes, some of them quite good, most of them harum-scarum, and Stafford had to go and address the clubs and associations she formed. Attlee would never have thought of forming a government without him. He was too important after his wartime experiences in Russia to be offered one of the lower offices of the Crown. Stafford always gave the impression that he was speaking with the direct authority of the Almighty and Attlee used to humour him. 'Why don't you submit a paper?' he would say. I think he regarded Stafford as a self-appointed saint, who, whatever his great abilities, was not a political animal at all.

Attlee felt that Nye Bevan had great qualities provided he could be kept under some sort of control. He handled him very well. 'The Cabinet will agree that this is too risky a procedure,' he would tend to say; 'indeed we have had this brought before us this morning with no estimate of the financial cost and I am quite sure the Chancellor would like to put a value on it if the Minister wishes to press the matter further.' The advancement of Gaitskell was certainly a counter to Morrison, whose real adversary was Ernie Bevin. I remember interceding with Ernie on one occasion after Morrison had tried to order the Cabinet about. 'Don't take too much notice,' I said, 'he is his own worst enemy.' Bevin said, 'Not while I'm around, he ain't.'

We were indeed a mixed band and the wonder is that Attlee succeeded in maintaining a united front for so long. He kept himself above the battle and exerted a quite extraordinary authority. Despite his sense of history, or possibly because of it, great events failed to move him. The story belongs to a later period, but after his premiership, while still Party Leader, he was chairing a meeting of Labour MPs which had assembled in a mood of great anxiety owing to the explosion of the first American thermo-nuclear bomb in the Pacific. There was great concern at the risks of possible nuclear fall-out, even thousands of miles away. As one pacifist ended an impassioned speech, Attlee picked up his papers and closed the meeting saying, 'Agree. We've got to watch it.'

He brought great clarity of mind to matters great and small. When the issue of Indian independence presented itself, he was the first to recognize the magic of the timetable. Fix a date, he decided, on which the British Raj would withdraw. It would be for the Indians to produce a definitive constitutional settlement for the sub-continent. It was his decision to appoint as Viceroy Lord Louis Mountbatten, who accepted providing he had plenipotentiary powers. To his surprise, Attlee said that this was just the proposition. All he was doing was laying down the timetable.

Mountbatten, never a man to miss an opportunity, recounted the story that at the end of the interview, he told Attlee that there was great concern among the Service Chiefs that X had been decided on as the next Chief of the Army General Staff. The right choice, he felt, would be Sir William Slim. To his surprise, Attlee agreed; Slim was the man he wanted. Mountbatten pointed out that X had been told that the choice had fallen on him. 'Untell him,' said Attlee.

He brought this gift of brevity to most occasions. Once, following a parliamentary recess, a junior minister turned up at a Cabinet committee meeting with a luxuriant beard. Attlee's immediate comment was, 'Move precious face' – a phrase derived from a device regularly used at Labour Party Conferences and National Executive committee meetings to stop discussion, instead of the traditional 'Move next business' or 'Move previous question'.

My wife was once asked by Mrs Attlee to go to Wimbledon with her and first went to lunch at Number 10. Clem had two main off-duty subjects of conversation, cricket and history. He asked Mary whom she liked in history. She said, knowing that he would not approve, 'The romantic ones, Charles II, Rupert of the Rhine, Byron.' His response was: 'Bad history, wrong people.'

There is a little-known Attlee story concerning John Strachey, at that time Minister of Food. A Cabinet rule in the manual *Questions of Procedure for Ministers* forbids any minister from publishing written work, such as a book or press article, without the specific authority of the Prime Minister. This is not usually withheld for a literary or historic work, such as Ian MacLeod's *Neville Chamberlain*. Strachey telephoned the Prime Minister – he should have gone to see him – 'Prime Minister,' he said, 'I see that under the rules I have to get your permission to publish a book. I have written a small collection of poems; there is nothing political or controversial in them. I take it you will agree to my publishing them.' Attlee would have none of it: 'Better send them to me.' A fortnight later, Strachey had not heard from him, which was unusual since Attlee normally completed his boxes every night and never deferred any correspondence. So Strachey phoned again: 'Clem, I take it you've no objection to letting me go ahead and publish those poems I sent you.' 'Can't publish,' said Attlee, and when Strachey asked for his reason: 'Don't rhyme, don't scan.'

Attlee proved that Labour could govern. He carried through the transition from total war conditions to those of peace in sharp contrast to the failure and lack of concern of 1918–22. There was virtually no unemployment. Attlee and his ministers linked the returning servicemen and displaced munitions and aircraft workers to the jobs that had to be done, not only to repair the ravages of war and the tasks postponed by the conflict, but to make up for the years of pre-war neglect in housing and education. His ministers were responsible for the completion of 400,000 permanent houses in three years after the end of the war, compared with 75,000 in the same period after the First World War. The 240,000 prefabs were in addition. He presided over the introduction of the Welfare State and very quietly dictated the priorities in public expenditure and parliamentary time which made the revolution possible.

In a world setting, his achievement was historic. It was he who initiated the peaceful transition from Empire to Commonwealth, taking personal charge of the entire operation. Most difficult of all was the achievement of independence and self-government for India, Pakistan, Ceylon and Burmah. This had not been an inheritance from the wartime coalition. Churchill had agreed to no such proposals and his Secretary of State for India was totally opposed to them. Beginning the process in July 1945, Attlee ensured that it was completed in just a few days over two years. Clement Attlee was the undisputed founder of the modern Commonwealth, now made up thirty-five nations linked in close association one to another with the Queen at its head.

One of his proudest moments was the ceremony in Westminster Hall, when the King formally opened the rebuilt House of Commons on 31 October 1950. Following the Lord Chancellor, Mr Speaker, and Presiding Officers of the Lords and the Commons, was a great assembly of Speakers of the Commonwealth, black, white, yellow and brown, many wearing the traditional Westminster robes and wigs, others the colourful robes of their countries. Among the Cabinet that day there were few dry eyes.

It is therefore painful to have to record the final disintegration of one of the strongest Cabinets in British history. Ernie Bevin was dead, Stafford Cripps was mortally sick, Dalton had blown himself up with his indiscretion. Bevan had taken himself out of the play and Morrison had made a fool of himself at the Foreign Office. It has been said of them that they could not carry their corn, a Yorkshire mill phrase applied to people who find themselves in a job higher than they had before. They are sure they know everything about everything, they do not consult and it goes to their heads. The majority in Parliament was so slim that the Conservative Opposition was able to harry the Labour Government almost to death. We were like a football team with ten minutes left and two goals down. Attlee never told me why he suddenly called his second election for 25 October 1951, but he was himself tired and felt that he could only carry on with some sort of improved majority.

In the event, it went the other way and Churchill was back with a majority of seventeen. Huyton was highly marginal and I decided against any national speaking tour to concentrate on my own bailiwick. Many leading Party colleagues came to help, including Nye Bevan, and I was undoubtedly assisted by a shift in the population to the new council houses in the constituency. Against the national trend, I was back with a majority of 1,193.

11

Bevanites Banned

Few could have foreseen that the election defeat heralded the beginning of thirteen years in opposition for the Labour Party. For the first nine years of that time, our internal affairs were to a considerable extent, and so far as press comment was concerned, almost totally dominated by the relations between Aneurin Bevan and Hugh Gaitskell. These ranged from complete mutual hostility to close co-operation, when Nye, strongly backed on that occasion by Hugh Gaitskell, became Deputy Leader of the Party. In my own case, there were periods of divergence, even dissociation.

The timing of our resignations had created serious problems for us. Having made a stand on what we and many other members of the Parliamentary Labour Party, as well as a large number of Party workers in the constituencies, considered an issue of principle, we could not remain silent. Even if the rest of us had taken a solemn vow to do so, it would have had no effect on Aneurin Bevan. He was in great demand in the constituencies and even on occasions when he had decided to speak with circumspection, his habit of extempore oratory, and the ease with which he could be goaded into attacking hecklers, would have saddled us with co-responsibility for all he said.

Critical as we were of certain aspects of government policy, particularly the bloated and unachievable rearmament programme, we had a duty to state our alternatives, while campaigning vigorously in support of Attlee and his team in their resistance to Conservative attacks. During this twilight period, no one knew, perhaps not even the Prime Minister himself, when the inevitable general election would take place and, in particular, whether it would precede or follow the Party Conference in October.

It was important for us to make a collective statement of our position. Nye's highlighting of the health charges as his reason for resigning hardly provided a policy in itself. In any case, many of our backbench supporters were more concerned, as I was, with the recklessly conceived rearmament programme. Some of us felt that instead of relying on unco-ordinated and in some cases contradictory weekend speeches by individuals, and instead of simply accentuating a negative approach to that of the official Labour leadership, we should issue a considered and positive statement of our beliefs.

We compiled a Tribune pamphlet under the title *One Way Only*, set in a much wider canvas than arguments about the health service. It had indeed an international rather than a national setting and its idealistic approach, combined with practical remedies, would have, we felt, a great appeal for young readers in the Party and indeed more widely. One of the articles, 'Neither Guns Nor Butter', which I had written, set out to show how the overloading of the economy by the arms programme had led to shortages of steel, coal and electricity, and had overstrained our transport system as well as harming our exports.

In what later became known as 'image' terms, we were fighting a hopeless uphill battle. Our carefully drafted and thoughtful pamphlets could not compete for the attention of the predominantly Conservative press with the day-to-day speeches of Aneurin Bevan. He was always ready to follow a heckler up uncharted tangents and could undo a month's hard work on our part by providing the richest of hostages for his critics in the press. Every speech produced prolonged analysis and endless repetition in the dailies, including Labour's small press, such as the *Daily Herald*, consistently critical of Nye and loyal to – indeed closely influenced by – Hugh Gaitskell and his intimates. Nye's reaction to our complaints varied from an eloquent defence of his latest speech to soon forgotten pledges never to sin again.

On the one occasion when we tried to take him in hand on the content and delivery of a speech, our efforts came to nothing. He had decided to take part in a debate in Parliament on economic affairs. Some of us urged that in view of the technicalities of the issue we should brief him and that he should then draft his speech on paper, at least in note form. He complied to the full, stuck to his brief, not putting a foot wrong, but his speech lacked all warmth and brilliance and was an oratorical disaster. The experiment was not repeated.

There were indeed undercurrents of which one had to be wary. Almost from the day of my resignation, I began to receive invitations from left-wing constituencies and local trade union branches to address mettings. These I treated with some reserve. While very few local parties were under communist influence, one had to watch out carefully for those who were. The same caution had to be applied to approaches from local trade union branches and federations. There were some extremely active left-wing operators, whose influence tended to be a direct function of small local membership and those of us who were supporting Nye Bevan had to be very careful not to become tainted by their company in the eyes of the right wing of the Party.

Attlee did not announce the dissolution of Parliament until the eve of the 1951 annual conference at Scarborough. The sessions therefore took on the nature of a rally. All sections of the Party buried their hatchets, some of them, to use the old phrase, in well-marked places. Labour Party Conferences are never confined to the seaside pavilions where they are held. The speeches from the Party high command, or from a humble delegate from a distant constituency, end at 5 pm. The intrigues go on far into the night in the conference hotels.

Scarborough 1951 was no exception. Indeed it set the pattern for many years of struggle in the Party, at Westminster, in the constituencies and trade union offices. The declaration of war came from the St Nicholas Hotel and its promoters were the leaders of the three most powerful unions. I must borrow Michael Foot's words in his biography of Aneurin Bevan to introduce the characters:

> The ringleader was Arthur Deakin, General Secretary of the Transport and General Workers' Union, a fierce, breezy, irascible, stout-hearted bison of a man, who genuinely believed that anything he could force through his union executive must be the will of the people and more especially the will of Ernest Bevin, whose requirements he had normally taken the precaution of finding out in advance. Bevin was now dead and Deakin lacked Bevin's redeeming powers of individual imaginative rumination. Leaders must be loyally followed: that was the Deakin dream of democracy and with Bevin gone he cast around for a new god he could serve with the same restless devotion. Meantime, the identity of the devil was plain enough. From Scarborough 1951 until the day of his death, Arthur Deakin was a man with a mission – to exterminate the infamous Bevan.

The other two were Will Lawther, President of the Mineworkers, and Tom Williamson, General Secretary of the General Municipal Workers, a more cultured and intelligent man who in later years came to provide statesmanlike leadership to the TUC. Between them, the big three commanded, almost literally, two million votes out of the then total vote of less than three million at Labour's Party Conference. Unfortunately for all hopes of electoral unity, Tom O'Brien, head of the National Association of Cine-employees, whom I knew well through my previous connection with the film industry, suffered even more than other trade union leaders in those gossipy days from the malady known as enuresis, defined as a propensity to leaking when pressmen are about.

The battle lines had been drawn and this duly had its effect on the Party as it endeavoured to adjust itself to the new role as His Majesty's Opposition. For some, both in Parliament and in the unions, this was an intense relief. Nothing was so dull as providing 'lobby fodder' for an Attlee Government. After all those years of self-denial, they could join in the more rewarding occupation of harassing a Tory Government. Because of the mass influx of 1945, only a relatively small minority on the Labour backbenches had been in Opposition.

The Churchill Government, however confused their economic policy, accepted with alacrity the presence of a divided Opposition, none more so than Winston himself, holding as he did the record for the still unequalled number of times he had crossed the floor of the House, and for his membership in government and Opposition of a succession of parties and of none.

'Churchill the warmonger' he had been called by many Labour candidates in the 1951 contest. A fairer assessment would have been based on his long experience of defence matters, in peace as well as in war, and his clear perception of the overstraining of the economy in general and the productive potentialities of the munitions industries. He had, after all, been Minister of Munitions a third of a century earlier.

In the first Defence Debate under the new regime, he referred to the outgoing Government's defence proposals for the current year. He had seen the books. Referring to Gaitskell's spending programme for the first year of rearmament, he said: 'We shall not, however, succeed in spending the £1,250 million programme and some of the late Government's programme must necessarily roll forward into the future year. The point was, I believe, made by the Rt Hon. Gentleman [Bevan] after his resignation.'

He went on to explain that he made no reflection on his predecessors. This was of the nature of things with armament programmes, of which he had seen many. Nye, never backward in seizing a parliamentary opportunity, leapt to his feet and pressed Churchill. Did this mean that the whole three-year programme would be rolled forward? Over how many years was it to be spread?

Churchill, savouring the mischief he had created, replied: 'I am not really wishing to embark on a debate with the Rt Hon. Gentleman. I was giving him an honourable mention in despatches for having been right by accident.' Nye rose to press him further, but Churchill was still at the box: 'I was giving the Rt Hon. Gentleman an honourable mention for having, it appears by accident, perhaps not from the best of motives, happened to be right.'

Nye, unfortunately and unusually, took this reply hard. In fact, Churchill had endorsed the line that Nye and the rest of us had taken, particularly the point I had pressed that Gaitskell's insistence on increasing the original programme would be nullified by lags in the delivery of arms. The Treasury in Gaitskell's time had thrown money at the armourers. Now Churchill was announcing that it could not be spent and rubbed this in by saying that the lag in production 'will of course be helpful to the Chancellor of the Exchequer in his fiscal problems' – the very issue on which Nye had resigned.

Nye should, as his friends hoped, have accepted, indeed embraced, Winston's words, which had put the seal on his victory over Gaitskell. But Winston criticized him, so he threw away the victory that mattered in order to take on Winston as well. Both Hugh Gaitskell and Nye Bevan were wrong to go on fighting the battles of yesteryear. The real fight should have been against the Conservatives, who were not only winding back defence expenditure but were determined, if not to destroy the social services in general, at least to roll them back as well. Some of us tried to bring Hugh and Nye closer together and turn their backs on 1951, but all to no avail.

As we moved further into the 1950s, entirely new problems and controversies came to dominate the political scene, provoking oratorial blasts and counter-blasts from one or other wing of a Party which met them, indeed welcomed them, as creating new opportunities and groupings. Nye's instant reactions could not be binding on his allies, particularly if he went on the record on issue after issue without consultation. Moreover, in Opposition, the central power shifted from the Cabinet and the House of Commons front bench to Party Headquarters and the National Executive Committee. More importance came to be attached to Party Conference, more controversy arose over the question of how far elected MPs were bound by monthly NEC decision, or even by the annual conference, dominated as it was by the trade union block vote.

The fifty or so Labour backbenchers, closely or more loosely linked with Aneurin Bevan, were in still more difficulty. We were not parties to the background briefing which a British Government frequently gives to the official Opposition, particularly on foreign affairs and sometimes, too, on economic questions and the shape of projected legislation. The truth is that a bunch of us were in the wilderness together and, since Moses was there and overshadowed the rest of us, we should have been more conveniently dubbed 'Moses-ites'. I disliked the word Bevanite as much as Nye did. I was a co-belligerent, not a satellite.

Not all the Labour MPs who survived the 1951 general election were unduly disheartened by the result. For six years, the life of Labour backbenchers had not been a path of roses. The Government which most of them supported had been forced by economic circumstances, from the disintegration of Marshall Aid onwards, to back measures in some cases, such as bread rationing, more painful than those of wartime days. They had found some difficulty in explaining these measures to bewildered and some-times angry constituency parties, most of which were loyal and understanding, with a minority controlled by the extreme left of the Party, which called for more nationalization and in some constituencies for measures based on the internal policies of our late, now self-distancing allies of the Soviet Union and for an open breach with the United States. Many of our backbenchers were analyzing Labour's shortcomings in office and calling for 'Socialism in our Time'.

The minuscule though articulate Communist Party was well placed to spread dissension in Labour's ranks, aided by the fact that the 1945 landslide had brought some hurriedly selected extremists into our ranks. They had a simple explanation for our defeat at the election. We had not been socialist enough. Jerusalem – or Moscow – had not been built in England's green and pleasant land. Nye, a woolly moderate, had in their eyes spent too much time ingratiating himself with the anti-socialist medical profession;

while a mere statistical machine, such as myself, had toured all over the country, including their constituencies, seeking to make capitalism work.

Now, as we sat in the unaccustomed seats to the Speaker's left and ex-ministers sought to attack the Conservative reversal of many of Labour's principal policies, they had to put up with an undercurrent of muttered barracking from behind them, the theme of which was that we should have enacted 'socialism' in such a way that no incoming vandals could destroy or even change it. Some of our detractors failed entirely to understand what parliamentary institutions involved. Others understood well enough – it was Labour's concessions to public opinion and fair play as between parties for which we have never been forgiven. We had spent too much time on law-making when we should have asserted power by short enabling legislation and filled in the details by Cabinet fiat and statutory rules and orders.

In this unhealthy atmosphere, the Gaitskellites were seeking their revenge. Their leader, far from discouraging them, was spurring them on, and some were aiming at expelling those who disagreed with him. A few of us, Barbara Castle, Ian Mikardo and myself, felt that we should form a small tight group to work out our strategy and our week-by-week tactics. I was elected leader. We met at half-past one every Monday. I set myself the task of resisting extremism and provocative public statements.

For MPs to meet in unofficial groups, getting together informally, as distinct from in committees and sub-committees set up by the House of Commons itself, is probably as old as Parliament itself. King John could have written a thesis on the subject. But this was too much for Hugh Gaitskell, who would have been better advised to acknowledge that he led an unofficial group of his own. Immediately after the annual conference at Morecambe in 1952 he found his voice.

In a speech at Stalybridge, he repeated an allegation that one-sixth of the constituency party delegates at Morecambe were communist or communist-inspired. He drew the conclusion that at a time when communist policy was to infiltrate the Labour movement, the Bevanites were assisting them by their disruptive activities. Then, in a direct reference to us and our pamphlets, he went on: 'It is time to end the attempt at mob rule by a group of frustrated journalists and restore the authority and leadership of the solid, sound, sensible majority of the movement.' He referred to 'the stream of grossly misleading propaganda, with poisonous innuendoes and malicious attacks on Attlee, Morrison and the rest of the leadership'.

I replied from my old stamping ground at Bebington a few days later: 'I was surprised and a little shocked at the intemperate outburst of Hugh Gaitskell. Phrases such as "mob rule" are hardly worthy of him. These continued personal attacks are harmful both to the Labour Party and to the country. The Morecambe conference showed that there was now a far better basis for agreement and unity in the Party on fundamental policy.'

My own position in the Party had been usefully reinforced at Morecambe. Hugh Dalton had never really recovered from his resignation as Chancellor and tended more and more to spend his time pushing the claims of his former kindergarten of potential Labour leaders. The booming of his voice, when quietly advising, warning or encouraging one of his flock, could be heard by any MP or visitor who happened to be within thirty yards or so of the Ways and Means corridor. In the election for the National Executive Committee, he was ousted and I was elected as fifth on the list. Nye Bevan and Barbara Castle were ahead of me.

The Shadow Cabinet took Gaitskell's side and followed up his words by aggressive action. They passed a resolution for the approval of Labour MPs, forbidding the Bevanites to continue meeting as a group. This was carried by 188 to fifty-one. A further fifty-three were either absent or abstained. Looking back on these extraordinary events, I am certain that if a government nowadays, Conservative or Labour, were to issue such a ukase, the matter would be raised in the House of Commons as involving an issue of privilege and its reference to the relevant committee would lead to strictures on, and possibly the expulsion from Parliament of, the instigators.

I chaired the final meeting of the banned organization and issued this statement: 'We deplore this resolution for three reasons. It is illiberal. It is based on allegations which are not true. It is prejudicial to Party unity.' I argued that the resolution was unprecedented in parliamentary history. For anyone to assert that MPs should not meet without approval from on high, gave to the Party machine a power which it had never sought to exercise before. We were not, I proclaimed, a 'party within a party'.

The leadership's move was completely based on insincerity. The Gaitskellites continued with their own meetings and it was hardly surprising that before long Nye Bevan and a few of his friends were having an occasional drink together at Dick Crossman's house in Vincent Square, or at Bevan's own home. Twice we met at our house in Hampstead Garden Suburb, including a 5th of November when Nye came to light the bonfire in the back garden. We were a bit far out from the centre for these social occasions and we found it more convenient to sit at the same table in the House of Commons dining-room or keep to ourselves at the Party Conferences. We were subjected to a certain degree of ostracism, particularly from the trade union delegates, but we felt in no way that we were a persecuted minority. We were always in high good humour, enjoying each others' company, and the only long-term consequence was that when I came to form my own administration a dozen years later, Mary found that she only really knew the Bevanite wives and none of the others.

The right wing of the Party reacted sharply to the Morecambe voting for NEC places, If, as they saw it, the constituency parties and some of the unions had gone out of their illiterate minds, a new force must be called into existence to redress the balance of the Conference. More specifically, the Parliamentary Party, where the hated left were in a minority, should be taken over. Although the Shadow Cabinet was much more right wing than the National Executive, it was felt that it should be further strengthened by a new voting procedure. With a determination which would have put a Tammany boss to shame, they decided to change the voting rules for the Parliamentary Committee. Each MP had to vote for twelve names, rather than 'plumping' for a lesser number. Only those who secured 50 per cent or more of the votes would be elected. To fill the remaining vacancies, there had to be a replay in the form of a second ballot.

This was widely interpreted as an anti-Bevanite move. There was criticism of this califugling even by moderate or right-wing MPs. The left thought that this was a plot to keep out Bevan and his friends, although it was asserted by those who thought they knew Attlee's mind that it was to ensure that Bevan had a second chance, if he failed the first time round. In the event he just made it. When the PLP came to elect its leader, Attlee was confirmed without opposition, but Nye challenged Morrison for the Deputy Leadership and surprised many of the pundits by polling eighty-two votes against Herbert's 194.

In the 1953 Party Conference in Margate, I moved up from fifth to third place in the NEC, with 934,000 votes against the previous year's 632,000. Nye and Barbara Castle headed the polls, with Hugh Gaitskell runner-up as eighth man. Morrison upset trade union leaders by his determination to stand against the ageing but popular Arthur Greenwood for the Treasurership. In the event, he was persuaded to drop his candidature by a concordat to change the Party rules by providing that the Deputy Leader should also be a member of the NEC, a wise and overdue reform since it enabled the parliamentary Leadership to be represented when the Leader was called away.

Back in Parliament, we had to deal with yet another election to the Shadow Cabinet. Nye was safely in, again as number twelve, but eighteen votes up on the previous year. I was runner-up as thirteenth man, just one vote behind, a position which was to lead to serious trouble in the following spring.

We already had troubles enough, most of them deriving from events abroad. Dr Cheddi Jagan had been deposed by the Westminster Government from his position of Prime Minister of British Guiana, together with his more left-wing Education Minister Forbes Burnham. Nye laid on a party for them at Cliveden Place. Seretse Khama, who had been ousted in an earlier *coup de Whitehall*, was also present and full reports reached the press.

Meanwhile, there was a crisis in Egypt. The Churchill Government had decided to evacuate their Middle Eastern base, in the face of a major revolt from their own Party and severe criticism from Shinwell and Morrison. Bevan supported Churchill's decision, indeed he had been pressing for evacuation for a long time. The *Daily Express* rejoiced in the decision of the Egyptian leader, General Neguib, to print Bevan's articles in his extremely foul Government's paper. Right-wing Tories attacked Bevan in Parliament, even suggesting that Nye had acted in breach of his Privy Counsellor's Oath. His supporters, including me, argued, in his own words: 'The presence of the troops of another nation on one's soil is a circumstance to be borne only when it is voluntarily conceded. A military base is useless if it is surrounded by a hostile population.'

The Party was further divided by the German rearmament controversy. Attlee was persuaded by the right to support the measures on which the unpredictable John Foster Dulles, the American Secretary of State, was insisting. I moved a resolution at a Party meeting opposing German rearmament. It was defeated by just two votes, 111 to 109. Few PLP meetings since the war, if any, have ended in such uproar, not least because Attlee had allowed Labour peers to vote. The National Executive voted the same way as the PLP, but with a somewhat larger majority. Hugh Gaitskell could always count on the support of the trade union barons.

To the German arms question and the anxiety about nuclear weapons was added a fresh Dulles initiative for creating a NATO in South-East Asia. Nye had had enough. He wanted to get back to his own people. Suddenly, in April 1954, he resigned from the Shadow Cabinet. I had supported him in his opposition to the Dulles move, but I could not agree with his unilateral decision to resign from the one position where he could and did formidably argue his case, and indeed mine.

He had placed me in an extremely awkward predicament. As thirteenth man in the PLP elections, I was automatically co-opted to fill the vacancy he had created. It was not open to me to refuse to serve on the Shadow Cabinet. I was on it automatically. If I wanted to support him I had to resign from it, and this I felt I could not do. There were wider considerations even than the German and SEATO questions. Someone in the Shadow Cabinet had to put the views of nearly half the parliamentary Party. I had the Easter recess to think about it, and to consult those whose opinions I valued most before meeting Attlee to tell him of my decision to remain.

Nye, inevitably, was furious, despite his failure to discuss the issue with me before his impulsive resignation. I became the subject of quite vicious attacks from those on the extreme left. My constituency chairman, Bob Foulkes, and a majority of the local Party supported me. Bob had telephoned me to say: 'Now, lad, tha's best signing on the dotted line.' In a very early television interview on *Press Conference*, I was asked if Bevan had agreed with my joining the Shadow Cabinet: 'Well,' I replied, 'naturally I discussed it with him and I discussed it with a very large number of members. Whether he agreed with it or not, I don't think is the real question. He did not have to agree. I made my own decision.'

Nye was carried away by his anger at my seeming apostasy. At a meeting at Dick Crossman's house he told me that I would be chucked off the National Executive at the next Conference. In fact, I received the top vote of 1,043,000 against 934,000 the previous year. Nye, who had topped the voting in 1953, did not stand for the constituency section. Instead, he challenged Gaitskell for the Treasurership, Arthur Greenwood having died the previous June. There was certainly a high degree of jiggery-pokery in individual union's decisions on their vote. The Amalgamated Society of Woodworkers, who had voted against rearmament both at their own conference and at the TUC, and were in fact so mandated, voted against Nye. His own miners voted against him, the usually statesmanlike leader Ernest Jones even going so far as to argue that the anti-German rearmament campaign was communist inspired.

It was an unhappy end to what had been an unsettling period, during which I had endured all the obloquy directed at those who had joined the Bevanite camp and now I found myself at odds with its rejected leader. Small wonder that my father, who followed all these events with avidity, said to Mary: 'If I were Harold I would give up, do something else.'

12

The Butskell Budgets

During most of the 1950s, my personal circumstances were much eased, indeed my continuance in public life on the miserable MP's salary of those days was made possible, by my acceptance of an offer from the international timber firm of Montague Meyer to become their political and economic consultant. They provided me with an office in their headquarters, which at least served as somewhere to store my copious correspondence, facilities still denied in the Palace of Westminster.

The arrangement derived posthumously from Ernie Bevin, who had known old man Meyer before the war when he had had to negotiate with him on trade union matters and had developed a high regard for his straight dealing. When the wartime alliance came under strain in the late 1940s, Ernie had never ceased his attempts at least to foster Anglo–Soviet trade, an initiative in which I had been called upon to play my part. Montague Meyer was one of the beneficiaries. They needed fresh supplies of timber and it was one of the few commodities the Soviet Union had for export. Once I was in Opposition, the firm approached me through an intermediary to see if I could help them to pick up the threads. I was to act as their diplomatic adviser and they, in turn, set out to educate me in the ways of the timber trade. I paid a visit to Canada and succeeded in arranging substantial shipments, then I undertook a trip to Moscow.

As a Privy Counsellor, I was under an obligation to inform the Prime Minister of this particular destination, so I sought Winston out on his favourite settee in the Members' Bar; he immediately invited me to share some liquid refreshment with him. 'Should I accept?' I asked. 'Shertainly, my boy, shertainly you should go. You'll meet some of the top leaders. What you must look out for is what they are doing in the way of conshumer goodsh.' So I went, and found myself involved in an embarrassing incident.

The Russian authorities had indicated that I was free to take a camera with me. Since my last official visit, they had built a huge department store on the other side of the Red Square from the Kremlin. This seemed good consumer goods' country to inspect and I saw a lady trundling a child's fairy cycle she had obviously just purchased. I trotted across the Square and was just taking a photograph of her when a heavy hand fell on my shoulder. It was a plainclothes policeman, who more or less frog-marched me down the road to a police station to try to relieve me of my camera. It was one of the few times in my life that I have lost my cool. I raised my voice and used abusive language; when this did not reduce his interest in my camera, I succeeded in conveying to him that I was seeing Mikoyan the following day and would give him an account of the whole incident.

This did the trick. I was allowed back to my hotel, one reserved for foreign visitors, with a resident Russian Foreign Office representative. I gave him an account of what had happened and he was so concerned that he sent for the Mayor of Moscow, who came with apologies and said that the uniformed policeman concerned would be disciplined. I told him it was a plainclothes man. He said there was no plainclothes man there. 'I was there,' I said, 'you weren't. I am seeing Mikoyan tomorrow and I am going to tell him the whole story. I am a regular visitor here and I shall want to see that chap to ensure that nothing has happened to him.' When I went back about ten months later, he was on duty in the street wearing a sergeant's stripes and all was well.

I also paid my first and only visit to China. I was attending a European economic conference in Geneva in my parliamentary capacity when the Chinese Peoples Minister in Switzerland made contact with me and gave me a formal invitation from Chou En-lai, the Chinese Foreign Minister, to visit Peking as their guest. The Chinese representative in London told me I had to be sponsored, and as Peking understood that I was an economist my hosts would be the Bank of China. I flew to Hong Kong and had to change for the flight to the Chinese capital. The aircraft was an incredibly ancient and noisy American product, presumably donated or lend–leased to the Chinese when relations were reasonably normal.

I had been warned by our people in Hong Kong that the Chinese were extremely wary aviators: one small cloud in the sky would involve a landing somewhere in the middle of that vast country and a long stay while waiting for perfect weather. The landing duly took place but, in a mercifully short time, the mini-cloud that had delayed us disappeared and we were on our way again.

I was met at the airport and driven to my hotel, which was perfectly comfortable but unpretentious, built many years before and managed by Englishmen. The staff were most accommodating, not to say servile, and while waiting to see the Foreign Minister, they arranged a shopping excursion. Apart from trinkets and the usual purchases, I bought a silk dress for Mary at a perfectly reasonable price by London standards. The shop was not in any way limited to foreign visitors and the diplomatic community, and most of my fellow shoppers were Chinese. My interest in the price charged was to feature in my discussions with the Chinese financiers.

My talk with Chou En-lai, including lunch, occupied seven hours. He gave away nothing about deteriorating relations with the Soviet Union, which our people in Hong Kong had advised me might be of interest, but he was very concerned to ask me about my recent visit to Moscow and particularly wanted my assessment of the Soviet economic situation.

I spent most of my time with my Bank of China hosts, mainly discussing world economics. On my last evening they gave a dinner for me. The food, they proclaimed, was typical Chinese fare, quite unlike anything I had ever been served in Chinese restaurants in London, which they said provided mainly Hong Kong dishes. The octopus eggs I could not stomach, and some of the other apparently choice specimens required chewing for minutes on end.

None of them spoke English, except my host and acquaintance of Geneva days, Dr Chi, who had won his doctorate at the London School of Economics. I said there was one economic problem which intrigued me. It was, in fact, triangular in its application. On my visits to Moscow, I said, I had not been able to buy at any of their shops a dress for my wife, except at something like ten or twelve times London prices. This was still in the days before the special price Soviet shops for tourists. In Peking, prices at the ordinary shops were about the same as those in London. So here was my triangle: London/Peking all right, London/Moscow all wrong; what then of the third rate, between Moscow and Peking?

At this they fell about laughing, almost tumbling out of their chairs, making what sounded like ribald comments at my expense, pointing at me and roaring with laughter. 'Do you know what they are saying?' Dr Chi asked. When I made it clear that I had no idea, he said: 'They are saying, "He's got on to it." ' A few weeks later back in London, I read of the break between China and the Soviet Union. It was certainly none of my doing, but it was confirmed to me later that economic exploitation, as Peking saw it, was part of the reason for the break in diplomatic relations leading to outright hostility between the two countries. I had reported the discussion to our own Foreign Office, who had expressed no surprise.

With more time on my hands in Opposition and a better-funded private economy, I was able to engage in a voluntary project I had long had in mind. It derived from my experience in Washington with the FAO and Sir John Boyd-Orr. I had been so struck by the findings of the Commission and the evidence of world food shortages and famine that I was determined to do something practical about it. I therefore wrote a book called *The War on World Poverty*, and set about forming the organization called War on Want to attract and disburse relief funds. Clem Attlee took a great interest in our work and gave us all the help he could.

In spite of the acerbities between the Bevanites and the rest of the Party, I was at pains to maintain a personal and political relationship with Hugh Gaitskell. I used to sit in the second row behind him in the House and we often used to meet behind the scenes or in the Party gatherings upstairs to discuss matters, particularly our response to the Government's financial legislation. As early as 1952, Hugh and I were collaborating closely on fighting Rab Butler's budget. The second reading of a Finance Bill goes into a committee of the whole House, at which stage amendments are in order on every line of the Bill, with no limit as in ordinary debates on the number of speeches an MP can make on each of them.

Hugh and I led the fight, passing the ball to one another for all the world as if we were a pair of well-trained American footballers. He would handle one clause, and I would handle another. We took it in turns to put on the pressure. If he opened the debate, I would wind up and vice versa. Some of the interventions were brief, particularly when the hour was getting late, and I see from *Hansard* that I inflicted on the House fifty-two speeches, some of inordinate length. Rab Butler must have been glad when the Bill finally left us for the Lords, who, of course, could not change it, following the passage of Lloyd George's

Parliament Bill of 1911. The Chancellor and his senior colleagues certainly earned their parliamentary salary in those days.

Hugh and Rab had much in common, including considerable respect for each other. They seemed to form a composite political personality, a characteristic duly spotted by the *Economist* which invented the phrase 'Butskellism':

> Mr Butskell is already a well-known figure in dinner-table conversations in both Westminster and Whitehall. The time has come to introduce him to a wider audience. He is a composite of the present Chancellor and the previous one. Whenever there is a tendency to excess conservatism within the Conservative Party, such as a clamour for too much imperial preference, for a wild dash to convertibility, or even for a little more unemployment to teach the workers a lesson, Mr Butskell speaks up for the cause of moderation from the Government side of the House. When there is a clamour for even graver irresponsibilities from the Labour benches, Mr Butskell has hitherto spoken up from the other.

The main difference was that the Butler half of the new composite Chancellor had followed orthodoxy by using the Bank Rate weapon, while the Gaitskell half had eschewed it. It was very much to Hugh's credit that as a Shadow Chancellor he was not afraid to bewilder his backbenchers with the most arcane analysis, even though his words were echoed very faintly in the constituencies. What the whole argument showed, and Nye and others were very quick to exploit this, was that he was more of a neo-classical economic theorist than a political leader.

These were three very unhappy years, the worst I have ever had to live through in nearly four decades in the House of Commons. Our own dissensions soured the atmosphere and, for those of us who knew and held him in high regard, there was the sad spectacle of the decline of Winston Churchill. His lapses were becoming more frequent. He still had flashes of his old impish sense of humour and there is one perhaps somewhat risqué story which should be recorded before it is forgotten.

Along the Ways and Means corridor on the left there is a lavatory reserved for Members of Parliament. Winston made his way there one day. In the stall to his left there was a young Tory MP, who is still in the House and vouches for the anecdote. Winston failed to fasten up his fly-buttons. His colleague, who had

147

never been a minister, wondered if he should say that Winston could not go out in that condition, or whether he might get his head bitten off if he drew close attention to it. Finally he plucked up his courage, cleared his throat and said, 'Prime Minister, the guard room door is open.' Looking down Winston said, 'And was the sentry standing to attention or lolling on a couple of sandbags?'

It is an open question whether he had been wise to undertake a further period in office. It was something of a derogation from his wartime stature, and from the Euoropean and world status he had the right to claim, that he should have to make little Party speeches about the merits of the decision to end the wartime nationalization of the Liverpool raw cotton market. As he perceptibly aged, it was pathetic to see him baited by Labour backbenchers such as Emrys Hughes and Sydney Silverman. He was increasingly becoming a misfit in the rapidly changing Britain of the post-war world.

The world itself was changing. The nuclear developments which had ended the Japanese war did not stop there. The atomic bombs on Nagasaki and Hiroshima were dwarfed by the thermo-nuclear weapon the United States had created. This had been detonated over Bikini in the Pacific. There were reports of clouds of noxious fumes capable of being blown 5,000 miles and threatening life over all that area. The House of Commons debated the issue. An ageing Churchill replied in terms uncharacteristic of a lifetime in the House of Commons, no doubt reflecting an unimaginative Foreign Office brief, but taken by the House as showing insensitivity. The reception to which he was then subjected totally unnerved him, and those of us sitting on the Opposition side close to the Speaker's chair saw him go out deeply upset on the arm of the Chief Government Whip.

It was time to go, and within six months the pressures of his Party's establishment, combining unimaginable public sympathy with the utter ruthlessness always shown to one who has served his term, saw him off the scene. To any parliamentarian, and there is no camaraderie, irrespective of Party, to compare with that of parliamentarians, it was a tragic period.

On 5 April 1955, he stood down and his successor, Anthony Eden, called a general election at the end of the following month. Labour, still in disarray, took a beating and the Conservative majority was increased to fifty-nine. Once again I was able to buck the trend, largely due to the activities of the housing authorities in Liverpool in shunting many more people into the Kirkby area of my constituency. My majority was up to nearly 4,000, and Huyton had almost become a safe seat.

We had to address ourselves anew in Opposition to the task of attacking the Government, seeking as far as possible to save from destruction the institutions we had created and the policies we had followed. The one decision of the Labour Government which the incoming Conservatives did not reverse was the nationalization of the coal industry.

In those days there were no regular Shadow ministers. For the most part, ex-ministers were given a watching and speaking brief on matters affecting or emanating from their old departments, and other spokesmen were selected *ad hoc* at the weekly meetings of the Parliamentary Committee to speak in individual debates. It was not until July that Shadow ministers as such, each with their clearly defined sphere of operation, were appointed by Attlee. His announcement made it clear that these front-bench spokesmen would in future stick to their own briefs and would not be allowed to speak or ask parliamentary questions outside the scope of their Shadow appointment. The main advantage of this was to prevent one frontbencher after another getting up to criticize a minister, a situation which had sometimes led to inconsistent assertions or demands by different occupants on the front bench.

In his first list of official spokesmen, Attlee, despite the divisions of the previous year, made it clear that I should normally handle Board of Trade matters, assisted by Arthur Bottomley, my former colleague as Secretary for Overseas Trade. This was my first experience of the Opposition front bench. Now I had the advantage of attacking the Government of the day without being open to charges of disloyalty, although on some issues such as arms policies, I was more than once out of step with colleagues who supported the incoming Government in the interests of 'continuity of policy', notably on certain aspects of foreign affairs and defence.

It was a watershed in my political life. I had been brought back into the main stream of the Party in Parliament. Hugh Gaitskell and I even had a reconciliation lunch with three or four colleagues, at which he invited me to take over the group of economists and managerial types who had been part of his own back-room coterie. I was becoming a Party machine-man, moving up in seniority with the length of time I had served on the National Executive.

I also became involved in the mechanics of Party organization,

both at Transport House and in the constituencies. Hugh Gaitskell
had been appalled by our election showing and was anxious for
me to hold an enquiry into its causes and remedies. At its meeting
on 22 June, the National Executive Committee appointed me as
the enquiry's chairman. Together with Jack Cooper, a senior trade
union official who had been MP for Deptford in 1950–1, Peggy
Herbison, MP for South Lanarkshire, and Arthur Skeffington, a
Labour and Co-operative Party MP, I was to investigate the
organization of the Party in the country and to report back by
September in time for the first post-election Party Conference.

Over three months we held forty-nine meetings to hear evidence
and exchange views with parliamentary groups of MPs, the
General Secretary and National Agent, parliamentary leaders and
regional staffs, regional convocations of constituency agents, the
National Union of Labour Organizers and Election Agents,
together with seven separate meetings with groups of individual
constituency parties in different parts of the country.

We analyzed the marginal constituencies, whether won by
Labour or Conservative, on the basis of particular percentage
increases in the turnout of Labour voters. We investigated such
issues as the percentage of voters canvassed – from nil in four
constituencies up to 90 per cent or more, and the number of cars
available during the election. On longer-term organizational
matters we took a complete return of borough Labour parties, the
affiliation fees paid per member by the trade unions, and
individual subscriptions direct to the borough or city. There was
every reason to think that a relatively high proportion of members'
fees went to the municipal parties, some of which were efficient,
others of which were almost totally preoccupied with city and
borough affairs and the aggrandizement of counsellors, aldermen
and, above all for a year, mayors and lord mayors.

One table covered all the seats with a majority of over 10,000
and the affiliation fees paid on the basis of membership to the
National Party. As I expected, the correlation was extremely
revealing. Some of the safest seats had some of the smallest
individual memberships, majorities of well over 20,000 with
membership of 300 or 400. There was reason to think, not only
that some of the recorded members had been long dead and
buried, but that the returns were inflated in other ways. The
reason, I knew, was that in safe Labour seats new, and possibly
active, members were resented. The main reason was the fear that
'comers-in' would begin to challenge the reselection of long-

serving municipal councillors just as the mayoral chair was ready for occupation.

In safe seats, it is council ambitions rather than national considerations which dominate so many of Labour's local parties. I suspect that Conservatives and even Liberals in certain areas may not be immune from this characteristic. Our detailed enquiry showed one historic South Wales seat where the register had fewer than 100 nominal members, those active being long-standing members of the council or aspirants. Meanwhile, hopeless seats and marginals were contributing the bulk of the income flowing into Party Headquarters from local associations.

Our enquiry showed that the safe seats had been failing to overspill their people to help the marginals next door. They were concerned only with local government, where we had a number of victories. It sounds contrary to common sense, but I have always held that the party which starts winning local seats is in trouble nationally. People on the whole are very cynical about members of the local council and tend to say, 'Old Tom there, what does he know about it? I'm not going to vote for the national leader if these are the sort of people he has built himself up on.'

I had to get very rough with the local government representatives, including those in my own area, particularly on Merseyside. Our report, with its eight appendices, filled 105 closely printed pages. It was very tough in tone, almost nasty, and it pleased the right wing of the Party, not up to that point my natural allies. Following acceptance by the National Executive Committee, it was published and was the subject of a debate at Conference in October, which took up a whole afternoon in private session. The text of the debate was therefore not printed with the Conference report. It had been enlivened by a number of fundamentalists, who argued vehemently that if the NEC and the Party would only put forward a programme for 'full socialism' we should not need any organization. The loudest cheers of the debate greeted those speakers who called on the Party to issue a truly socialist manifesto, nationalizing everything and nearly everybody, with the intended consequence that the undeniable purity of our approach would lead to victory after victory and drive the Tories, the Liberals and the moderate socialists into oblivion.

Our report had been published as an 'interim' document. In fact, we covered so much ground and our findings had been so widely reported that we felt there was no need to add to it. It was action that was required now. The newly elected NEC, at its first meeting after the Conference, reconstituting its sub-committees for the first year ahead, appointed my colleagues to the Organization Sub-Committee and elected me its Chairman. The four of us became the nucleus of a small action sub-committee charged with the task of turning our recommendations into reality.

I had been greatly assisted in all this work on Party organization by a young lady on the staff of Morgan Phillips, the General Secretary in Transport House. Her name was Marcia Williams. The following year she joined me as my full-time political secretary to deal with my enormous mailbag. She worked first out of my office at Montague Meyer and stayed with me through all the vicissitudes of the following twenty years.

Meanwhile, back at the parliamentary range, Rab Butler's autumn budget was pursuing its stately progress through Parliament. In November we reached the committee stage, where we had given him trouble on previous occasions. Hugh Gaitskell, as Shadow Chancellor, was in charge of the proceedings, with me as his principal lieutenant. It soon became clear that a measure which involved many pages of individual tax rates on items ranging from dustbins, buckets and pails, brooms and mops, baths and wash tubs, pots and scourers and steel wool, to pastry boards and rolling pins, laid itself open to 'prolonged parliamentary scrutiny'. That is an Opposition term. 'Time wasting' or 'filibustering' are the phrases used by ministers and their back-bench supporters on such occasions. The group of Labour MPs, including the experienced lawyers and accountants who advised me, applied themselves to the Bill. Since the Schedule occupied several pages of the Commons Order Paper, we were in for a field-day, or rather a succession of field-days and field-nights.

Since this became a famous parliamentary occasion, with important consequences for me, I hope I may be allowed to resuscitate brief details from *Hansard* to chart its course. We began with an amendment moved by Elwyn Jones, a lawyer and MP for Edmonton, who later became a distinguished Lord Chancellor. He was concerned, no doubt for sound constituency reasons, with rabbit fur skin: 'I beg to move, in page one, line nineteen at the end, to insert: "except insofar as it applies to articles made wholly or partly of rabbit fur skins".' His opening paragraph showed what 'a tangled web they weave' when the Treasury seeks to ensure that an already complicated tax structure should become still more incomprehensible:

(ABOVE) With President and Mrs Truman, *c.* 1950

(TOP) At a lunch with Joseph P. Kasper (centre) and W. J. Kenney to encourage the sale of British goods in America, July 1950

(LEFT) As Leader of the Labour Party at an anti-apartheid rally in Trafalgar Square, March 1963. Amongst the supporters were the Rt Rev. Mervyn Stockwood (seated, second right) and my son Robin (seated far left).

(BELOW LEFT) At a Labour rally with George Brown, September 1963

(RIGHT) With President Kennedy just before his assassination

(BELOW) At home with Robin and Giles. The above photo is on the cabinet behind us.

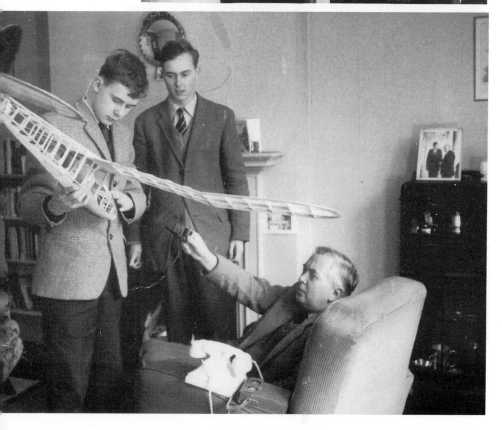

(LEFT) Making a keynot
speech at the Labour Pa
Conference, Scarboroug
October 1963

(BELOW) Talking to
Clement Attlee at the sa
conference

(RIGHT) With my father
1964

(BELOW RIGHT) Relaxin
with the family in the Is
of Scilly, 1964

(ABOVE) Prime Minister: at Transport House after the Labour Party victory, October 1964

(TOP) Campaigning in the general election for a 'New Britain', September 1964

The purpose of the first amendment is this. Under the D-Scheme, rabbit skin garments in the main were free of Purchase Tax. In the case of coats of rabbit skin fur, the wholesale prices range from £6 to £16 with the bulk selling at £12, which was the D-line limit. The effect of Clause 1, therefore, is to impose generally a 50 per cent tax where none was chargeable before and means, in effect, an increase of £9 on the retail price of coney fur coats hitherto retailing at £18. In the case of garments of this type selling at £16, which hitherto bore a Purchase Tax of £1, the tax now becomes £7, which is a tax increase of 700 per cent, which must be a high record for any Chancellor of the Exchequer to have achieved.

After this simple introduction, he went on with all the eloquence of an experienced advocate to deal with the more complicated aspects of the subject, with particular reference to the sufferings of the British Coney Fur Association and the dire consequences for their planned export drive. The debate on rabbit fur skin continued from 3.42 pm to 6 pm, at which time a division was called.

At 6.15, Austen Albu moved a resolution to exempt furniture, which lasted until 9 pm, when the resolution was rejected by a majority of 277 to 228. It was clear, indeed it was in our plans, that this debate would go through the night, and with Hugh Gaitskell's agreement I divided my Finance Bill front-bench team into two groups, one of which would pair with government supporters and go home at a reasonably early hour ready for a late sitting the following night.

Anthony Greenwood then rose to oppose the increase in tax from the existing 25 per cent to the 30 per cent proposed on a range of goods which for the convenience of the House he grouped into a single list. It included haberdashery and most head gear, carpets and linoleum, wallpaper, office and garden furniture, and so on through twenty items. But this, he made clear, was not the only or indeed the major reason for opposing the Bill. The Chancellor had included in the 30 per cent tax bracket many essential household items which had never previously borne tax: household brushes, brooms and mops, dustbins, buckets, pails and lids, pedal-operated sanitary bins, coal hods and coal scuttles. It was the debate on these items that created the name which history has applied to Rab Butler's budget – 'The Pots and Pans Budget'. By the time we were through this list, we were well into the small hours.

The next day we were still in full flood. Well into our second all-night sitting it was clear that little progress was being made. Indeed, we were busy tabling further amendments to later parts of the Bill. Hugh Gaitskell rose to move that we should 'report progress'. The Chairman of Ways and Means, Sir Charles MacAndrew, refused to accept the Motion. No progress had been made and a procedural argument raged. *Hansard* contains the following entry dated at eight o'clock in the morning:

Mr H. Wilson: on a point of order: 'Sir Charles Erskine-May lays down that, where a difficulty has been reached about a Motion to report progress, there is an alternative way in which the debate in a committee of the whole House can be brought to a conclusion if that is the wish of the committee. I think that the case instanced in Erskine-May is a debate on the Government of India Bill 1858 when, for a technical reason, it was impossible to move that the chairman of the committee should report progress. Erskine-May, as I read it, in this instance provides that an alternative Motion can be moved and is quite often accepted, to the effect that the Chairman do leave the chair.

'I should like to ask whether you would accept as an alternative the Motion "that the Chairman do leave the Chair forthwith". It being understood that it would be moved in the spirit of Erskine-May's suggestion that this is an alternative way of bringing a debate in committee to a conclusion when there has been a refusal of the Motion to report progress. If it is in order I should like to move that, so that we may get out of this very serious impasse.'

I have to admit that my historical precedent was to a certain extent snatched out of thin air, although there had been a case of that sort. Sir Charles, desperate by this time, agreed that my suggestion would be in order. The point was of course, and the Government front bench failed to realize the implications of what I was doing, that my Motion did not ask leave to sit again. The Bill, in parliamentary terms, would be non-existent, as if it had never been introduced. Unfortunately, just as I looked like getting this through, that expert proceduralist, Sydney Silverman, most unhelpfully rose to point out that the Bill would be dead. Those of my colleagues who were aware of what I was up to screamed at him, and one or two tried to pull him down. Their persuasion worked, the House accepted my Motion, indeed the Leader of the House, the Lord Privy Seal, Harry Crookshank, commended it. The Serjeant-at-Arms came to remove the Mace, symbol of parliamentary authority, from its position in front of the Clerk's Table.

The following day, or what was left of it, he and the other members of the Government realized what had happened and knew that they had suffered a nasty defeat. Their morale sank to a new low, particularly during Smoking Room inquests after Parliament began the following day's work. A leading newspaper commented: 'The Finance Bill is now in limbo and that is no place in which a Finance Bill should be.' I suddenly acquired an undeserved reputation for knowledge of parliamentary procedure, but my colleagues were ready to accept my proposal that we should not resist the restoration of the Bill to its place in the Commons Order Paper.

If all this should appear a somewhat frivolous piece of parliamentary horseplay, it had serious and determining consequences. On 7 December, Clement Attlee announced his resignation as Party Leader. A close colleague of his, Arthur Moyle, who had been his PPS for many years, told me that after the general election he had wanted for some time to retire and that when the procedural triumph over the Finance Bill had shown him how well Hugh and I were working together, he had no fears for the future of the Party and felt that he could safely step down.

A week later Hugh Gaitskell was elected Leader of the Labour Party and of Her Majesty's Opposition. He obtained 157 votes, Nye Bevan attracted seventy and Herbert Morrison forty, so Attlee had organized his come-uppance at last. I was appointed Shadow Chancellor. A week after that there was a Cabinet reshuffle. Harold Macmillan became Chancellor and Rab Butler Home Secretary. The Butskell days were over and a new pair of adversaries, 'the two Harolds', took charge of the economic debate.

13

First In, First Out

Apart from acquiring an entirely unwarranted reputation as a master of parliamentary procedure as a result of the rout of Rab Butler over his Finance Bill, I had for ten years been one of the dullest speakers in the House of Commons. I always knew my facts and produced them doubtless at excessive length. Nye Bevan, with his marvellous gift of spontaneity, often tried to persuade me to lighten things up a bit, but the real opportunity presented itself when Anthony Eden appointed Harold Macmillan as Chancellor of the Exchequer in December 1955 and Hugh Gaitskell made me his front-bench shadow the following month.

I already had a perfectly genial relationship with Harold Macmillan, a clubbable person by nature, and we often used to find ourselves in conversation in the Smoking Room. For the first nine months of the Eden Government he had been Foreign Secretary. 'After a few months learning geography,' he complained to me, 'now I've got to learn arithmetic.' He was a consummate parliamentarian and quickly mastered his brief, as he had in every previous senior office he had held. There must have been a chemistry at work which brought out the best in both of us, and the debates on his first budget and Finance Bill became popular occasions. I suddenly developed an aptitude for dealing with serious economic and financial problems in a humorous and personal way, to which Macmillan responded.

He and I had a happy and stimulating relationship. In those days, even on the committee stage of the Finance Bill, the House would fill up to listen to the most abstruse amendments and hear us knocking each other about. After a gladiatorial exchange, the Chancellor would pass me a note, usually suggesting a drink in the Smoking Room, occasionally congratulating me on my attack on him, sometimes asking a question about how I had prepared my speech. 'Do you have a discard box?' he asked on one occasion, a reference, I discovered, to his own custom of preparing a speech. If a favourite idea or phrase seemed inappropriate, he would put the rejected piece of paper in a box for use on a subsequent occasion. He would ask me where I had picked up a particular story or reference and, in return, would tell me where he had gathered some of his own anecdotes.

Patrician that he was, Macmillan had always been a good constituency member, first at Stockton and then at Bromley, and he had the knack of talking to ordinary people and injecting their ideas and remarks into his own speeches. We never quarrelled and our relationship was an example of the cameraderie of the House of Commons at its best. It does not mean betrayal on either side of deeply held principles, but it does mean that their expression need not destroy personal friendship. It got to the point where I used to have the House laughing so much that a colleague took me into a corner and said, 'Harold, that was wonderful fun, but you must not overdo this or people will just think that you are an entertainer and not serious.'

All this was immensely agreeable to Hugh Gaitskell, who cheered and laughed with the rest as our relationship went through one of its best periods. It was an immense relief to Hugh to have a Treasury and economics spokesman who really knew his stuff. This meant that he could spend more time on work within the Party, but also that he could concentrate more on studying foreign affairs, an essential area of knowledge for a Leader of the Opposition. I found myself more frequently than before in his office discussing strategy and tactics, especially as I had come out on top of the Shadow Cabinet poll with 185 votes.

Hugh's principal target was the Prime Minister. Anthony Eden had never really been a parliamentary adversary of mine. My first sight of him had been at Oxford getting an Honorary Degree on the occasion when I gave my Gladstone Memorial Lecture. During the post-war years, with the Conservatives in Opposition, I have a curiously muted memory of him in the House. He was Churchill's trusted foreign affairs expert, and was generally assumed to be heir apparent to the leadership of the Tory Party, but somehow there was a feeling that Churchill was waiting for him to emerge as a stronger character, while ostensibly grooming him for the succession.

On their return to power in 1951, Eden immediately became Foreign Secretary again. It was a matter for regret that he had never had the opportunity to show what he could do on the home front. He had never been given the Treasury, Labour or Housing. He never seemed to have had time to enjoy Parliament, although his period as Leader of the House during the war showed his parliamentary potentialities. He appeared to have little time to meet his fellows, of all parties, in the Smoke Room or Tea Room.

As Foreign Secretary, Churchill was prepared to leave more to his discretion than either Chamberlain before him or Macmillan after him would have been prepared to do. He had a serious bile duct operation in 1953, from which he never seemed fully to recover. Illness had dogged him through much of his last period at the Foreign Office, and it seemed as if Churchill, who was his senior by twenty-three years, began to have doubts about Eden's physical staying power. Churchill had begun the grooming process nearly twenty years after Baldwin should have started it. Nevertheless, Churchill still wanted Eden and might himself have gone in 1953, when he was also seriously ill, but waited to give Eden time to complete his recovery.

He was still not fully fit at the time of his election and this made him unsure of himself. On foreign affairs he thought, quite reasonably, that he knew where he was. But a Prime Minister has to deal with economic affairs, home affairs, unemployment and constituency problems raised by other members. Eden just did not fit in with this routine. He had the replies written out for him and just read them out. He was really rather a pathetic figure, very sophisticated, on the whole too much Foreign Office-trained, perfectly nice and hardly ever capable of saying boo to a goose. When he did say boo, he chose the wrong goose and said it far too roughly.

In 1956, the British political scene, and, still more important, Britain's role and standing in the world, were transformed and devalued by the attempted invasion of Egypt as a response to the action of Gamal Abdel Nasser, the Egyptian President, in seizing the Suez Canal. The consequences, even clearer after three decades than at the time, included:

– The tragic end of a great career in the retirement through ill health of Anthony Eden, the man who had resigned as Foreign Secretary over his resistance to Neville Chamberlain's policy of appeasing Hitler.

– The ending of Britain's role as a world power, which she had held since the days of the Younger Pitt, leaving her, with France, as a still significant influence in world affairs due to her long experience, but no longer a dominant force.

– The consummation of a development created by the Second World War: the unchallenged role of the USA and the Soviet Union as the world's two principal super powers.

– A challenge to Britain's role as the dominant force in the Commonwealth, as Australia and Canada began to take a more independent line in world affairs, and such leaders as Robert Menzies and Lester Pearson began to exert real personal influence in the United Nations and in 'regional' associations north and south, east and west.

– The censure of Britain by the almost unanimous agreement of the United Nations, including Commonwealth countries.

– The arrival at the centre of affairs of Harold Macmillan, whose patrician skulduggery had made him virtually the inspiration of the attack on Suez, the failure of which led to him assuming the premiership.

– The emergence of Hugh Gaitskell to the rank of a world statesman, as day by day he dissociated his Party from the Government's actions, with a long series of speeches combining statesmanship with a power of oratory few had associated with him.

It was on 26 July that Nasser announced his 'unilateral' nationalization of the Suez Canal. Anthony Eden heard the news towards the end of a Downing Street dinner to honour King Feisal of Iraq and his premier, Nuri-es-Said. The guest list is important. In addition to Hugh Gaitskell, it included the French Ambassador, Chiefs of Staff and the US Chargé d'Affaires. The guests tactfully withdrew, Nuri-es-Said not making himself any more popular in Eden's eyes by pointing to the portrait of Disraeli among the others, now numbering about fifty, of ex-Prime Ministers and saying, 'That's the old Jew who got us into all this trouble' – by borrowing the money from the House of Rothschild when he heard that the Canal was for sale.

Eden was at first a reluctant warrior. Macmillan was putting the heat on from the start. At a separate dinner, he and Lord Salisbury were entertaining Robert Murphy, the US Defence Secretary. Macmillan took an extremely tough line about Nasser's action, which, he later explained, was designed to stiffen the American administration. Murphy was left to draw the conclusion that Britain would certainly go to war to secure the Canal and ensure free passage for the world's ships. In the whole history of the Suez fiasco, nothing has become clearer than the effect of Macmillan's tough line with Murphy both then and throughout the following weeks, when Eden was going through the torment of preparing to use force to recapture the Canal.

American leaders, from President Eisenhower downwards, took Macmillan's comments as representing a decision of the British Cabinet. There is surprisingly little in Macmillan's memoirs to indicate the hard line he was taking or the continuing effect of his musings in Washington. It was not until it was becoming clear that the invasion was turning into an almost farcical failure, with Harold already the odds-on favourite for the succession to the sick and exhausted Eden, that he again assumed the statesman's mantle.

The war was delayed by the almost full-time intervention of the American Secretary of State, John Foster Dulles, who took the lead in securing strong resolutions from the first. It was he who successfully moved the creation of the Suez Canal Users Association, which, when analysed, was little more than a consumer's co-operative society to whom Canal dues should be paid and frozen until the problem was solved by diplomatic action. But he was far from consistent. At one moment he quietened Eden's worries by urging that Nasser must be made to 'disgorge'. 'Those were forthright words,' Eden was to say, 'they rang in my ears for months.' Britain accepted SCUA, yet, within days, Dulles was saying that payments to the organization should be entirely voluntary. In the event, he was taken to hospital suffering from incurable cancer in the very week of the Anglo–French invasion, and died shortly afterwards.

British and French military preparations could not begin and relations with the United States reached an all-time low. The American attitude was not so much one of denunciation; the administration just thought that the leading members of the British Cabinet, Eden in particular, had gone off their heads. One of the best books on the Suez affair was written by Chester Cooper – *The Lion's Last Roar*. He had been appointed the CIA contact man in London with the Foreign Office's intelligence staff. In the book, he describes the way the Foreign Office officials froze up when he appeared. In fact he, and most of Washington, knew as much about the Cabinet plans as the Foreign Office. For one thing, he records, British officers in the US Exchange of Duties programme had spoken quite freely about the forthcoming invasion. As a result, the American who knew most about Anglo–French intentions was President Eisenhower. With Eden still believing that his secret was safe, the President sent two messages warning him against any resort to invasion.

The first was a telegram addressed not only to 'The Head of Her Majesty's Government', but also to 'My long-term friend'. He asked Eden to explain

> exactly what is happening betwen us and our European allies – especially between us, the French and yourselves. We have learned that the French have provided Israel with a considerable amount of equipment . . . in excess of the amounts of which we were officially informed and in violation of agreements now existing between our three countries. . . .
>
> Egypt has not yet formally asked this Government for aid. But . . . if the United Nations finds Israel to be an aggressor, Egypt could very well ask the Soviets for help . . . and then the Mid-East fat would really be in the fire . . . we may shortly find ourselves with a *de facto* situation that would make all our present problems look puny indeed.

This was followed up by a telephone call to Number 10 when the President, as reported by the Americans, gave Eden 'unshirted hell'. In fact, Eden was not at the other end of the line. The call was taken by a private secretary who bore the brunt of the President's outburst, until Ike slammed down the telephone.

The Israelis were taken for a ride. Britain and France were not intervening as their allies, not even as co-belligerents. In October, D-Day was put back from the 8th to the 20th, and again deferred. Macmillan had been to the United States, where his hopes of moving the Administration were disappointed. His meeting with Humphrey, the Secretary for the Treasury, was a disappointment. Humphrey only wanted to discuss finance with the Chancellor. On his return, it is said, worried by the temporizing, Macmillan threatened to resign if, assuming the UN failed to accept the British demands, force was not used. Eden was ill, and his bile trouble flared up, creating a temperature of 105°–106°. The Defence Minister, Walter Monckton, resigned, ostensibly on health grounds, but really because he disagreed with the invasion plans. The Foreign Secretary, Selwyn Lloyd, was trying to find a peaceful solution, encouraging Pineau, the French Foreign Minister, to negotiate with the Egyptian Foreign Minister Fawzi. Throughout October the plans were developed and refined.

Eden and Lloyd went to Paris to meet the French. Eden accepted pressure from the French Premier, Guy Mollet; Lloyd was desperately worried. Mollet and Ben-Gurion, the Israeli Prime Minister, met at Sèvres. They were joined by a 'responsible British minister', identity not disclosed, but said to be 'an old-fashioned family lawyer' — it was, in fact, a still unhappy Selwyn Lloyd. The plan was for Israel to attack Egypt, and then for Britain and France to appeal for a cease-fire and to intervene in the isthmus.

At the meeting in France on 1 October, there was still doubt whether Britain would join in, yet her bombers, a component in which France was deficient, were essential to the operation. The second meeting took place in Paris on 21 October. The proposal put to the Israelis was that Britain and France would demand that both Egypt and Israel should withdraw from the Canal area. If either refused, Britain and France would intervene to keep the Canal open. The plan was that Israel should attack the Canal zone while Britain and France should go in as policemen, demanding Israel's and Egypt's withdrawal, and would then take over the Canal.

It was one of the most cynical international scenarios in history, nor was it revealed to Parliament even after hostilities had begun. An Israeli proposal for a sortie was rejected by Britain. A small-scale encounter would be no good. It must be 'a real act of war' (real enough for Britain to condemn). In the succeeding days the plans were worked out to the day, the hour and the minute. The Israeli invasion took place on 29 October. The French and British bombed Egyptian airfields on 31 October, aircraft having been moved up over a period of several weeks.

We now know, particularly from the Israeli General Moshe Dayan's *Story of My Life* published nearly twenty years later, that it was the French and particularly her Foreign Minister, Christian Pineau, who masterminded the attack on the Egyptians, with Israeli and British connivance. In the event, Dayan never got within ten miles of the Canal. He marched in its direction for long enough to provide what W.S. Gilbert characterized as giving 'verisimilitude to an otherwise bald and unconvincing narrative', turned smartly to the left and went down to occupy the Sinai.

This all happened just a week before the voting in the American presidential election. Eisenhower, his electorate and the world, including the smug operators in the Kremlin, were witnessing a reversion by Eden and Ike's old North African colleague, Macmillan, to a bygone world of British hegemony. When US Ambassador Aldrich went to Downing Street to register his protest, he was met with the suggestion that Britain was planning to arraign Israel at the UN as an aggressor. This was probably the all-time low in Britain's attempts to fool Washington – probably the lowest point in Anglo–US relationships in this century. Selwyn Lloyd handed him the text of the Anglo–French ultimatum, an insult to his intelligence as well as the deception of a friend.

In explanation of the two Governments' decision to mount their invasion, a patently dishonest statement was issued:

The Governments of the United Kingdom and France have taken note of the outbreak of hostilities between Israel and Egypt. This event threatens to disrupt the freedom of navigation through the Suez Canal on which the economic life of many nations depends. The Governments of the United Kingdom and France are resolved to do all in their power to bring about the earliest cessation of hostilities and to safeguard the free passage of the Canal.

They accordingly request the Government of Israel to stop all warlike action on land, sea and air forthwith; to withdraw all Israeli military forces to a distance of ten miles east of the Canal.

The communication has been addressed to the Government of Egypt, requesting them to cease hostilities and withdraw their forces from the neighbourhood of the Canal and to accept the temporary occupation by Anglo–French forces of key positions at Port Said, Ismailia and Suez.

The United Kingdom and French Governments request an answer to this communication within twelve hours. If at the expiration of that period one or both Governments have not undertaken to comply with the above requirements, the United Kingdom and French forces will intervene in whatever strength may be necessary to secure compliance.

Quite apart from the immorality of the invasion and the lies issuing from the Government, was the sheer incompetence of the planning. Cyprus waters were too shallow for some of the bigger ships entrusted with the operation, so that the invasion fleet had to undertake a six-day voyage from Malta. The continuing tragi-comedy of the invasion was highlighted, in more senses than one, when a ship of the invading fleet crossed in front of one of the US warships, which illuminated it with their searchlights.

Eden wrote to Eisenhower giving as his excuse for not having consulted or even informed Washington 'the constitutional and other difficulties in which you are placed', going on to say that 'our two Governments have tried with the best will in the world all sorts of public and private negotiations in the last two or three years and they have all failed. This seems an opportunity for a fresh start. . . .'

The French Prime Minister Guy Mollet was more frank, indeed to the point of rudeness, telling his Assembly in Paris: 'When our American friends asked us "why", I told them "you would have stopped us". I even added, "We did not want you to be late: we did not want to go through the same periods of waiting that we went through from 1914–17 and from 1939–41." '

Eisenhower was not having any of this. He issued a public statement:

> As soon as the President received his first knowledge, obtained through press reports, of the ultimatum, he sent an urgent personal message to the Prime Minister of Great Britain and the Prime Minister of the Republic of France. The President has expressed his earnest hope that the United Nations Organization will be given full opportunity to settle the issue by peaceful means instead of by forceful ones. . . .

The Shadow Cabinet meetings during the early part of the crisis were a model of statesmanship, thanks partly to Gaitskell's leadership and partly to the remarkable co-operation of George Brown. George had been for many years a passionate pro-Arab. It was an unhappy and tough moment for him when Hugh informed the meeting that George had, after much discussion between them, come to accept the existence of the Israeli state. George smiled wryly and said nothing. Within the next few weeks he was as vigorous as Hugh in supporting the Israeli nation's right to exist.

During these crisis weeks, Hugh Gaitskell made speeches on the conflict between Egypt and Israel which were models of con-struction, moving in their oratory and utterly consistent. He strongly rejected Egypt's claim to have the right to prevent free passage through the Canal, but was equally vigorous in opposing the British Government's decision to seek to force the Canal by an invasion. When it began, and right through the period of the fighting, his speeches ranked as the greatest of his life. He asked me to take over responsibility for economic affairs to free him to concentrate on the Middle East.

During the long sequence of parliamentary debates, suspicion deepened that the whole operation, particularly the prior collusion with the Israelis, was a conspiracy and that the statements purporting to justify it were simply fraudulent. Little was known at the time about the role of the French, although one Labour backbencher, Harold Davies, MP for Leek in Staffordshire, interviewed during one of the long succession of Suez debates, blew a story which an increasing number of MPs had come to suspect. When Philip Noel-Baker was pressing the Foreign Secretary about consultations with Washington, Davies interrupted: 'No, the Rt Hon. Gentleman has a card up his sleeve with Pineau.' The interesting fact was that in his reference to Pineau, Davies somehow knew that it was he, far more than the French Prime Minister, who was the organizing political genius of the invasion.

Selwyn Lloyd reveals little in his memoirs of the French connection. Indeed, it is doubtful how much he knew, or for that matter perhaps wanted to know. It is certain that he was excluded, or contrived to exclude himself, from some of the key meetings where the conspiracy was planned. But interesting evidence exists at Chequers.

Years afterwards I had occasion to look at the Visitors' Book. On the critical Sunday the guests were listed, but strangely a civil servant's name was included, contrary to the usual practice. It seemed to me that a name had been scratched out by a sharp instrument, such as a razor blade, and the official's name written in over it. In the Long Gallery there is a powerful, electrically lit magnifier for visitors to use when examining a ring worn for years by Queen Elizabeth I and taken by a courtier, who became the first Earl of Home for his services, to prove to James VI of Scotland that she was really dead and that he could come to claim the throne. This magnifier confirmed that the rough surface had, in fact, been caused by a razor-like instrument. I concluded that the name excised had been that of an Israeli general. I was wrong. It was that of General Challe.

Hugh Gaitskell showed great courage in leading and organizing a nationwide campaign against Suez. He was an obvious target for the Conservative press, who were loyally supporting their Prime Minister, for, as past history since the Boer War has shown, calm statesman-like criticism of a government's action during a war is quickly branded as treachery and a betrayal of HM forces.

We all took part in the operation, christened the 'Law not War' campaign. At one Shadow Cabinet meeting I reminded my colleagues of the occasion during the Boer War (when the Liberal Opposition was split on the issue) that Lloyd George had had to be smuggled out of Birmingham Town Hall disguised as a policeman to save his life. I said that I hoped that the luck of the draw would not lead to my being sent to Birmingham.

I was, in fact, sent there. The main hall was packed, as was a smaller hall which was linked to the platform by a public address system. Roy Jenkins, himself a Birmingham MP, rightly accused the Government of causing 'enormous damage' to the chances of success of the simultaneous Hungarian revolt against Russia 'for the sake of a squalid adventure in the Middle East'. In fact, I did not have to don police uniform and, together with Roy, was cheered to the echo.

In Labour's measured but increasing criticism of the Government, second only to Gaitskell was Aneurin Bevan, in complete harmony with his leader, in his speeches in the House and in the country. During this period, he took the greatest care in preparing his interventions at Question Time. In one of the later Suez debates, he made an unforgettable speech. By then, the sinister role of the French was being emphasized in the British and world press. It was this which led to Nye's most quoted intervention:

> The fact is that all these long telephone conversations and conferences between M. Guy Mollet, M. Pineau and the Prime Minister are intelligible only on the assumption that something was being cooked up. . . . What happened? Did Marianne take John Bull to an unknown rendezvous? Did Marianne say to John Bull there was a forest fire going to start and did John Bull then say, 'We ought to put it out'? But Marianne said, 'No, let us warm our hands by it; it is a nice fire.' Did Marianne deceive John Bull or seduce him?

My only contribution in the Commons was to lead for the Opposition on 12 November during a debate on the Queen's Speech when, by agreement between the two front benches, the argument was about the economic consequences of the Suez adventure, already becoming too menacingly plain:

> For the past fortnight, the House has debated the cost in political and moral terms of the Government's action in Suez. Today we have to count the reckoning in economic terms as well. When I say 'in economic terms' I do not mean merely the cost in terms of government expenditure. We are no longer in the days of nineteenth-century colonial wars, when the cost of these ventures could be reckoned in terms of another tuppence on the income tax or another penny on tea. . . .
>
> . . . I hope that the Chancellor or the Minister of Supply will tell the House frankly today what, in the view of their advisers, will be the economic consequences of this military action. After all, it was long prepared. What estimates did the Government make of its costs and its economic consequences? What estimates do they make now?

The greatest personal tragedy of the Suez operation was that of Anthony Eden. The strain of the crisis had aggravated his already serious internal complaint. On 23 November, a fortnight after the decision to withdraw from Suez in favour of the United Nations Force which had been created, he left London for a rest cure in Jamaica, having with difficulty survived a debate in which the first substantial charges of collusion with the French and Israelis were levelled at the Government.

There were two more debates before Christmas in his absence. Selwyn Lloyd, far from the most inspiring of speakers at the Government Despatch Box, opened with an anodyne report on a virtually useless UN debate. He had resisted an Afro–Asian resolution demanding an immediate withdrawal by the British and French forces. The Belgians tabled an amendment more acceptable to him. The voting was twenty-three in favour, thirty-seven against and eighteen abstentions, including the USA. Reporting the figures, Selwyn Lloyd tried to present this as a victory: 'In other words the majority of the Assembly either voted with us or abstained. Had he pursued his arithmetical exercises he could have concluded that an even larger majority had 'voted against us or abstained': fifty-five versus twenty-three rather than the forty-one to thirty-seven in his formulation.

It was Aneurin Bevan who moved the amendment which

restored matters to a more proper plane. 'Recognizing the disastrous consequences of Her Majesty's Government's policy in the Middle East, [the amendment] calls on Her Majesty's Government to take all possible steps to restore Commonwealth unity, recreate confidence between our allies and ourselves and strengthen the authority of the United Nations as the only way to achieve a lasting settlement in the Middle East.'

Eden returned to make an astonishing defence of his ill-at-ease Government:

> I want to say this on the question of foreknowledge, and to say it quite bluntly to the House, that there was not foreknowledge that Israel would attack Egypt, there was not. But there was something else. There was, we knew it perfectly well, a risk of it, and certain discussions and conversations took place as, I think, was absolutely right and as, I think, anybody would do. So far from this being an act of retribution, I would be compelled, and I think my colleagues would agree, if I had the same very disagreeable decisions to take again, to repeat them. . . .

There was a relatively small attendance in the House, which is usual on Motions for the adjournment; the Opposition called for a Division, the Government side prevailing by 165 to eighty-five. That was Eden's last speech in the House of Commons. His resignation was a sad occasion. His illness had thrown him out of his stride and he became agitated and a terrible worrier. I cannot help feeling that what emerged in him was an inferiority complex due to having lived so long in the shadow of Chamberlain and Churchill. In his retirement there were many of all Parties who had reason to be grateful for his friendship and courtesy. I, for one, shall not forget that in 1976, when he was desperately ill and forbidden by his doctors to go to Windsor for the annual Garter Ceremony in which I received the honour, he wrote to me to say that although he would have to miss the investiture ceremony, he would be there for lunch and the installation in St George's Chapel.

While Selwyn Lloyd floundered, the star of the long-running show, Harold Macmillan, certainly one of the main creators of the Suez adventure, had begun to overtake the aspirations of his only possible rival in the inevitable contest for the succession to Anthony Eden, Rab Butler. I had characterized his record as 'First

In, First Out', when, on the day the actual fighting began, he had issued a demand for the withdrawal of the British troops. His Treasury officials were informing him of Washington's expertly prepared Wall Street run on sterling. His versatile responses to a changing situation had already ensured that he, not Butler, would be Eden's successor.

Kingsley Martin, editor of *New Statesman and Nation*, summed up the outcome of the Conservative Party's struggle for power when he said that the Party, after Suez, were like a group of men who had been out on a drinking party and, sitting round the next morning with severe headaches and mouths 'like the bottom of a parrot's cage', they turned in their wrath not against the man who had taken them on the night's dissipation, but against the man who went along with the party and spent the evening drinking tomato juice.

Britain's role in the world changed totally in the weeks before Macmillan went to Number 10. Our last imperial adventure had failed humiliatingly. Britain could not go it alone, or even for that matter in alliance with France. She could not withstand the censure of the United Nations with a Canadian Prime Minister in the lead. Still less could she withstand a scowling US President, briefed by an obsessive and complicated Secretary of State. If she tried, Eisenhower could almost anonymously mount financial sanctions which could bring sterling to peril point.

It is an open question how far Suez contributed to Britain's changed position or how far it registered a decline which had already occurred. That Britain could no longer impose her will on other countries without the law was manifest to the world, to a growing number of people in this country, but to none more than Macmillan. It is to his credit that he did more than anyone to adjust Britain's role to her circumstances, to seek to change things by influence rather than force. He recognized, and this is still true today, that Britain's strength lies above all in the wealth of experience still residing in her race of statesmen, administrators, industrialists, craftsmen, diplomats, traders, exporters and ship-owners, and in the vast accumulated knowledge and expertise of the City. None embodied these qualities more than Macmillan himself.

His most immediate problems were the oil crisis, the closure of the Canal and the consequence on the balance of payments. The Canal was cleared with surprising speed and reopened for traffic in April. But Britain's industry had serious anxieties about shortages of fuel and feedstock, and the crisis was surmounted only by recourse to a strict system of petrol rationing, the first in peacetime.

The main problem in diplomacy was to restore relations with the United States. In this, Macmillan speedily succeeded, thanks in part to his personal association with Eisenhower during the North Africa campaign. On Eisenhower's suggestion, there was a meeting in Bermuda only nine weeks after Macmillan became Premier. One of the agreements reached there was that the United States should supply Britain with nuclear missiles.

Macmillan, who, as much as anyone, had masterminded Suez, had profited from it by seeing Eden off under the post-Suez financial pressures and had secured for himself the inheritance. Now he invited the country to rally round to deal with those pressures. As Prime Minister, he never lost control of the Treasury, which he saw as the means of creating a favourable financial system for winning elections. Had the trade cycle never existed, he would have invented it and used it for his electoral purposes. As Chancellor under Churchill, Butler had begun it: sixpence off income tax before the election: an emergency budget afterwards to ward off the resultant crisis by increased indirect taxes to claw the money back. But whereas Butler was the apprentice, Macmillan was the craftsman. As Chancellor and Prime Minister, he played the cycle. In 1958–9 he introduced vast tax remissions to stimulate the economy in time for the 'You've never had it so good' election of 1959. He was right. He had played the cycle and saw, even ahead of Gaitskell, the further electoral significance of an economic situation based, not in a cyclical but a secular sense, on the sudden impact of the virtual first introduction to Britain of hire purchase.

It was impossible not to admire the skill with which he engineered the recovery in his Party's fortunes. He survived the resignation of Peter Thorneycroft and Nigel Birch from his Treasury team, when they objected to his fiscal policies, and was able to take advantage of the change in the public mood brought about by the greater availability of consumer goods in contrast to the sour memory of rationing and shortages under the previous Labour Government.

In spite of all my efforts, the Tories' constituency organization in the country was much stronger than ours and this played its part. When general election time came in October 1959, few on either side of the House, recalling the President's anger in the autumn of 1956, could have foreseen Macmillan's success in persuading Eisenhower to come over for an official visit on the eve of the election and parade him round London as a prize exhibit to help in the winning of the campaign. In spite of Labour's new-found coherence and a strong front bench, the Conservatives had staged a remarkable recovery in the short period available to them. They were returned with 365 seats, to 258 for Labour, six Liberals and one other, a majority of ninety-nine.

14

Confrontation with Gaitskell

The outcome of the 1959 general election was a severe blow to the Labour Party, and for a period had a seriously disrupting effect on the unity of its members. We had endured eight years in the political wilderness and now faced another five years out of office. I had been worried during the whole of the campaign, which was the first to be fought in the new-found freedom of television coverage. I had been more or less kept off the screen by those running the Party's appeal to the electorate and it did seem to me that Hugh Gaitskell had been far too didactic in his speeches and public appearances, adopting more the manner of an Oxford don explaining economic theory than seeking to identify himself in homely terms with the electorate.

Our organization in the country had been much improved, but it had a curiously negative effect. We had been doing well in local elections and this had given us considerable hope of a successful result. But as I had noted in the comprehensive study we had made of constituency affairs, an increase in the number of local Labour councillors was not transmitted into national support. They were the visible representatives of the Party and voters tended to blame them for shortcomings in their lives and to look elsewhere for solutions in a general election. It is a phenomenon I have observed over the decades and it works both ways, affecting local Conservatives when Labour is in power in very much the same way.

I am obliged to acknowledge that I was a personal beneficiary of the election result. In the new Parliament I was appointed Chairman of the Public Accounts Committee, which is a position of considerable influence. It is always held by a member of the Opposition, and I had indicated to Hugh Gaitskell that I would be pleased to be nominated if he saw fit. The Prime Minister always accepts the recommendation of the Leader of the Opposition, and

Harold Macmillan was well disposed. It had been a long time since I had been the administrator of a large department like the Board of Trade and I felt that I was getting further and further away from the facts of public life and that I needed to refresh my recollection of the conduct of affairs.

The Public Accounts Committee is the most feared organization in the whole of Whitehall because it can send for papers, call witnesses and bring its members in very close touch with the administration. In fact I became the centenary Chairman, the post dating back to the days of Palmerston and Gladstone. It also had the sovereign advantage of providing the Chairman with an office in the House of Commons, a rare privilege for a Member of Parliament. In order to avoid any possible conflict of interest, I also resigned my consultancy with Montague Meyer, which had been a very pleasant relationship and helped to keep me afloat in public life.

This was almost the only agreeable transaction I had with Hugh Gaitskell during the difficult year that followed. My relations with him during the later 1950s had been very much improved but now a further crisis, or rather a series of crises, arose between us. He had been very badly shaken by the election result and his intemperate reaction to what he considered to be its causes in terms of Party policy found us seriously at odds. I was in no sense a member of his 'Hampstead' or 'Frognal' set, apart from a brief weekend membership during the Suez crisis. He now tended to withdraw in the company of his small clique of cronies to refashion policies through them rather than in the Shadow Cabinet, and the atmosphere in the Party became uncomfortably divisive and exclusive.

The Gaitskell group had come to the conclusion that it was inherited Labour Party policies which had lost us the election. Douglas Jay was the first to erupt. A regular contributor to the weekly *Reynolds News*, he came out on the eve of our 1959 Conference with an article in which he suggested that we should change the name of the Party (Labour being too plebeian) and drop all consideration of nationalization. Patrick Gordon-Walker wrote a similar piece for the extreme right-of-left *Forward* and revealed this at a Shadow Cabinet meeting. I reminded him of the self-denying ordinance which members of the Parliamentary Committee had agreed to observe. He immediately rushed out of the meeting, telephoned *Forward* and demanded that they cancel the article – or, as he said, 'I've had it.'

The timing of the election had compelled us to cancel the Party Conference and the NEC had agreed that we should have a short weekend conference in Blackpool in November, this being essential for electing a new National Executive. It was at this that Hugh Gaitskell, without any prior warning to either the Shadow Cabinet or the National Executive Committee, came out with his denunciation of Clause IV with its commitment to the 'nationalization of the means of production, distribution, and exchange'.

Barbara Castle chaired the two-day conference. In her opening speech, she hit out at the campaign already launched by Hugh Gaitskell's coterie. It would be a fallacy, she said, if Labour abandoned the attempt to take over more industries into public ownership. The previous year we had 'met in the bright hope of victory', now 'we meet in the shadow of electoral defeat'. She then called on Hugh Gaitskell, the early part of whose speech was analytical:

> We are told that we have succeeded so well in reforming capitalism that we have made it not only civilized but practically indestructible. We are told . . . that our best bet is to accept it almost completely in its present modified form, abandon the attempt to take over any more industries, and use public ownership merely to ensure that the community gets a cut at the capitalist cake. Such a policy would lead us slap bang into the fallacious belief that one can separate moral issues from economic ones. . . .
>
> Nevertheless, we can probably expect a further improvement in living conditions of the same kind as that experienced in recent years. To full employment we can add the Welfare State – another of our achievements which has had profound consequences. We point out rightly how much remains to be done. Indeed, we fought the election very largely on the improvements in the Welfare State which are so urgently needed. But this is not to deny that for the majority at least, the protection of the Welfare State has made a profound difference. Unfortunately, gratitude is not a reliable political asset.
>
> Moreover, the recent improvements in living standards have been of a special kind. There has been an especially notable increase in comforts, pleasures and conveniences in the home. Television, whether we like it or not, has

transformed the leisure hours of the vast majority of our fellow citizens. Washing machines, refrigerators, modern cookers have made women's lives a great deal easier. Incidentally, I suspect that our failure this time was largely a failure to win support from the women.

He then turned all the speculation about the Hampstead manœuvrings over Clause IV into bitter reality; since this was to cause a major schism in the Labour Party, we should remind ourselves of the public record:

Now I turn to public ownership and nationalization. Why was nationalization apparently a vote loser? For two reasons, I believe. First, some of the existing nationalized industries, rightly or wrongly, are unpopular. This unpopularity is overwhelmingly due to circumstances which have nothing to do with nationalization. London buses are overcrowded and slow, not because the Transport Commission is inefficient, but because of the state of London traffic which the Tory Government has neglected all these years. The backward conditions of the railways are not due to bad management but to inadequate investment in the past, which has left British Railways with a gigantic problem of modernization. Coal costs more, not because the Coal Board has done badly, but because in the post-war world we have to pay miners a decent wage to induce them to work in the pits.

Above all, we must face the fact that nationalization will not be positively popular until all these industries are clearly seen to be performing at least as well as the best firms in the private sector. When we have achieved that goal, then we can face the country with complete confidence. . . .

We should make two things clear. First, that we have no intention of abandoning public ownership and accepting for all time the present frontiers of the public sector. Secondly, that we regard public ownership not as an end but as a means, not necessarily the only or most important one, to certain ends: full employment, greater equality, higher productivity. We do not aim to nationalize every private firm or create an endless series of state monopolies.

We shall try to express in the most simple and comprehensive fashion our ultimate ideals. The only official document which now attempts to do this is the Party Constitution, written over forty years ago. It seems to me that this needs to be brought up to date. For instance, can we really be satisfied today with a statement of fundamentals which makes no reference to colonial freedom, race relations, disarmament, full employment or planning?

Then, of course, there is the famous phrase 'to secure for the workers by hand or by brain the full fruits of their industry, the most equitable distribution thereof that may be possible upon the basis of the common ownership of the means of production, distribution and exchange and the best obtainable system of popular administration and control of each industry or service'.

Standing as it does on its own, I think this is misleading. It implies that we propose to nationalize everything, but do we? Everything? The whole of light industry, the whole of agriculture, all the shops, every little pub and garage? Of course not! We have long ago come to accepted a mixed economy. . . .

It was a courageous speech, embodying some important home truths, but this was the bible of the Labour movement being challenged, the religion for miners, cotton workers and many others. It was as if Methodists or Baptists had been told by somebody who was trying to win an election that there was no God. He also failed to foresee the avidity with which the predominantly Conservative press would use it against the Party or, unwisely advised, he did not consider such a question to be of any importance.

In Conference itself all hell was let loose. Hugh was denounced not only by the left, but even by right-wing trade unionists. My worry was about Nye Bevan, particularly after he had seen the Sunday newspapers with the Conservative majority in Fleet Street exulting in the split which they had rightly forecast would develop. *Reynolds News*, disagreeing with Hugh, nevertheless pleaded sadly for unity within the Party. Nye decided to kick over the traces at the evening public rally, and I had to work on him all day.

I was not going to be disloyal, but I was not going to back Gaitskell on a position where the Party was split and I knew that Nye was liable to go into orbit at any moment. We had to hold him down by his ankles. Nye had told all his friends on the way down by train — I went by car — that he was going to move in on

Gaitskell and take over the leadership. He never said that to me, but we did have a meeting. Nye and I were pressing for the removal of Standing Orders in the Shadow Cabinet and there was a row between Gaitskell and Nye so vigorous that Nye, when he went out of the room, said he was going to resign and campaign in the country.

I said, 'You are not going to resign, Nye. You're winning, but if you resign you will put yourself beyond the pale once again. You stay and fight it out here. We are going to win on this issue in the Shadow Cabinet. And there is a much bigger issue coming up. Once you resign, he wins.' In the event he threw the mantle of his protection around Gaitskell and everybody knew it. Nye stayed.

Further articles by Douglas Jay and Patrick Gordon-Walker not only confused, or angered, wide sections of the Party, but they also convinced more and more Labour backbenchers that we were now not administered by the Parliamentary Party, still less by Transport House, but by a coterie operating in the Hampstead area.

It was that fact more than any pressure from parliamentary colleagues which persuaded me that I had to stand against Hugh in the next convenient annual PLP election for the Party Leader. First I had to deal with Nye. His immediate reaction was to embark on a nationwide campaign against Hugh. He told all of us that he had decided to resign from the Shadow Cabinet and 'fight it out' with Hugh in the country. In the end I persuaded him that this was just what the Hampstead set were hoping for and he cooled down. We agreed that I should make the challenge when the right time came. Sections of the press were, of course, demanding to be told where I stood. Their argument was politically illiterate: 'Where does Wilson stand? Is he in favour of outright nationalization or opposed to it? Is he for Gaitskell or against him? He is sitting on the fence. . . . etc., etc.'

I was in favour of neither outright nationalization nor a complete ban on all further nationalization. The question, I told my colleagues, and such of the press as were listening, is 'daft'. It was a matter of degree and of proving a case. I was, and still am, an egalitarian and not necessarily a nationalizer. I looked at each industry to see whether there was a case for taking it into public ownership. It has never been any part of my political attitude to tear society up by the roots and replace it with something entirely different. I do not look at problems from that kind of perspective. I consider that the best style of government is like rowing – the ideal solution is to get the boat along as quickly as possible without turning it over.

In July 1960 Nye died, unexpectedly and tragically. I recall one of my last Smoke Room chats with him. My son Robin was by this time sixteen and Nye asked me what I thought he was going to be. When I said that he looked like becoming a mathematician, Nye responded in a flash, 'Just like his father. All bloody facts. No bloody vision.'

So the 1960 Conference took place at Scarborough without Nye, and nothing was the same. A great deal of work was put in to secure trade union block-vote support for the compromise we had reached on defence policy. Hugh and Frank Cousins, General Secretary of the Transport and General Workers, were the protagonists. One of those active in the discussions advised Hugh: 'Don't press Cousins too far, he's agreed with the document so far.' 'That', said Hugh, 'is the one thing I am afraid of.'

I had not expected the TUC to have any truck with unilateralism at their annual Congress at Douglas, Isle of Man, in September. In fact, they incurred the scorn of the press by the fact that two resolutions were carried. The first supported the official policy drawn up by the TUC Council:

> First priority must be given to securing an agreement to end all nuclear tests. In any case no further tests should be conducted by this country. To break the present deadlock, the Government should launch a new British disarmament plan, along the lines laid down last year in the joint Labour Party–TUC declaration.

This 'official' resolution was carried by 4,356,000 to 3,213,000.

The second resolution, moved by Frank Cousins for the Transport and General Workers Union, was carried against the General Council's advice by 3,448,000 to 3,213,000 and declared:

> This Congress, believing that the great majority of the people of this country are earnestly seeking a lasting peace and recognizing that the present state of world tension accentuates the great danger of an accidental drift into war, is convinced that the defence and foreign policy of the future Labour Government should be based upon:
>
> 1 A complete rejection of any defence policy based on the threat of the use of strategic or tactical nuclear weapons.

2   The permanent cessation of the manufacture or testing of nuclear and thermo-nuclear weapons.

3   The continuation of the opposition to the establishment of missile bases in Great Britain.

On the pre-Conference Sunday, Tony Benn resigned from the National Executive because of Hugh Gaitskell's refusal to accept the vote for the TGWU resolution on disarmament. He had seen Hugh the day before and pressed him to accept it, and Hugh had refused with what Tony considered 'brutal rudeness'. Tony told me what he had then said:

> Look, you are always talking about improving the image of the Party. I am one of the young men you talked about. Young. Not cloth cap and all that, but I am bound to say now that I consider that your leadership is disastrous. You've made these two terrible blunders. Clause IV and now this one.

Hugh, in Tony's account immediately afterwards, surprised him by saying, 'Yes, I recognize Clause IV was a blunder.' For one moment Tony thought Hugh was admitting that he had been wrong. He was, he said, quite 'warmed' by the admission. But his temperature cooled as Hugh went on: 'I went into the Clause IV row without making sure that I had got the support of the big trade union leaders. I hadn't got it and that's why I went under. But in this I've got them all behind me, so this is the issue on which to fight' – meaning, as Tony interpreted it, that a fight on the ground Hugh had chosen was definitely going to take place.

On that Sunday the NEC met to decide its attitude to the various motions on which Conference would vote. Most unions were already 'mandated', that is to say under instructions from their own conferences or their governing bodies on how to vote. Where a resolution corresponded broadly with a similar one which had been debated at the TUC a few weeks earlier, there was usually no difficulty. But a great deal had happened in the intervening period and new textual formulations were before them. Not only that, on some issues the NEC, albeit by majority votes, had taken its decisions on the advice to be given to Conference. And overshadowing all this was the question of personalities.

Though I did not learn of this until afterwards, some weighty trade union leaders had formed the view that Hugh was becoming 'unstuck', and messages reached me saying there was a growing feeling that I would have to take up the challenge. This irked Sam Watson, the arch-priest of Gaitskellism, who turned particularly sour. Ray Gunter on the other hand, a Labour frontbencher and a right-wing member of the NEC nominated for the trade union section, was profoundly unhappy and told pressmen that it was all going my way.

It was unfortunate that I had been chosen, by a combination of NEC voting and the recognition of 'Buggin's turn', to address the pre-Conference rally, where Nye in past years had been so successful a performer that the NEC had altered the rules to limit any individual to one appearance in three years. Looking back on it, I feel that my speech was too close to the issue dividing the Conference. There were banners inside and outside the hall demanding that 'Conference must decide'. My speech was somewhat sanctimonious in its reference to the fact that on German rearmament, the Bevanites had agreed and announced that despite our opposition we would accept the decision of Conference however it might go.

It was clear that we were in for a miserable week and that the Party could suffer immense damage. The situation was made all the worse by the fact that the NEC and delegates missed the wisdom and guidance of Morgan Phillips, who had suffered a severe stroke in August. His loyalties were undivided – the Party first, second and all the time. I knew that his intention was to stiffen the powerful trade union element in the Conference and he would have had a ready response to his insistence that the National Executive was, under the Party's constitution, the custodian of Conference decisions.

Behind the scenes, Hugh was making clear his decision to 'fight, fight and fight again' to reverse any Conference vote with which he did not agree. Some of his friends were engaged in whipping up feeling against me, because it was being widely asserted that if Hugh were to trip I was the only possible successor now that Nye had gone.

Hugh did not help his cause by his remoteness. While the NEC was staying at the Royal Hotel, Hugh and his coterie were in the Grand. They did not know that a personal friend of mine, not at all involved in the Party, was also at the Grand and was able to absorb the atmosphere. Hugh caused further affront when he called a hand-picked meeting of certain members of the Shadow Cabinet. This came to my knowledge and I asked the Secretary of the Shadow Cabinet if he had been aware of this. He was not. By this time Hugh had got his friends together and had, we were told, promised James Callaghan the Chancellorship when Labour won.

Hugh had, in fact, after the Conference decision on the Wednesday, called certain members of the Shadow Cabinet to a meeting at his hotel. Tony Benn, himself a member of the Shadow Cabinet, challenged Jim about his attendance at that meeting. Jim denied attending, but ten days later, so Tony told me, admitted that he had misled Tony about this. Meanwhile, George Brown had been won over. Hugh either sent for him or sent an emissary to him. I was not clear which version was correct, perhaps both were. The message was: 'If you will get up on the rostrum and denounce Frank Cousins, you're in and you will be Deputy Leader.' George took the hint.

It was clear to me also that some of the hatchet men around Hugh were determined to get me off the Shadow Cabinet when the PLP elections took place at the beginning of the new session of Parliament. The division between Hugh's heavy squad and me was a simple one. I wanted to fight to work for Party unity, including Gaitskellites and erstwhile Bevanites. He wanted to divide. I was against 'fight, fight, fight'; he was determined on it.

Back in London a group of MPs, headed by Tony Greenwood, Dick Crossman, Barbara Castle and Jennie Lee, met with me and tried to persuade me to run against Hugh Gaitskell for the leadership of the PLP. In those days the Party Leader had to submit to annual re-election. I refused. It was not only that it would be a deliberately divisive action, I argued, but I would be to a considerable extent dependent on unilateral votes, though I resented Hugh's attacks on them as irresponsible neutralists.

I was not in any way exercised by the argument that in standing against Hugh I would be identified again with the Marxists in the Party as the Bevanites had been ten years earlier. I had taken charge of Party organization and neutralized their influence effectively. A number of my public speeches had been patently anti-Russian. If the Marxist element had offered their help, it would have been rejected. I was certainly not in the business of creating a party within the Party.

However, in the next few days, my hand was forced. Tony Greenwood let it be known that if I did not contest the Leadership, he would. Tony was a very nice man, a well-liked figure, but he did not carry anything like the weight of his father, Arthur Greenwood, although he would have attracted the support of the left. His argument was a strong one. Hugh's intimates were putting it about that the Leader had decided that the unilateralist issue had to be pushed to finality, even if he had to expel fifty or sixty MPs. The CND, Hugh was reported to have said, was a conspiracy to take over the Labour Party and had to be destroyed.

I was intensely worried. I did not want to force an unnecessary contest, but Tony Greenwood by this time was determined to run. I had to pay a duty visit to Cumberland, and on my return was involved in a further meeting of colleagues urging me to oppose Hugh. I was still against it, but in the end I agreed, for the unhappy reason that if Hugh was unopposed, he would claim an undeniable mandate to act against a substantial number of the loyal members of the Parliamentary Party.

On the other hand, if Tony stood, the votes would be a straight division between Bevanites and others further to the left, while middle-of-the-roaders would be driven into the Gaitskell camp. However strong the argument, it was the most miserable decision I have ever had to take. I knew it would be a mucky election, not because I thought Hugh would fight dirty, but because some of his friends were determined to do so and the press, one could confidently assume, would make even the Gaitskellites' effort seem puny by comparison.

So we went through the prescribed routine. I was defeated by more than two to one, 166 votes to eighty-one. I have always said that I had a love–hate relationship with Hugh Gaitskell. I admired his many qualities and had been an unwilling challenger. However, although his position remained secure, the Party now had two standard bearers.

What Hugh never recognized was that, from the Party's earliest days, a great number of converts had joined Labour because they believed that socialism was a way of making a reality of Christian principles in everyday life. The same is true of a large number of Conservatives, and it is intimately bound up with the history of the Liberal Party. Hugh's background and introduction to politics, despite his noble work when young in slum settlements, denied him any knowledge of how ordinary people thought. He undoubtedly learned far more from university in Leeds than he had learned from Winchester, but even there, it was from the right-wingers that he chose his tutors.

15

Party Leader

My challenge to Hugh Gaitskell for the leadership only caused a temporary further estrangement. He made the mistake of trying to whip up the National Executive Council against me. On the whole, there were as many left as there were right on the Executive. The Party was split in the House as I had never seen it before, and it was also split on the Executive. Instead of thinking about how to beat the Conservatives at the next election, too many constituency parties were devoting themselves to debating Gaitskell pro or contra. I would guess that in the very small local parties of those days there was more contra than pro.

This soon died down, although I did drop to eighth place in the voting for the Shadow Cabinet. Hugh Gaitskell was sufficient of a political realist to recognize that, with Nye dead, he needed to have people like me around in order to restore some semblance of unity in the Party and get out the Labour vote at the next general election. Divided, he knew the Tories would be attacking us all the time. I was in a strong position and had come top of all the votes at the Party Conference for three years running, so Hugh and I made concourse.

Nineteen sixty-one was my Pooh-Bah year. After the Party Conference, I became chairman of the National Executive Committee. By this time I was holding five offices – Party Chairman (for one year), Chairman of the Home Policy Committee of the National Executive, as well as being NEC nominee to the TUC General Council; I still retained the chairmanship of the Public Accounts Committee and, in November, Hugh appointed me Shadow Foreign Secretary on the front bench. Dick Crossman warned me that he had heard – I think from a pressman – that if Labour did win the next election and Hugh was Prime Minister, he was not going to give me one of the main offices of state, but try to neutralize me as Attlee had neutralized Morrison by making me Leader of the House. In the meantime, I relished this appointment as a new sphere of interest and was soon on my feet.

At the beginning of February 1962, the House debated, on a Labour initiative, a speech which had been made at the end of December by the Foreign Secretary, the Earl of Home. At a meeting in Berwick-on-Tweed, he had indulged in an almost hysterical attack on the United Nations. Hugh Gaitskell, moving a formal vote of censure on the Government, took issue with the claim by Lord Home that the speech had not been an attack on the UN as such.

His address had been basically critical of the United Nations as it was then functioning, or as ministerial imagination conceived it to be functioning. The real problem for him and a strong and articulate section of his Party was, it seemed to me, that when the roll was called at the UN, there appeared to be a majority of foreigners among the nations. What was more, eighty-two of them were behind in their financial contributions. I pointed out that since we too had been laggardly in meeting our quota in respect of recent UN action to stop the fighting in the Congo, we were one of those defaulters. The Prime Minister gloried in the fact that Britain spent £12 million on the direct and indirect services of the UN which, as I said, was about one-fifth of the funds we had invested in the Blue Streak missile, soon to be scrapped. The Government was dithering and delaying, while the three Scandinavian countries, with a total national income of about a third of ours, were contributing £10 million, nearly as much.

The United Nations Association, which we all supported, and which the Prime Minister, an Honorary Vice-President, had glorified in recent speeches, and which even had a Conservative MP as its President, had issued a withering statement attacking the Government: 'We do not believe that there is a "crisis of confidence in the UN", but consider that such a crisis can be induced by an assumption that it already exists. We fear that these statements may suggest that Great Britain's support for the UN depends on the extent to which our policies prevail there.'

Harold Macmillan had cited a few words by the Foreign Secretary commendatory of the United Nations. 'A master butcher addressing a vegetarian gathering', I commented, 'would at the end of his speech have found time to say a few words in praise of lettuce.' The Prime Minister had backed the Foreign Secretary in criticizing the United Nations for not attacking communist tyranny, but they had in fact passed resolution after resolution against communist action in Tibet, Hungary and elsewhere. 'I say this seriously to the Rt Hon. and Hon. Gentlemen opposite,' my recorded intervention states:

> In their rush to get into Europe they must not forget the four-fifths of the world's population whose preoccupation is with emergence from colonial status into self-government; and into the revolution of rising expectations. If this is so, is the world organization not to reflect the enthusiasms and aspirations of the new members and new nations entering into their inheritance, often through British action, as the Prime Minister said, and who want to see their neighbours also brought forward into the light? It must be recognized that this is the greatest force in the world today, and we must ask why it is so often that we are found, or thought to be found, on the wrong side.
>
> The record of this country since the war, under both Governments, is good enough to proclaim to the world – India, Pakistan, Burmah, Ceylon, Ghana, Nigeria, Tanganyika and Sierra Leone and, even after the agonies, Cyprus. Why do we contrive it that in the eyes of the world we are so often allied with reactionary governments, whose record in the scales of human enfranchisement weigh as a speck of dust against real gold and silver as far as our record is concerned? Why is it that the British Foreign Secretary speaks in accents of the dead past, as though he fears and resents the consequences of the very actions which his Government as well as ours have taken?
>
> Not only in this country but abroad people are asking, 'Who is in charge? Whose hand is on the helm? When is the Prime Minister going to exert himself and govern?' I do not believe that he can. The panache has gone. On every issue, domestic and foreign, now we find the same faltering hand, the same dithering indecision and confusion. What is more, Hon. Members opposite know it, and some of them are even beginning to say it.
>
> The MacWonder of 1959 is the man who gave us this pathetic performance this afternoon. This whole episode has justified our insistence eighteen months ago that the Foreign Secretary should have been in the House of Commons. But we were wrong on one thing. We thought that the noble lord

would be an office boy. The Prime Minister was able to restore his tottering position today only by a fulsome tribute to the noble lord. Indeed, to adopt the saying made famous by Nye Bevan: 'It is a little difficult to know which is the organ grinder and which is the other.'

This is why the Rt Hon. Gentleman has refused to disavow the speech of the Foreign Secretary. Personal ties apart, and the Prime Minister's almost sub-idolatory for the hereditary Earl apart, his duty today was clear. He should have disavowed the Foreign Secretary. When we go into the division lobby tonight it will be with a clear and united demand for the Foreign Secretary's resignation. No doubt we shall be outnumbered by the votes of those who, every election, hand on heart, appeal for votes because they support the United Nations; but we shall have with us the support of millions of the people in this country who believe that Britain has reached the parting of the ways, that the crisis of confidence is not in the United Nations, but in the Government's support of it, and that it can now be resolved by the unequivocal repudiation of the minister who has put it in doubt.

I have included these lengthy passages from a still lengthier speech to give readers a picture of British Party democracy, and also to put on record an argument for which Attlee and his supporters had fought and which we were putting forward as representing the philosophy which an incoming Labour Government would be expected to take. Still more important, I wanted to give a small impression of something the House, in a generation of granting independence to previous subject colonies, had not yet lost – namely its sense of responsibility for the many millions in five continents for whom Britain is still the protector and the legislative authority.

Edward Heath replied for the Government. Despite his great abilities, no one had, or has ever, right up to today, criticized him for any marked attachment to Commonwealth countries or the Commonwealth ideal. His enthusiasm, until very recently, came to a shuddering halt at the boundaries of the members of a European Economic Community. When the House divided, the Ayes had 208 and the Noes 326.

As Chairman of the National Executive Committee for the year 1961–2, my final task was to chair the annual conference, held in

Brighton during the first week of October, an assembly which I described in my first sentence as 'the greatest democratic conference in the world, with 1,300 delegates from every part of the country'.

> We are here not to represent ourselves, but as trustees for a great democratic movement; most of us are democratically mandated on every great issue which is to come before us. . . . We claim, and it is a proud claim, that we are truly representative of the British people as a whole.
>
> It is our task this week to speak for Britain. There is no one else to do it. We meet this year on the threshold of victory. Month by month, evidence has mounted of the total collapse in support for our Tory opponents. No socialist Party can be satisfied with an electoral victory based on a mere swing against the Government. This Party is a moral crusade or it is nothing. That is why we have rejected timorous and defeatist proposals for a Lib–Lab alliance. We are not going to sail into power under any flags of convenience, so now let us concentrate on putting that socialism before the people.

I ended with some well-known lines from James Russell Lowell, written just a hundred years before:

> Man is more than Constitutions, better rot beneath the sod,
> Than be true to Church and State while we are doubly false
> to God.
> We owe allegiance to the State: but deeper, truer, more
> To the sympathies that God has set within our spirit's core.
> Our country claims our fealty: we grant it so, but then
> Before man made us citizens, great Nature made us men.
> He's true to God who's true to man; wherever wrong is done
> To the humblest and the weakest, 'neath the all-beholding
> sun,
> That wrong is also done to us, and they are slaves most base,
> Whose love of right is for themselves and not for all their race.

It is a mark of how the Labour Party has fallen in recent years that if at any Party Conference held these days anyone had sought to quote these sentiments from the rostrum, he would have been jeered out of court by members of what for some reason is called a militant 'tendency'.

It was a busy year in Parliament, particularly in foreign affairs.

The world is rarely quiet for long and to the normal round of 'wars and rumours of war' were added the strains based on the Commonwealth, and indeed on the North Atlantic alliance, by growing ministerial and Civil Service preoccupation with the European Economic Community. The question whether Britain should seek membership of the Common Market, as it was more frequently called – even assuming that President de Gaulle could be persuaded to remove the *massif central* which he had built against our entry – was highly divisive, not so much between parties as within parties.

Both Labour and Conservatives were sharply divided between pro- and anti-marketeers, Labour possibly the more so because of fears by a number of trade unions that tariff reductions and the creation of a Common Market would threaten employment. At the same time, those of us on the NEC and Shadow Cabinet, who were involved in meetings with our colleagues in European socialist parties, were under strong pressure, whenever we went abroad, to become less 'insular' and to join them in making the EEC a success.

Those with a significant rural population tended to be as keen as the Gaullists on developing restrictionist protection for their own agriculture and, country by country, were putting pressure on us to sacrifice our own agricultural interests, which over a wide area of products were at least as efficient, frequently more efficient, than their counterparts across the Channel and the North Sea.

De Gaulle was obdurate. He did not want Britain in. While far from attracted by some blueprints of the Community which certain other European colleagues wanted to see created, he was willing to go a long way in building an integrated economic system in Europe, provided that he dominated it and made the rules. He was quite outspoken in saying that the European Community would be organized on the basis of '*Un coq: cinq poules*'. British entry would mean '*Deux coqs*'.

Britain was a world power and he resented it. Worse, some of our 'colonies' as he regarded them, such as Australia and New Zealand, were more efficient agriculturalists than his French farmers. Indeed on some key products, English and Scottish farmers were more efficient, to say nothing of the Welsh and Northern Irish. His hopes for a tightly knit, protectionist economic Western Europe would be greatly at risk if we were in a position to lower continental tariff barriers. It would be worse still if we were to poison his neighbours' minds on political issues to the point, perhaps, where they came under American domination as much as he conceived that Britain had done. His reasoning was implacable and, in January 1963, he imposed his veto on British entry in spite of Edward Heath's devoted implementation of the policies of the Macmillan Government.

On a number of occasions in the late 1950s and early 1960s, I had been in the habit of visiting the United States on short lecture tours. These were organized for me by Senator William Benton. Bill was an interesting and very American character. In his youth he had set up a small shop in the centre of New York and was a dollar millionaire before he was thirty. His heart was in academics and in politics. He returned to the university where he had graduated, Chicago, and became an administrator.

One of his earliest tasks concerned the *Encyclopedia Britannica*, then the property of Chicago University and losing money. The University authorities sought means of getting rid of it and Benton bought it, speedily turning it into a profitable concern and extending its scope by publishing annually a topical volume, the *Encyclopedia Book of the Year*.

In 1945 he resigned from the University to become Assistant Secretary of State in President Truman's administration, where he initiated the *Voice of America* broadcasts, including those to the Soviet Union. He led America's entry into the UN Educational and Scientific Organization. He was also responsible for the Smith–Mundt Act, the Fulbright legislation on international educational interchange programmes. In 1950 he became a senator, representing the state of Connecticut. The incumbent had died and the state party organization nominated Bill to fill the vacancy. Not the least of his senatorial achievements was to introduce the resolution calling for Senator Joseph McCarthy's expulsion from the Senate and the subsequent censure of McCarthy. He was a senator, in fact, for only two years, and was defeated in the election of 1952, though in accordance with US practice he was entitled to be called Senator Benton to the end of his days.

He took a great interest in Britain and came to the House of Commons regularly. At our first meeting, he invited me, all expenses paid plus an honorarium – very small in comparison with the more lush fees paid nowadays on the American circuit – to visit Chicago for a short course of lectures. This invitation was repeated each autumn. For February 1963 I asked Bill if he would cut my usual programme of five lectures down to two, as I wanted to study Chicago's system of extra-mural teaching, which was in high esteem in the academic world. I had already begun to formulate the idea of what I later created as the Open University.

The Chicago lecture hall was packed out upstairs and down. As far as I can recall, I was speaking from the front of the upstairs gallery and had barely begun my speech when I found myself being heckled. Stretched out on the far end of the floor behind me, with his back to the inner wall, was a figure looking somewhat old for a student, but clearly accomplished in the art of interruption. To see him the better I remember I put on my glasses. I surmised that he was one of those perennial students not unfamiliar in my pre-war Oxford days who managed to stay on year after year, occasionally taking an examination or persuading a tolerant college to agree to a fresh course of studies. I decided to put my notes on one side and take him on for a few minutes. I might not be a great authority on contemporary economics but I knew, or thought I knew, all about dealing with hecklers. I would wait for the end of his interruptions, catch them as it were in mid-air, and throw them back in familiar British House of Commons style. My first return ball was widely cheered, as was the second, the third and all the rest. The speech had become a dialogue. As we left the hall to a further round of cheers, the President of the University said, 'That was great entertainment – my, you were very rough with Milton Friedman tonight.'

From Chicago I flew straight to Idlewild, as I was due to address the Foreign Affairs Institute in New York. As always, this was a small and intimate gathering, a short speech followed by questions and discussion. During and indeed after dinner, I was called from the table seven or eight times to take telephone calls from London. Hugh Gaitskell had not been well when I left, but it was generally assumed that he was suffering from some lingering bug. It had turned into something much more serious and the alarming and unexpected news was that he was dying. These calls were from friends and associates who wanted to make sure that I would be prepared to make a short statement and attend interviews, paying tribute to the Party's Leader.

I arranged to go from the Institute meeting to Bill Benton's flat. He was also an old friend of Hugh's but was matter of fact. 'Hugh's dying,' he said, 'Will you stand in his place?' I naturally said that I really could not discuss issues of that kind at such a time. 'Having said that, will you stand?' he insisted. I intimated that this was very possible and that would-be supporters had already been on the phone.

Suddenly a new thought struck him. 'Say . . . this is like an American presidential election, where the Party has to choose its candidate.' *Mutatis mutandis* and the rest, I agreed. 'But what is this going to cost?' he asked me; 'our last Democratic convention cost $25 million.' He was going, he said, to write me out a cheque for $10,000 towards my expenses. I told him that I could not accept any donation from him or from any American, or for that matter from a fellow countryman of my own. What was more it would not cost $10,000.

He was quite taken aback by this forecast. I undertook, however, to send him, when the contest was over, an exact financial statement, certified by a parliamentary colleague who was a chartered accountant. In due course this statement reached him. My total expenses were four old pence, the cost of two telephone calls to enthusiastic supporters who, I heard, were engaged in canvassing Labour MPs for their vote. I had decided that canvassing would be counter-productive, and so it proved.

Fortunately, my return flight to London was booked, and I flew back immediately to be met by Mary, whom Marcia Williams had driven out to the airport, within a matter of hours of Hugh's death. We were inevitably assailed by journalists and photographers, but after issuing a short statement, to which I was not prepared to add or subtract, we made our way home and holed up. The Party was in turmoil and, although I spent long periods on the telephone, I refused to campaign for the succession. Events would have to take their course.

There would have to be an election and, almost by common consent, there were three runners: George Brown, who was the Deputy Leader, Jim Callaghan and myself. Straw polls indicated that I had a substantial lead over George Brown, but no majority over their combined votes. Jim was allowing his name to go forward, but there was anxiety about George and his drink problem: it was felt that he might not attract sufficient right-wing votes, in spite of the solid support of the unions.

We had one parliamentary trial of strength to endure first. We had all been to the memorial service for Hugh Gaitskell in the morning and in the afternoon debate in the House of Commons it had been arranged that all three of us should speak. Harold Macmillan, whose Government was going through a difficult time, thought he saw advantage in the situation and, knowing me of old as his most consistent opponent, had planned a trap. George Brown had not made much impact in the debate, nor had Jim Callaghan. The Prime Minister was winding up, looking mighty pleased with himself.

He challenged me to state whether I agreed with a particular pronouncement Hugh Gaitskell had made. Patrick Gordon-Walker got up and complained that it was exceedingly bad taste to ask such a question on the very day that we had all been to Hugh's memorial service. Macmillan was not to be deterred. Did I agree with what Hugh Gaitskell had said? I was completely relaxed. I had my feet up on the table, but then stood up and said, 'The Rt Hon. Gentleman has correctly quoted what Hugh Gaitskell said.' I went on to point out to the Prime Minister that Hugh had said there were two possible approaches to this problem and that the Prime Minister had failed to mention the other, which I told him he would find on a particular page of the published version of Hugh Gaitskell's speeches. This for once had Macmillan flurried. He did not have the reference and had no possibility of checking it. I always think that this exchange is what really won me the leadership, because what the Labour Party wanted was someone who could put Harold Macmillan down.

The vote duly took place. Jim Callaghan got forty-one votes in the first round and had to drop out. In the second round the voting was Wilson 144, Brown 103. George was civil and courteous and congratulated me. After all the in-fighting the Party rallied round.

16

Prime Minister

I was acutely aware as Party Leader that nothing short of a war could prevent a general election within, at the most, eighteen months and I was determined that the Labour Party should go into the contest with a more positive approach to wipe out the disappointments of the three previous occasions. In the early spring of 1963 I began formulating three main areas of policy with which to rejuvenate the economy and the administration, and to provide new openings and opportunities for those prepared to become technically skilled.

I had now spent over twenty years in Whitehall and Westminster watching, and wherever possible, countering the wily and dominating ways of the Treasury. I was determined that this department should be cut down to size with a new machinery of government to handle economic affairs in a Labour Cabinet. I therefore told Jim Callaghan, the Shadow Chancellor, and others of my decision that, while the Chancellor of the Exchequer would be responsible for all actions necessary in the monetary field, foreign exchange, internal monetary management and government expenditure and taxation, Britain could hope to win economic security only by a fundamental reconstruction and modernization of industry under the direction of a department at least as powerful as the Treasury. This new department, which I proposed to call the Department of Economic Affairs, would be concerned with real resources, economic planning and strengthening our ability to export and save imports, with increasing productivity and our competitiveness in domestic and export markets.

There is a legend that the DEA was all worked out in a taxi with George Brown on the way back from a meeting with the TUC at St Ermins Hotel to a division at the House of Commons – a distance of less than a mile. This is just not true. I had already formulated detailed plans and the only thing that happened in that taxi was that I first suggested to George Brown that the right job for him would be Secretary of State for Economic Affairs.

My second concern was science and technology. It was Hugh Gaitskell who first deployed me on these questions. During the long Opposition years, he would attend small dinner parties given by Patrick Blackett, later President of the Royal Society, and some of his colleagues. As the burdens of leadership took more and more of his time, he asked me to take his place. The scientists set out the arguments, hard going for me despite the family's scientific background, and I tried to formulate the political implications.

In addition to the DEA, I proposed to set up another major new department with the title of Ministry of Technology. I had long felt that we needed a ministry to discharge two functions which existing departments were inadequate to perform. It was to be a ministry of industry, starting with a relatively small number of industries but taking on a wider and wider sponsorship, with a very direct responsibility for increasing productivity and efficiency, particularly within those industries in urgent need of restructuring or modernization. Its second task would be to speed the application of new scientific methods to industrial production.

Britain has always been good in the scientific laboratory, but all too often the results of fundamental research done here had been clothed with the necessary know-how by foreign industrialists. This had been a not unfamiliar process before the war. During the war some of our major inventions, such as jet propulsion, radar, other electronic developments and antibiotics, had been handed over to the United States under the Lend–Lease arrangements from 1941–5. The process had continued apace after the war, and I decided something must be done about it.

I once described my intended Ministry of Technology, while we were still in Opposition, as 'NRDC writ large'. The National Research Development Corporation, an idea of Sir Stafford Cripps, had been set up by me in 1948 after I had succeeded him at the Board of Trade, to develop to the production stage inventions by British scientists and research workers. Over its sixteen years of life it had achieved considerable success on a modest scale. I felt not only should the NRDC be transferred to the new Ministry, but that over a far wider field this kind of activity should become a central theme of the Ministry's work.

My third brain child, perhaps of a lesser category but for me of fundamental importance, was to set up a 'University of the Air' to bring higher education to those who had not or could not find the time to attend a full university course. The idea was not brand new. It had been mooted as early as 1926, when the educationalist and historian, J.C. Stobart, wrote a memorandum advocating 'a wireless university' for the infant BBC. It has always attracted me and I had spent part of the time in Chicago studying the University's extra-mural system, which was based in part on television.

During my several visits to the Soviet Union I had discovered that 60 per cent of their engineers had got their degrees in part from distance teaching. Then, in March 1963, a Labour Party study group under the chairmanship of Lord Taylor presented a report on higher education in general and commented on the continuing exclusion of the lower-income groups. They also proposed an experiment on radio and television for serious planned adult education.

I was extremely busy with election preparations, and visiting local parties all over the country, but Mary and I spent Easter Sunday in the Isles of Scilly. Between Church and lunch I wrote the whole outline of a proposal for a University of the Air. I did not get a chance to make use of it until 8 September, when I was speaking at a meeting in Glasgow. Always when I went to Scotland, I would devote half a speech to Scottish problems and the other half, accompanied by a handout, to covering the whole country:

> Today I want to outline new proposals on which we are working, a dynamic programme providing facilities for home study to university and higher technical standards, on the basis of a University of the Air and of nationally organized correspondence college courses.
>
> These will be intended to cater for a wide variety of potential students. There are technicians and technologists who perhaps left school at sixteen or seventeen and who, after two or three years in industry, feel that they could qualify as graduate scientists or technologists. There are many others, perhaps in clerical occupations, who would like to acquire new skills and new qualifications. There are many in all levels of industry who would desire to become qualified in their own or other fields, including those who had no

195

facilities for taking GEC at O or A level, or other required qualifications; or housewives who might like to secure qualifications in English Literature, Geography or History.

To my disappointment, the handout setting out the full scheme was hardly reported at all, except in the local Scottish papers. There was virtually no interest in the idea in the daily press or among my colleagues. I discussed it with a few of them, Ted Short for example, but I did not circulate copies within the Executive or the Shadow Cabinet. Significantly, it was taken up and supported by the *Economist*, then edited by Sir Geoffrey Crowther. He played a substantial part in working out the detailed plan, which, in fact, went much further than my own somewhat limited proposals. It certainly was not official Labour Party policy at this stage, except in the sense that I was running the Party in a slightly dictatorial way, and if I said something was going to happen, I intended it to happen.

I was able to return to the theme three weeks later in the much wider context of my first speech as Party Leader to Labour's annual conference. This was at 10 am on Tuesday, 1 October, and as it was regarded as a major event in my political career and a turning-point in the attitudes and fortunes of the Labour Party I may perhaps record some of the things that I said.

I had been singularly improvident in preparing for such a major occasion. On the Sunday evening I had to deliver a major speech on foreign affairs to a large fringe meeting. On the Monday I felt that as this was the first Conference since my election, I should sit through all the debates. In the evening there was the usual tour of the affiliated organizations, trade unions and Scots and Welsh receptions. I had still prepared nothing for the following day and I told Marcia Williams, my secretary, that I was too tired, was going to bed and was going to have an alarm clock to wake me up at 5 am to write the speech.

'You are not, you know,' she said. 'You are not going to get up at five o'clock', and she made me stay up. She was quite right. I dictated that speech, which is rare for me as I am not good at it and have to keep stopping the machine to search for a word. I had no idea whether the text was going to last fifteen minutes or ninety-five. Marcia and her assistant sat up all night typing it and I got up at seven and read it through; parts of it were still being typed while I was at breakfast. I told my staff the Conference would be disappointed with it but that they might nevertheless react with sympathy to a beginner out of traditional loyalty to the Party Leader. Expecting a tub-thumping speech about Tory iniquities they would hardly welcome a disquisition on science and technology. I told the Conference:

The problem is this: since technological progress, left to the mechanism of private industry and private property, can lead only to high profits for a few, a high rate of employment for a few and to mass redundancy for the many, if there had never been a case for socialism before, automation would have created it. Because only if technological progress becomes part of our national planning can that progress be connected to national ends.

So the choice is not between technological progress and the kind of easygoing world we are living in today. It is the choice between the blind imposition of technological advance, with all that means in terms of unemployment, and the conscious, planned, purposive use of scientific progress to provide undreamed of living standards and the possibility of leisure ultimately on an unbelievable scale.

Now I come to what we must do, and it is a four-fold programme. First, we must produce more scientists. Secondly, having produced them, we must be a great deal more successful in keeping them in this country. Thirdly, having trained them and kept them here, we must make more intelligent use of them when they are trained than we do with those we have got. Fourthly, we must organize British industry so it applies the results of scientific research more purposively to our national production effort. Russia is at the present time training ten to eleven times as many scientists and technologists. And the sooner we face up to that challenge the sooner we shall realize what kind of a world we are living in.

Until very recently over half our trained scientists were engaged in defence projects or so-called defence projects. Real defence, of course, is essential. But so many of our scientists were employed on purely prestige projects that never left the drawing-board. Many more scientists are deployed not on projects that are going to increase Britain's productive power, but on some new gimmick or additive for some consumer product which will enable the advertising managers to rush to the television screen to tell us all to buy a little more of something we did not even know we wanted in the first place. This is not strengthening Britain.

What we need is new industries, and it will be the job of the next Government to see that we get them. This means mobilizing scientific research in this country to produce a new technological breakthrough. We have spent thousands of millions in the past few years on misdirected research and development contracts in the field of defence. If we were now to use the technique of R and D contracts in civil industry I believe we could within a measurable period of time establish new industries which would make us once again one of the foremost industrial nations of the world.

Relevant also to these problems are our plans for a University of the Air. I repeat again that this is not a substitute for our plans for higher education, for our plans for new universities and for our plans for extending technological education. It is not a substitute; it is a supplement to our plans. It is designed to provide an opportunity for those, who, for one reason or another, have not been able to take advantage of higher education, to now do so with all that the TV and radio state-sponsored correspondence courses, the facilities of a university for setting and marking papers, conducting examinations and awarding degrees, can provide. Nor, may I say, do we envisage this merely as a means of providing scientists and technologists. I believe a properly planned University of the Air could make an immeasurable contribution to the cultural life of our country, to the enrichment of our standard of living.

The journalist G.E. Noel filed this report:

At exactly ten o'clock in the morning of 1 October . . . he rose to speak. There was fairly prolonged applause; he sat down again exactly three-quarters of an hour later to a standing ovation of nearly three minutes. Writing about it within a matter of hours, one had an unmistakeable impression that a significant turning-point in Britain's social and political history had just been witnessed. The very absence of fireworks in a speech which some might even describe as 'dull' somehow put the seal of world leadership on the young Oxford don of a short generation before. . . .

Robert Mackenzie, reporting on the BBC at lunchtime, said, 'Harold Wilson has moved the Labour Party forward fifty years in fifty minutes.'

Ten days later came the unexpected and distressing news that Harold Macmillan was ill and, on 18 October, he resigned. It had been a bad year for him. The de Gaulle veto on Common Market entry had been a severe setback. The Profumo affair had raised questions about his judgement, the economy was faltering and his supporters were becoming restless. He had missed his own Party Conference at Blackpool on 10 October with prostate trouble.

I have to say that I consider that the Tory Party behaved in an unfeeling and ungenerous manner. Prime Ministers often run into trouble after some years in office. Backbenchers without preferment look to a new face to provide it. Macmillan had not always spared critics on his own side, causing resentment, and in the callous way of politics a faction seemed set on finding a new leader. They could have given him time to recover. A prostate operation is only temporarily disabling and, when we look at him as I write more than twenty years later, no one can say that he has not retained all his faculties.

I was going to miss him. He was a Tory radical whom I could understand and, in spite of our jousts in the House of Commons when neither had spared the other, I had a warm affection and admiration for him, both as a Conservative leader of high gifts and a political operator of extraordinary skill. In a clever balancing act, he had brought the Tory Party up to date, while preaching the old Tory legends. He had maintained a good front-bench team most of the time, and, although he was not a modernist in the Thatcher interpretation, he picked some good people with no Tory background in the old sense and gave them positions of consequence, in spite of his own patrician attitudes. He was a substantial figure and ranks high among the Prime Ministers of this century. He rallied his Party after Suez and held it together for seven years, which was no mean achievement.

The long Macmillan tenure of 10 Downing Street had been a fascinating premiership. His opponents enjoyed his consummate style as much as did his friends. But behind that public nonchalance was the real professional. He brought the style of the Edwardian age but of other ages too, including that of the great Whig families, to the study of nuclear technology and nuclear disarmament.

He was an accomplished parliamentarian, with a great sense of timing. Whenever he was about to produce a telling remark, he kicked the front of the table below the Despatch Box. If he was winding up an argumentative, perhaps noisy, debate, he would spend twenty or twenty-five minutes of the final half hour making serious points, sometimes consciously boring the House. A few minutes before ten o'clock he would look pained and say that he had not expected the Leader of the Opposition to treat so serious a subject in a controversial, indeed, he might say, partisan manner, but since he had done so it was necessary to reply. He would then take out of his left-hand jacket pocket a carefully typed speech, probably composed the night before.

Few Prime Ministers have worked so hard, and even fewer derived so much enjoyment from it. Few have had so wide-ranging a grip on every aspect of government, or so clear or easy a command over their colleagues. Few rivalled his sense of history, few felt as identified as he was with that history, and of those who did, even fewer savoured the challenges, the tasks and the protocol as much as he did.

The Tories should have elected Rab Butler to succeed him. I expected them to do so and I would have enjoyed renewing the contest of the 1950s. But Rab did not have enough of the killer instinct to take over and his colleagues knew it. Instead, they chose the Earl of Home, who demoted himself to the House of Commons for the purpose. Politically I was pleased. Instead of the formidable Macmillan, with his deep knowledge of politics and administration, I was getting an opponent with very little experience of Parliament and much ignorance of economics.

He was to prove much more formidable than I expected. When the election came we only just scraped in and I am often asked whether we might have lost if Macmillan had been restored to power. It is very hard to say, but I doubt it. Macmillan had provided us with so much ammunition that I consider that we would have made mincemeat of him, whereas with Alec Douglas-Home our barrage was perhaps more subdued.

At the beginning of November I flew to Washington to see President Kennedy. I had first met him in 1940, when his father was still the American Ambassador in London. He had come over to take a short course at the London School of Economics and was invited down to Oxford to stay with Beveridge, who asked Mary and myself to join them for tea at University College. He had already received Alec Douglas-Home at the White House, but his embassy people in London were sending reports on the political situation in Britain indicating that Labour was likely to win the general election. The Ambassador came to see me and said that if I were to go to Washington the President would certainly see me. It seemed a useful contact to make and we had a pleasant conversation. He recalled our previous meeting, and showed great interest in Labour's plans for 'getting Britain moving again'.

He emphasized how much he envied the position of a British Prime Minister. 'I know', he said, 'exactly what needs to be done to get this economy moving again. But I have no hope of getting Congress to adopt my policies until my fourth year. Then they'll be thinking, most of them, about keeping their seats and they'll see my programme through.' He then opened up with great frankness about his own plans for stimulating and modernizing the stagnant US economy. His brains trust had drawn up detailed plans for economic expansion, but it would have to wait for the Lower House to be re-elected, together with a third of the senators, who would then 'be clinging to his coat-tails' to ensure their return to Washington.

There is a press photograph of our meeting. He had very serious back trouble as a result of a war injury and we conducted the whole conversation standing up. I believe that sitting in a normal fashion caused him very considerable pain.

On 22 November he was assassinated. I was on a speaking tour in North Wales when the news came through, accompanied by a peremptory message from my secretary asking me to go to the nearest BBC station, somewhere in West Lancashire, to record my reaction. I stopped at a fish and chip shop for a bite to eat on the way. The owner recognized me and, when I told him of my mission, he absolutely refused to charge me a penny, which was his contribution to the memory of Jack Kennedy.

I had rather expected Alec Douglas-Home to go to the country in the spring or early summer of 1964. Instead, he did something which has rarely occurred in British history – he took us through the full five years of Parliament before calling his general election. In fact, it was five years and two weeks, only just constitutional. I had thought I was going to have the time of my life with him in the House, but I was proved quite wrong. He knew very little about industry, even less about economics and, I suspect, very little about ordinary people, apart from those who worked on his Scottish estates. But he was literate and quickly asserted himself as a formidable leader of the Tory Party.

I assumed that he would have all his speeches written for him in

Tory Central Office, but that was another miscalculation. He established himself as a very useful debater and held his own. He did not acquire the mastery of the House that Churchill and Macmillan had enjoyed, but his short, clipped manner of speaking was effective. I do not know if anyone ever used a stop-watch on him, but I suspect that his speeches were on the whole 30 per cent shorter than any other holder of the Prime Minister's office.

In what is loosely called the business of the House, I found his behaviour impeccable. There always have to be exchanges between the Party Leaders behind the Speaker's Chair, particularly when the Chief Whips cannot agree on some matter of procedure or the formal timing of a debate. I always found him absolutely fair and reliable, and his integrity was such that there could never be any question on my part of letting him down on something we had agreed. He was quite properly determined to keep the upper hand in the House, and our relationship was easy and agreeable. It was even possible to revive to a minor degree the custom of having a drink together in the Members' Bar, which had been such a feature of my relationship with his predecessor.

He has charming manners and is a man of generous instincts. Nearly twenty years later, when I had myself been elevated to the House of Lords, the Labour peers gave a small party for me. They had just proposed a toast when Alec came into the room. He had quite simply gate-crashed, poured himself a glass and, standing just behind me, made a charming speech of welcome.

Mary and I had shared a staircase at Oxford in the early stages of our marriage with Elizabeth Douglas-Home's brother, Giles Allington, who became Dean of University College and died young. We were both very fond of him, and when our second son came along we named him Giles. Mary and Elizabeth always had an affectionate relationship and when the time came for us to move into Number 10 Downing Street, Lady Douglas-Home went out of her way to make things agreeable with the staff for the new incumbent wife.

In the end the call came, with polling day set for 15 October. The campaign is so much part of the public record that I hardly need to recapitulate the details. Alec was being teased about being the fourteenth Earl and made his very neat come-back about my being the fourteenth Mr Wilson. I have never really found out whether he thought that up himself or whether it came from some bright spark at Tory Central Office.

The opinion poll auguries were good, although inevitably the Tories started to catch up. It has been suggested that I took the first ten days in rather too stately a fashion, and that I altered my tactics half-way through to adopt a more popular style. I was not conscious of it myself; I made my points to a set plan, and was always conscious that it was the speeches of the final week and the last appearance on television which would have the greatest impact.

We certainly seemed to generate immense enthusiasm. There was a large eve-of-poll meeting in St George's Hall in Liverpool and the crowds outside were so enormous that when Mary and I left to go back to the Adelphi Hotel, we were simply swept apart in the press of people. Mary's feet hardly touched the ground and, if she had not been closely supported by friends, she might well have come to serious harm. In the end we got up to our suite, looked down from the window and saw the street below was thick with people shouting.

The count was a cliff-hanger. Labour was making gains in the urban seats, but nothing was clear, and after not more than three or four hours' sleep Mary and I caught the milk train to London, making straight for Transport House, where there was still no firm result. We were maintaining a lead over the Conservatives, but they were creeping up and the Liberals were doing better than for some time. There was always the possibility that the figures might enable the Conservatives to do some deal with the Liberals to remain in power and it was not until three o'clock in the afternoon that Labour registered the seat that put us over the top with a majority. In the end the figures were Labour 317, Conservatives 303, Liberals 9, and the Speaker. We had fourteen seats more than the Conservatives and an overall majority of four. It was Winston Churchill who said, 'One is enough,' and I was duly summoned to the Palace.

The next task was Cabinet-making, which went right on through that afternoon and evening; by the end of the day I had made my main appointments. It is worth recording the difficulties I faced. Most of the old stalwarts of the Attlee Government had passed on or faded away. Apart from myself, only three Labour MPs had held any previous office. Patrick Gordon-Walker had been Attlee's Commonwealth Secretary from 1950–1, but he had failed to win his seat at Smethwick and would have to be found another if he was to serve, as I intended, as Foreign Secretary. George Brown had held secondary office in the Ministry of Works, not in the Cabinet, and Jim Callaghan had been Financial Secretary at the Admiralty.

I was also perfectly well aware that not more than three of the dozen members of the Shadow Cabinet had voted for me as Party Leader. For my part I was prepared to draw a line under previous attitudes on the assumption that appointment to office in a Cabinet of twenty-two would dilute any previous differences of opinion there might have been. I was also absolutely determined that our narrow majority should not give scope for interest groups within the Party, whether of the extreme right or left or with some particular doctrine in mind, to be placed in a position to bring pressure to bear with some hint of rejection or abstention. In the event, none of these dangers presented themselves during our first period in office. The will to stay in power covers many divergencies.

I had spent the final months in the previous Parliament watching all my colleagues very closely and making a note of those who coped best with their opponents on the Government front bench. With one or two exceptions I was able to allocate jobs pretty much in accordance with the Shadow Cabinet appointments which had originated with Hugh Gaitskell, and this had a mollifying effect.

I had to make one appointment with particular speed if my plans for a technological revolution were to be given effect. The group of scientists with whom I had remained in touch right up to the election had been warning me that the British computer industry, essential to all our plans, was facing financial collapse. The Treasury was about to order an American computer system and, if this had gone through, we would never have recovered.

The first evening I summoned Frank Cousins, Secretary of the Transport and General Workers Union, and confirmed that he was to become the first Minister for Technology. I told him that he had, in my view, about a month to save the British computer industry and that this must be his first priority. He succeeded. First of all we had to find him a seat and he was never happy in the house of Commons. I knew the rationalization schemes we had in mind would cause difficulties with the unions and I wanted one of their own to deal with them. Frank proved an able administrator but never quite accommodated himself to the role of poacher turned gamekeeper and, in due course, he resigned. I might have done better with a different trade unionist.

George Brown, as First Secretary and Head of the Department

of Economic Affairs, and Jim Callaghan, as Chancellor of the Exchequer, already knew what their respective roles were to be. They had accepted the broad division of function between the two departments, but an immediate need arose, in the light of the advice each was getting from his departmental advisers, to settle a concordat as to the division of duties between them. It had to be settled that Friday night. The draft I was given, which had been prepared by civil servants, set the division as between short-term responsibilities (Treasury) and long-term planning (DEA).

This was not what I had in mind. The concordat which emerged from my meeting with the pair of them later that evening made clear that the fundamental distinction was between monetary responsibilities on the one hand, which must come under the Treasury, and, on the other, the co-ordinating responsibility for industry and everything to do with the mobilization of real resources, productivity and exports.

I was taking a risk with George Brown, with his erratic habits. The drink problem was always with us. It was not that he drank more than anybody else but that he could not hold it. For a time he was on his best behaviour. He had high ability and a very sharp mind, enjoyed a solid position of trade union support in the Party and would I knew face down the Treasury whenever the occasion arose. Jim Callaghan I felt I could handle. He was a substantial figure in the Party, with strong trade union support, and always a potential rival. But I knew more about the Treasury and the economy than he did and the Prime Minister is also First Lord of the Treasury and holds the whip hand.

I made Denis Healey Minister of Defence. He is a strange person. When he was at Oxford he was a communist. Then friends took him in hand, sent him to the Rand Corporation of America, where he was brainwashed and came back very right wing. But his method of thinking was still what it had been: in other words, the absolute certainty that he was right and everybody else was wrong, and not merely wrong through not knowing the proper answers, but wrong through malice. I had very little trouble with him on his own subject, but he has a very good quick brain and can be very rough. He probably intervened in Cabinet with absolute certainty about other departments more than any minister I have ever known, but he was a strong colleague and much respected.

Patrick Gordon-Walker was a problem. We found him another seat to fight at Leyton by offering a peerage to the incumbent, but the electorate would have none of it and we lost our first by-election, something we could not afford. The fact has to be faced that constituencies do not like this sort of manipulation and we paid the price. In his place I moved Michael Stewart from the Ministry of Education to the Foreign Office, where he proved an outstanding success.

I brought Barbara Castle into the Cabinet as Minister for Overseas Development in a substantially enlarged department. This had been another hobby horse of mine ever since I had started the War on Want movement in the Attlee days. Barbara proved an excellent minister. She was good at whatever she touched. I doubt if any member of the Cabinet worked longer hours or gave more productive thought to what they were doing. I was also able to repay a a long-standing political debt to Nye Bevan's widow, Jennie Lee, who had been denied all preferment during the Attlee years. I made her Minister for the Arts and asked her to take over my University of the Air. It was her total commitment and tenacity which gave it form and being.

On 19 October we held our first Cabinet. We had learned that we had inherited an annual trade deficit of £800 million from the previous administration. Khrushchev had just been toppled in Russia and the Chinese had just exploded their first nuclear bomb. We were going to need to keep all our wits about us, as indeed was the case for the next dozen years, when I finally decided that I had come full circle.

Index

Index